About the Author

Kader Abdolah (Iran) is the author of three other Dutch novels released in English translation: *The House of the Mosque*, *My Father's Notebook*, and *The King*, that has been longlisted for the International IMPAC Dublin Literary Award 2016.

Having arrived in the Netherlands in 1988 as a political refugee, his efforts to learn the language paid off. He started writing in Dutch and was the recipient in 1995 of an incentive grant for promising new authors. He went on to write many award-winning novels. *The Messenger* and *The Qur'an* (2008), originally published in Dutch as a two-book set, have been received in the Netherlands with high regard.

Additionally, the author has been honoured with many distinctions including the Mundial Award for his achievements in the area of international cooperation, peace, and security, and the Order of Orange-Nassau to recognize his contributions to society and the world of literature. Abdolah's writing talent has not gone unnoticed: his work has already been translated into thirty languages.

About the Translators

Nouri and Niusha Nighting met when they were graduate students abroad. While travelling in the Middle East in that period, they experienced the Hajj firsthand. This later inspired them to explore Islamic culture and literature. They have translated many related academic essays and books, but have always been keen to tackle more literary work. Kader Abdolah's *The Qur'an* and *The Messenger* are their first collaborative efforts.

D0235000

Kader Abdolah

The Qur'an

A Journey

Translated from the Dutch by
Nouri and Niusha Nighting

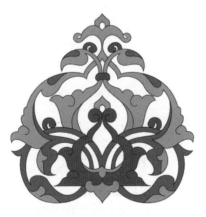

World Editions

Published in Great Britain in 2016 by World Editions Ltd., London

www.worldeditions.org

Copyright © Kader Abdolah, 2008
English translation copyright © Nouri and Niusha Nighting, 2016
Cover design Multitude
Image credit © Jerónimo Alba Age/F1online

First published as *De Koran* in the Netherlands in 2008 by De Geus BV, PO Box 1878, 4801 BW Breda

British Library Cataloguing-in-Publication Data
A catalogue record for this book is available on request from the British Library.

ISBN 978-94-6238-023-3

Typeset in Minion Pro

The publisher gratefully acknowledges the support of the Dutch Foundation for Literature.

N ederlands
N letterenfonds
dutch foundation
for literature

Distribution Europe (except the Netherlands and Belgium):
Turnaround Publisher Services, London
Distribution the Netherlands and Belgium: Centraal Boekhuis, Culemborg, the Netherlands

ACKNOWLEDGEMENTS

My gratitude is due to all those who read the various drafts of the manuscript with painstaking care and provided welcome suggestions and observations.

Sincere thanks are also due to the staff at World Editions and to the translators for what they have done for my two books.

KADER ABDOLAH

LIST OF NAMES

Anneh	Anna (mother of Mary)
Ayoub	Job
Aziz	Potiphar
Binyamin	Benjamin
Dawud	David
Qabil	Cain
Habil	Abel
Hajar	Hagar
Harun	Aaron
Hawwaa	Eve
Hud	Eber
Ibrahim	Abraham
Idris	Enoch
Ilias	Elijah
Isa	Jesus
Ishaq	Isaac
Isma'il	Ishmael
Jabra'il	Gabriel
Laya	Leah
Lut	Lot
Maryam	Mary
Madyan	Midian
Musa	Moses
Namrood	Nimrod
Nuh	Noah
Qarun	Korah
Rahil	Rachel
Saleh	Shelah
Sheth	Seth

Shuayb	Jethro
Sulayman	Solomon
Talut	Saul
Uzayr	Ezra
Yahya	John the Baptist (Yahya is used a few times for Jesus in the Qur'an)
Yajuj & Majuj	Gog & Magog
Yaqub	Jacob
Yunus	Jonah
Yusuf	Joseph
Zakariya	Zachariah
Zulayka	Potiphar's wife
Zulkifl	Ezekiel

Introduction

Allah is all-knowing, says Muhammad.

Kader Abdolah knows nothing.

I treated the book with great affection because it was the book of the house of my father and of people dear to me.

If any part of my explanation and reworking does not tally, it is due to my ignorance and to my love for Muhammad's prose. I use the name Muhammad as it is written in the Qur'an, and out of reverence for the prophet.

This translation can be seen as a journey through the Qur'an: I have tried to take you, the reader, with me to every corner of the book. There are many translations of the Qur'an. All, of course, are worthy of consultation, and I bow my head to the labour of those who created them. I have always cherished their work, treated it with respect, and given it a prominent place in my library.

I have to confess a few things at this juncture:

It is impossible to translate the Qur'an; the beauty of Muhammad's language is lost in the process.

Every sentence in the Qur'an is evocative. You can translate them in different ways, and you can make mistakes.

I confess that I have made many mistakes. There was no other way. Without these mistakes, I could not continue.

There are many ambiguities in the Qur'an, but in each instance I have tried to bring clarity to the text.

I consider it a great shame that I cannot pass on the original flavour, smell, and feeling of the words of Muhammad's recitation. What I have done, nevertheless, is make a hole in the wall that allows you to look at the gardens of Muhammad.

It pleases me, Kader Abdolah, that I have been able to show my readers something of Muhammad's divine prose. Enjoy it.

Modus Operandi

I translated the book directly from the original Arabic Qur'an that belonged to my father.

After translating each sentence, I immediately looked at four Persian translations and then at five Dutch translations.

In addition, I consulted the five volume medieval commentary of the prominent Qur'anic exegete Tabari and used it as a foundation. When I encountered something I did not understand, I turned to him for his opinion; his judgement was always pure and original.

If Tabari was not enough, I picked up the phone and asked my elderly uncle Aga Djan for advice. Without his interpretations and explanations, I would have lost my way in the book.

Besides Aga Djan, I also consulted devout men and women in my family, men and women of advanced age; like ancient trees, the first to fall to the ground when the wind is strong.

I thank them; I thank them for their generous hearts.

Chronology of the Chapters or Suras

There are many repetitions in the Qur'an.

Repetition is part of the character of the book. The Qur'an is a recitation that was intended for illiterate people. Repetition was essential in those days.

I have removed a great deal of the repetition, but inevitably some of it has remained.

I have made four important decisions:

Muhammad's recitations, or suras, are of two different types.

The first type of suras came into existence when he was living in Mecca and the second when he was living in Medina.

There are eighty-two suras from Mecca and thirty-two from Medina.

The compilers of the Qur'an mixed the suras together in such a way that their chronological order was lost. As a result, a sort of chaos has taken hold; a chaos, nevertheless that has given the book a divine character.

I have restored the suras to their chronological order, to allow us to better follow the development of Muhammad and his Qur'an.

In addition, I have provided most of the suras with an introduction, to pave the way to the heart of the text, and I have added one of five elements—the cow, the tulip, the windmill, the rain, and the clog—at the beginning of each sura to underline the book's new identity. To immortalise my prose, I have added a sura to the Qur'an, sura 115.

I confess from the outset that my work has its roots in the ancient Persian literary tradition. Great Persian masters such as Hafez, Saadi, Khayyam, and Rumi each disseminated the Qur'an in their own unique way.

In the last fourteen hundred years, the Qur'an has served as a source of inspiration for the great eastern poets, writers, and architects. Arabic and eastern literature as a whole are deeply rooted in this book.

This new journey through the Qur'an has the potential to influence English literature. Up to now, most English writers, poets, and artists have turned to the Bible for inspiration, but now they can include the Qur'an. For them, it represents an ancient and mysterious world.

The prose of this journey is the combined prose of Muhammad ibn Abdullah and Kader Abdolah. It is not the kind of prose one would expect in the English speaking world.

I wish you a pleasant journey through the Qur'an and through the fascinating life of Muhammad.

Read and admire.

May Muhammad ibn Abdullah be pleased with this journey.

With respect and pride,
Kader Abdolah

1

The Closed Drop

Muhammad waited years for a sign from above.
He thought that Allah lived on the seventh level of heaven; that
He saw him and would choose him as His messenger.
Muhammad turned forty and still he waited patiently, but it
seemed that no one in heaven was thinking about him.

One night he was sitting on the top of Mount Hira again, wait-
ing. When he looked up at the sky in a moment of emotion, he
saw a beam of light descend upon him like a falling star.
The light took the form of a winged angel, and it landed beside
Muhammad on the rock.
It was the angel Jabra'il, the messenger of Allah!
Muhammad jumped to his feet in surprise.
The angel showed him a short text and said, ''Iqra', Muham-
mad! Recite!'
'I cannot,' Muhammad answered.

The sura speaks of Abu Jahl, one of Muhammad's enemies, who
threw stones at him while he was praying and wounded his head.

In the name of Allah
He is love
He gives
He forgives

1

Muhammad! Recite!
Recite in the name of Allah, the Creator.
He created humankind from a single closed drop of blood.
Recite! Your God is the most loving.
He who taught humankind by the pen.
He who taught them what they did not know.
Humans tend to rebel when they experience a little independence.
But they always return to their creator.

2

Have you seen the man who impeded our servant's prayer?
Did he not know that Allah sees all things?
If he does not stop, We shall tug the forelock on his head.
That deceitful, guilty head.
Let him call on his comrades.
We shall summon the watchers of hell.
Muhammad! Do not listen to that man.
Pray, and draw closer.

2

The Pen

'Nun wa-l-qalami wa-ma yasturun.'
These are the words with which the original sura begins.
The text opens with the letter N (nun), and a solemn promise is made by the pen.
It is one of the most beautiful suras in the Qur'an because Allah swears by the pen and by the ink.
The letter N (nun) has no clear meaning, but it makes the invocation mysterious.

Allah swears by the pen and immediately thereafter by what is written by it.

In doing so, He restores Muhammad's confidence.

This oath is seen as the crown jewel of the Qur'an because it reveals a broad-minded Allah who swears by 'whatever the messenger writes'.

The Qur'an has one hundred and fourteen recitations, otherwise known as suras.

Eighty-two of these suras were revealed in Mecca, the remaining thirty-two in the city of Medina.

The recitations from Mecca are gentle, poetic, lyrical, rhythmic, and probing.

These are the suras Muhammad recited at the beginning of his mission, at a time when he was still without power and did not believe in violence.

But after he flees to Medina, his language changes completely. In Medina, he becomes a man of power who brandishes the sword, and his words acquire harsh overtones.

In the name of Allah
He is love
He gives
He forgives

1
Nun (N.)
By the pen and what you write with it.
And by the elegance of your Creator, no, Muhammad, you are not mad.
Rather, your behaviour is worthy.
A great and eternal reward awaits you.
Soon you will see, and soon they will see who is mad.

2

Muhammad! Above all, do not listen to that liar, that wretched swearer of oaths.

He gossips, he is sly.

He leads people away from the right path.

He is a sinner.

He is violent.

He is a bastard.

3

When Our signs are recited he says, 'Old fables, every one of them.'

He does this because he is wealthy and has sons.

But soon We shall carve a sign on his face with a sword.

4

Be sure! We put unbelievers to the test, just as We tested the two sons of the fruit farmer.

His sons had decided to pluck the fruit of their garden early in the morning so that the poor would not see them. And they had made no reservation. They had not said, '*in sha' Allah*. If it is Allah's will.'

We thus let their garden be afflicted while they were asleep. It was transformed into a pile of ashes. In the morning when they woke they said to each other, 'We must go to the garden to pick its fruit without delay.' They did not know what had happened.

They stole away and agreed as they went, 'No needy person shall enter our garden.'

5

When they saw the garden, they were startled and said, 'Oh, we are erring spirits.'

And one said to the other, 'We have been robbed. Didn't I insist that we say, "'*in sha' Allah*?"'

They showered each other with accusations and said, 'Ah, woe to us. We have been arrogant.'

They then turned to God, 'Praised be the Creator. We were unjust. Perhaps you will give us a better garden than this.'

6

In this way We punish the unbelievers in this life. And the punishment after death is even worse. But for the devout there are gardens of delight.

No, We shall not treat believers as We treat unbelievers.

Muhammad, say to them, 'What has happened to you? Why do you do such things? Do you not have a book in which you can read it all?'

Leave the unbelievers to Us.

We shall quietly destroy them.

We now give them space to do what they want.

But Our intention is firm.

7

So have patience, Muhammad. Wait upon the judgement of your Creator, and do not be like the man who called out to his God from the belly of the fish, impatient and desperate.

You know that he would have found himself humiliated in some barren place, if God had not helped him.

Muhammad! When the unbelievers see you recite Our signs, they shall want to smite you with their gaze. They say, 'He is mad!'

But you are not mad, Muhammad. And the Qur'an is a warning to humankind.

3

The One Wrapped in a Blanket

It is night. Muhammad is lying under a blanket. The angel Jabra'il appears and wakes him, 'You there under the blanket, get up!'
He asks Muhammad to stay awake part of the night to recite the suras of the Qur'an.
He says, 'Muhammad, we did not give you the Qur'an to walk around with it all day long, sharing it with people, only to end up with blisters on your feet. Take rest at night and recite the verses thereafter.'

In the name of Allah
He is love
He gives
He forgives

1
You, with the blanket pulled over your head.
Get up halfway through the night or a little before.
Recite the verses of the Qur'an at that moment, calmly, with beauty and clarity.
Muhammad, We are entrusting important words to you.
Getting up in the night is an exceptional experience and reinforces the efficacy of the Word.
You have done many other things in the course of the day. Rest at night, therefore. Let everything go, remember Allah, and be with Him completely.

2
He is the Creator of the east and of the west. There is no God but He. Ask him, therefore, to protect you.

Bear everything the unbelievers say with patience, and politely distance yourself from them.

And leave Me alone with the liars, who think their life is a delight.

We have set aside fire and chains for them.

3

Muhammad! Your Creator knows that sometimes you pray two thirds of the night with a group of your followers. Sometimes half the night and sometimes a third.

Allah determines the length of the night and of the day. He knows that you cannot extend it.

Recite, therefore, as much of the Qur'an as you are able.

Perhaps some of you are sick, others on a journey, and others still fighting for Allah.

Choose, therefore, an easy sura, and recite it for as long as you consider convenient.

Pray five times per day, give away part of your income, and offer untainted loans in the name of Allah. He shall return everything to you in abundance.

Do good deeds and ask Him for forgiveness.

He is kind and He forgives.

4

The One Wrapped in a Mantle

Muhammad has just been appointed messenger in the cave of Hira.

Hesitant, covered in sweat and forlorn, he returns home.

His wife sees him standing in the doorway, a broken man. She senses immediately what has happened, pulls his mantle over his head, leads him inside, and lets him rest his head on her lap. Then the angel Jabra'il appears anew and says, 'You, the one wrapped in a mantle! Get up! Begin!'

In the name of Allah
He is love
He gives
He forgives

1
You, the one who pulled a mantle over your head.
Get up and warn!
Proclaim that your Creator is great.
Put on clean clothes.
Avoid idols.
Do not strive for more.
And be patient on the way to your God.

2
When the trumpet is blown, that day will be a difficult day for the unbelievers.
Leave Me alone with the person I created.
I gave him much wealth and sons.
But he still wants more of Me.
Out of the question; he resists Our signs.
We shall soon punish him severely.

3
Look! Disobedient persons contrive and deliberate.
Led astray are they.
Cursed are they.
They look around, frown peevishly, stretch their necks, and say, 'This is nothing more than trickery.'

These are the words of humans.
Without delay I shall roast them in the fire.
Do you want to know what the fire is? It leaves nothing behind
and lets nothing escape. It scorches the skin.
And it is guarded by nineteen guardians.

4
By the moon.
By the night when the sun is gone.
And by the dawn as it comes in radiance.
This is one of the greatest events.
A warning for humankind.

Why do they refuse to listen?
They are like donkeys fleeing from a lion.
Without doubt! They are not afraid, but they have been warned.
And every person is responsible for what they do.

5

Al-Fatiha

*This sura is one of the most important in the Qur'an. It is a
text that Muslims recite seventeen times a day, turning toward
Mecca: twice in the morning before dawn, four times at noon,
four times late in the day, three times as the evening begins, and
four times late in the evening.*

*Believers say these words whenever and wherever they have to
make important decisions, 'bi-smi llahi ar-rahmani ar-rahim.'
'In the name of Allah. He is love. He gives. He forgives.'
Even the devout bridegroom who shares his bed with his bride*

for the first time says them softly before he touches her. Likewise, the bride says them to herself when she receives him. These are the most commonly used words spoken by devout students before they begin an exam or test. They are the first words on the lips of believers when they start their car.

In the name of Allah
He is love
He gives
He forgives

1
'Alif Lam Mim.
All praise to Him, the Creator of the worlds.
The King of life after death.
We pray to You, and we ask only Your help.
Lead us on the right path.
On the path of those You have granted grace, not on the path of those You do not favour or who have gone astray.

6

The Book *In the Beginning*

The book In the Beginning *is in the hands of Allah.*
Allah knows all the secrets of the world, and He noted every calculation in that book by hand.
'I am illiterate,' Muhammad asserted, 'I cannot read or write. The texts I recite to you are not my own. They all stem from the book In the Beginning.*'*

In the name of Allah
He is love
He gives
He forgives

1
By the heavens where the highest towers are.
By the promised day.
By the witness and by what is declared as testimony.
Death to those who make a pit of fire.
A fire of wood.
And death to those who stood by the pit, those who were wit-
ness to what they did to the believers and looked on.
They took revenge on them because they believed in Allah.

2
The punishment of God is great.
He is the One who started with creation and who can recreate.
He is the Owner of the universe.
And He does what He wills.
Did the story of those armies not yet reach you?
The armies of Pharaoh and Thamud?

3
The unbelievers continue to deny everything.
But God surrounds them.
Without doubt! The Qur'an is a majestic document.
And it has its roots in the book *In the Beginning*.

7

A Rope of Fibres

Abu Lahab was Muhammad's uncle, one of his avowed enemies,
and a fierce opponent of his Qur'an.
His wife also detested Muhammad.
Abu Lahab considered Muhammad an embarrassment to their
clan and did everything he could to obstruct him.
At one point he devised a plan to kill Muhammad.

In the name of Allah
He is love
He gives
He forgives

1
Ruined are the hands of Abu Lahab.
May he himself also perish.
His possessions and his deeds shall not benefit him.
He shall be brought to a blazing fire.
His wife likewise, she who carries wood for the fire.
With a rope around her neck, woven from the fibres of a date palm.

8

When They Go Out

Qur'an was a new Arabic word. Muhammad shared his revela-
tions little by little and referred to them together as the Qur'an.
The word Islam was also used for the first time in this period,

and it acquired the meaning 'Submit!'
'To whom should we submit?' people asked.
'To Allah,' said Muhammad.
'How should we picture Allah?'
'The letters "lah" in the word "Allah" mean "no" or "no more".
Allah is thus One and nothing more. He has no father and no
mother. He has no need for food. No one is like Him, and He is
like no one.
'He is not empty inside.
'Sometimes he slices off a part of the night and adds it to the day.
And vice versa.'

In the name of Allah
He is love
He gives
He forgives

1
When the sun grows dark.
When the stars go out.
When the mountains begin to move.
When the heavily pregnant and cherished camels are abandoned.
When the wild animals are assembled.
When the seas seethe and swell.
When the souls are gathered together.
When the girls are asked for which sin they were buried alive.
When the heavens are torn asunder.
When the fire of hell is kindled.
When paradise is made ready.
And when the scrolls are opened, in which the deeds of every person are inscribed.
Then everyone will know what he has done.

2

I swear by the recurring stars, which finish their course and go down.
And by the night when it disappears.
And by the morning when it appears.
These are the words of an outstanding messenger, who has an exceptional place next to Allah, who is obedient and reliable.
No, Muhammad is not mad.
He encountered the angel Jabra'il on the clear horizon.
And the angel passed on the complete message.

Where are you going?
The message is nothing other than an exhortation for the dwellers on earth, those in search of the right path.

9

The Night Star

In the culture into which Muhammad was born, most things were passed on orally.
The book and the pen were preserved for the elite of Mecca.
Poets placed a wooden stool on the market square, climbed onto it, and recited their poems by heart.
When the texts of the Qur'an were assembled, the oral tradition was transformed into a literary culture. The Qur'an became a book for everyone.

In the name of Allah
He is love
He gives
He forgives

1

By the sky and the night star.
How do you know which star is the night star?
It is a radiant star.
Every soul is watched over.
Humankind should be aware of what they are made.
They are made of leaping fluid that runs from the back of the
father to the ribs of the mother.
Indeed, He is able to call back humankind.
On the day the secrets are revealed.
Then humankind shall be powerless and have no helper.

2

By the heavens from which the rain falls.
By the soil, split by a plant.
The Qur'an is a recitation, conclusive in all respects.
And the book is not an invention.
They are devising a scheme.
And I am likewise devising a scheme.
But Muhammad! Give the unbelievers a little more time!

10

He is the Most High

*Out of nothingness Muhammad called out, 'Allahu 'akbar! Allah
is Great!'*
He said, 'la 'ilaha 'illa llah. There is only One: Allah.'
The form and composition of his statements were new.
Muhammad said, 'As-salamu alay-kum! My Salaam for you.'
No Arab had ever greeted anyone with As-salamu alay-kum.
*(According to al-A'sha, a great poet and contemporary of
Muhammad)*

In the name of Allah
He is love
He gives
He forgives

1

Repeat the name of the Creator, the Most High.
He who created all things and governs it all.
He who apportions fate and shows the way.
He who brings forth vegetation.
And thereafter makes it dry and withered.

2

Muhammad!
We shall soon teach you to read so that you shall not forget the
will of God.
He knows what is hidden and what is revealed.
We shall make your task easy.
Warn the people so they will benefit from the warning.

3

You opt for this present life.
But life after death is better and eternal.
This was also said in the previous heavenly books.
In the scriptures of Ibrahim and Musa.

11

The Night

*Muhammad sometimes uses the 'I' form in his recitation; one 'I'
for himself and the other 'I' for Allah, and it is not always clear*

to the reader who is speaking, Allah or Muhammad.
Sometimes the prophet uses the 'he' form, which can refer to both himself and Allah.
He also uses the 'we' form, referring sometimes to himself and other times to Allah.
He mixes a variety of perspectives, and in so doing—consciously or unconsciously—he creates a holy confusion in his work: the reader's thoughts travel in every direction. The recitations in the Qur'an thereby transcend what is human.
Ordinary people do not do this, but Muhammad does. His Qur'an thus acquires a divine and mysterious character.
(According to the medieval poetry collection Hafez, *by Shams edine Shirazai)*

In the name of Allah
He is love
He gives
He forgives

1
By the night when it veils all things.
And by the day when it shines brightly.
And by He who created male and female.
Your endeavours are different.
We shall clear the path to happiness for those who give, and fear, and are just.
But for those who do not give, and are self-satisfied, and are not just, We shall show the path to misery.
And when they perish, their possessions shall be to no avail.

2
Our task is to give guidance.
This life and life after death belong to Us.
We warn you.

12

Early Morning

'Muhammad, tell stories. Give the people food for thought, and keep repeating them,' says Allah to Muhammad.
With every step he takes, with every move he makes, he says, 'Bi-smi llahi ar-rahmani ar-rahim. *Allah is love, Allah gives. Allah forgives.'*
Muhammad also repeats the life stories of the ancient prophets without ceasing.
With these repetitions he draws everyone's attention in one direction, toward Allah.

In the name of Allah
He is love
He gives
He forgives

1
By the early morning.
By the ten nights.
By the even and the uneven.
And by the night when it vanishes.
Does this not contain a sign for those who have understanding?

Do you not know what your Creator did with the ancient people of 'Ad?
The people had palaces with pillars.
Elevated buildings, to be found nowhere else.
And with the ancient Thamud people, who made homes in the rocks.

And with the Pharaoh, the lord of the pegs.
They were all oppressors who spread death and destruction in their land.
Therefore, God let the scourge of punishment descend upon them.
He knows all things.

2

When God tests a man by giving him something he says, 'God has exalted me.'
But when God puts him to the test by limiting his bread, he quickly loses patience and says, 'God has humiliated me.'
No, nothing of the sort.
You do nothing for the orphans.
And you do not feed the needy.
And you greedily devour the inheritance in its entirety.
And you are too attached to possessions.

3
But you, the soul who has found rest!
Return to Me.
Be one of My servants.
And enter My paradise.

13

The Radiant Day

After his first encounter with the angel Jabra'il, Muhammad waits three years for a new sign, but nothing happens. It seems that no one in heaven has time for him.
Muhammad is a broken man, and he begins to doubt whether he

is really a prophet, and whether he really encountered the angel.
Did he imagine it all?
Then, on the point of despair, the angel appears again and reassures Muhammad.

In the name of Allah
He is love
He gives
He forgives

1
By the radiant day.
And by the night in which one rests.
Muhammad! Your Creator has not abandoned you and has not forgotten you.
The hereafter shall truly be better for you than this life.
He shall uplift you so that you feel happy.
Did He not find you an orphan and give you shelter?
Did He not find you lost and give you guidance?
Did He not find you needy and give you prosperity?
Never speak harshly to the orphan.
Never turn away the beggar.
And speak with respect about the favours of your God.

14   ٶ

The Expansion

This sura comes at a time when Muhammad no longer has doubts and has become a familiar figure in Mecca.
He considers himself a true prophet, and seems equal to everything.

In the name of Allah
He is love
He gives
He forgives

1
Muhammad!
Did We not expand your heart?
And did We not remove the heavy burden resting on your shoulders?
And did We not grant you renown?
Remember! After a time of difficulty, a time of ease always dawns.
When you have found rest, turn, then, to your Creator and focus on prayer.

15

Time and Life

In the name of Allah
He is love
He gives
He forgives

1
By time and life.
Humans do damage to themselves.
Except those who believe, and do good deeds, and urge one another to be righteous and patient.

16

Those that Run

The prose of the Qur'an is the crown of the Arabic language. No one can reach higher, no one can produce anything more powerful, nothing is more mysterious than the Qur'an.
It is not human prose. It is the prose of Allah. And it is all in the book In the Beginning.
(According to Naged Andelesi, the Qur'an expert)

In the name of Allah
He is love
He gives
He forgives

1
By the running, fighting horses, their breath short and panting.
And by the sparks that fly from their hooves.
And by the warriors in the early morning.
Who then cause dust to rise.
And thus clear a path through the middle of the battle array.
Humans are ungrateful to their Creator.
And they know it.
And they are mean and possessive.
Do they not know that every grave shall be dug over?
That secrets shall be exposed?

17

A Wonderful Pond

A large part of the Qur'an deals with the Jews, sometimes directly, often indirectly.

Muhammad and the Jews have a mutual bond.
Without the presence of the Jews in Mecca, and especially in Medina, Muhammad would never have completed his mission.
Medina was under the control of the Jews. The Arabs felt subordinate in their own country and in their own city. The Jews had a book and a prophet, but the Arabs had nothing.
Muhammad responded to this dissatisfaction and gave the Arabs the Qur'an, and with it a strong personal identity.
He fought against the Jews to convince the Arabs of his leadership. It was only after the Jews in Medina had been defeated that the Arabs accepted Muhammad as the messenger.
(According to Abu'l-Fadl Bayhaqi, a medieval poet)

In the name of Allah
He is love
He gives
He forgives

1
Muhammad!
We have given you a wonderful pond of abundance.
Praise your God, therefore, and bring Him sacrifices.
Not you but your enemies shall die out.

18

Wanting More

In the name of Allah
He is love
He gives
He forgives

1

Your greed preoccupies you.
Until you are buried in your graves.
Be warned! You shall soon come to know.
Again, be warned!
And woe to you, when you behold everything with your own eyes.
Yes, look carefully.
On that day you shall be questioned about the squandered gifts.

19

Giving

In the name of Allah
He is love
He gives
He forgives

1

Have you seen the one who denies this faith?
He is the one who sends the orphan away.
He is the one who gives no bread to the poor.

Woe, therefore, to the believers.
Those who are careless with their prayer.
Or those who flaunt it.
And refuse to give.

20

The Unbelievers

How many prophets did Allah send? One hundred and twenty-four thousand!
He started with Adam and after him came many more, including 'Ad, Hud, Saleh, Ishaq, Shuayb, Ayoub, Idris, Ilias, Yunus, Nuh, Yaqub, Yusuf, Musa, Dawud, Sulayman, Zakariya, Yahya, Ibrahim, Isma'il, and Isa.
Muhammad is the last of the prophets. He does not cease to tell stories, for Allah said to him, 'Muhammad, tell stories and keep repeating them. Give the people food for thought.'

Muhammad thus recounts:
'Hawwaa, the wife of Adam, bore two sets of twins.
'In both instances a son and a daughter.
'Their sons were called Habil and Qabil.
'Habil loved the land. He gathered seeds, plucked fruit, and brought home vegetables.
'Qabil loved the animals. He jumped on the back of horses, took care of the cattle, and slaughtered them when necessary.

'Adam gave the twin sister of Qabil to Habil as his wife, and the twin sister of Habil to Qabil.
'Qabil wanted to marry his own twin sister, but she was not granted him, and hatred grew in him.

'When the wife of Habil bore him a son, Qabil was overcome with jealousy, and he killed Habil with a stone.
'He did not know what to do with his brother's body. Then he saw a crow with a walnut in its beak! The bird dug a pit in the ground and hid the walnut in it.
'Qabil followed the bird's example, dug a hole and hid his brother's body in it.'

Muhammad tells another story:
'Sheth was the son of the son of the son of Habil.
'He was the first genuine prophet, for now that there were so many people on earth, they needed someone to lead them. Sheth warned the people for two-hundred and seventy years, but he was unable to steer anyone onto the right path. The people were hungry, and they constantly had to fend off the animals. They had no time for God. Sheth himself, moreover, did not know precisely what God was.'
(According to Abu Ali Sina)

Muhammad also recounts:
'For a thousand years, no prophets came.
'There was still no question of a god, not even of an idol.
'The people were afraid of everything: of death, of sickness, of the night, and of the cold, but they did not know what to do about it. In the midst of this great ignorance, a man named Idris stood on an elevation and cried out, "People. I am a messenger of God."
'But humans were still unable to make themselves completely understood, because language was still in its infancy and inadequate. Thus, Idris did not succeed in imparting his message to his people. When he died, he did not have a single disciple.'

In the name of Allah
He is love

He gives
He forgives

1

Muhammad, say, 'Oh, you unbelievers.
'I do not serve what you serve.
'And you do not serve what I serve.
'And I shall not pray for what you pray for.
'And you shall not pray for what I pray for.
'Your faith is for you.
'My faith is for me.'

21

The Elephants

Muhammad was born in the year 570 CE.
At that very time, the king of neighbouring Habasha and his
warriors invaded the city of Mecca on elephants, intent on
destroying the Kaaba.
But God sent flocks of birds to crush the king's army.

In the name of Allah
He is love
He gives
He forgives

1

Have you not heard what God did with the army of elephants?
Did He not frustrate their plan?
Did He not send flocks of birds to stone them with small stones?
Thus, he made them as harmless as chewed straw.

22

The Dawn

In the name of Allah
He is love
He gives
He forgives

1
Muhammad!
Say, 'I take refuge in the Creator of the dawn.
'From the evil side of everything He created.
'And from the evil of the night when it approaches.
'And from the evil of witches who blow into knots.
'And from the evil of those who are jealous.'

23

Mankind

Human beings dwell on earth, like the jinn do.
The jinn are invisible, said Muhammad.
They have their own life and their own prophets.
The jinn can see and hear human beings, but human beings can-
not see or hear the jinn.
They are everywhere, and in large numbers.
During the day, they rest on the banks of the river, in aban-
doned houses, and in old bathhouses, but as soon as darkness
falls, they come out en masse. The jinn think that human beings
are blind. When they see a human being approach, they say to
one another, 'Make way, a blind person is approaching.'

The jinn enter into the lives of human beings in various forms.
A black dog suddenly appeared, instantly transformed into a
black crow, and flew off. Who or what was it?
A jinn.

In the name of Allah
He is love
He gives
He forgives

1
I take refuge in the Creator of humankind.
In the King of humankind.
In the God of humankind.
From the evil of those who whisper secretly and enticingly.
Those who murmur in people's innermost hearts.
Both the jinn and the human beings.

24

Submission

Everything in heaven and on earth praises Allah.
'Even the stones lying on the ground?' people asked.
'The stones on the ground, the mountains, the stars, the moon,
the trees, and the sun; all of them praise Allah.'
'And solid iron?' people asked.
'Iron too.'
'Why, then, don't we hear the iron?'
'Humans were created with limitations. They cannot perceive
everything,' said Muhammad.

In the name of Allah
He is love
He gives
He forgives

1

Muhammad!
Say, 'Allah is One.
'Allah is the Eternal.
'He was not fathered nor does He father.
'And there is no one equal to Him.'

25

The Star

Allah wanted to meet Muhammad personally.
He sent a winged white horse to collect him, and received him on the seventh level of heaven, where they spoke to each other behind closed doors.
When they were finished, the angel Jabra'il gave Muhammad a tour of paradise.
On one path, Muhammad encountered Musa. The prophet with the staff opened his arms with a smile, embraced Muhammad, and kissed him on the head.
A little further, he found Sulayman under an almond tree, surrounded by a cluster of animals, 'Good day, Muhammad!'
And in a garden of fragrant flowers, he met Isa. There, smiling young female companions placed a crown of colourful flowers on his head.

In the name of Allah
He is love
He gives
He forgives

1

By the star at the moment it falls,
Your fellow human being Muhammad has not gone astray and
has not been misled.
And he does not speak what he desires.
And it is nothing other than a clear revelation.
The angel Jabra'il taught it to him.

2

Allah is resolute. He possesses power.
He stood on the farthest horizon.
He came closer, and He descended.
To a distance of two bows or less.
He revealed to Muhammad what he had to reveal.
His heart did not lie about what he has seen.

3

Do you dispute what he has seen?
Truly! He saw Him beside the tree of Sidrah on the distant
horizon, next to the gardens of happiness, when the tree was
covered with the light that ought to cover it.
Muhammad did not look away nor did he stare.
Truly! He saw the tremendous signs of the Creator.

4

Have you seen the idols al-Lat and al-'Uzza, and the other, the
third, Manat?

Do the daughters belong to Allah and the sons to you? Then the apportioning is unjust.

These are just names you and your forebears have given them. Those who do not believe in life after death give female names to the angels. At the same time, they give their idols male names.

Their knowledge is based on speculation. They are ignorant.

5

Muhammad! Turn your face away from those who do not think about Us and are only concerned with this life.

Everything in heaven and on earth belongs to Him.

Those who show remorse for minor and major sins are forgiven by God.

He already knew you from the time He made you from earth, and you were still in the bellies of your mothers.

He knows who is God-fearing, and who is not. So do not simply count yourself among the devout.

6

No one shall carry the sins of another.

And humans get what they want.

And they quickly see the consequences of their deeds.

That they are recompensed completely for them.

That everything ultimately returns to Him.

That He is the One who causes smiles to appear and tears to flow.

That He is the One who causes death and gives life.

That He has created a male and a female part in the seeds that fall.

That He makes life after death possible.

That He created the stars and the firmament.

That He destroyed the ancient people of 'Ad and left nothing

of the people of Thamud, and, before that, wiped the entire people of Nuh from the face of the earth.
He caused the ancient cities to perish, and covered them with what ought to cover them.
Which gifts of Allah would you call into question?
Muhammad is one who warns, in line with others who warned before.

7
What must come is on its way.
Are you still surprised at this news?
Do you laugh? Do you not cry?
Kneel before Allah, and praise Him.

26

He Scowled

A blind beggar used to visit Muhammad regularly.
On one occasion, when he entered his house, Muhammad was in conversation with a group of wealthy merchants from Mecca. The beggar called out, 'Muhammad, do you have something more for me to learn today?'
Muhammad was not pleased with the way the beggar spoke to him in the presence of prominent men from Mecca. So he scowled and gestured to his servant to send him away.
The beggar left dejected.
Later Muhammad had a gnawing sense of guilt.

In the name of Allah
He is love
He gives
He forgives

1

He scowled and turned away.

Because the blind man came to visit.

Perhaps he wanted to better his life.

Or perhaps he was seeking the right path. And you could have helped him.

Why spend your time with those who think they do not need you, when you are not responsible for their deeds?

And someone who comes to you so eagerly, you send away.

2

Muhammad, that is not allowed!

This is a warning!

And those who are so inclined can learn a lesson from it.

It is written in the beloved scriptures.

Written by the exalted angels who quote Us.

3

Woe to those who are ungrateful.

We made them from a single drop and formed them in harmonious proportions.

We then level the way for them.

Thereafter We let them die and be buried.

After which We cause them to return.

No, humankind still does not listen.

Look at the food.

We cause water in abundance to fall.

We cause the earth to split open.

We cause grain to grow on it.

And vegetables and olive trees, palm trees, mature gardens, fruit and grass, for you and your animals.

4

But when the Cry sounds, humans shall run away from their brothers, their mothers, their fathers, their spouses, and their sons.

On that day, some faces will be filled with joy; they shall laugh. But other faces shall grow sombre. Those are the faces of the unbelievers.

27

The Night of the Qadr

In the name of Allah
He is love
He gives
He forgives

1

We sent down the Qur'an on the night of the Qadr.
And how do you know what the night of the Qadr is?
The night of the Qadr is better than a thousand months.
On that night, Jabra'il and the other angels will descend with Allah's approval to fulfil the dreams of humankind.
It is the night of joy and well-being, until the early morning.

28

The Sun

There are seven moving stars in the heavens, and there are thousands and thousands of fixed stars.

'And the moon and the sun?' the people asked Muhammad.
'The moon stops in twenty-eight houses. Each night it stays in a
different house.
'The sun has twelve houses. It changes house every month.'

In the name of Allah
He is love
He gives
He forgives

1

By the sun and when it shines.
And by the moon when it follows.
And by the day when it is illuminated.
And by the night when it covers all things.
And by the sky, and by He who built it so high.
And by the earth, and by He who made it so vast.
And by the soul, and by He who nourished it, and bestowed on it the bad and the good.
Happy those who keep their soul pure; those who humiliate them will themselves be humiliated.

2

The people of Thamud denied everything.
When the most wretched among them revolted, the messenger of God said to them, 'This is a she-camel of God. Set it free. And let it drink.'
But they declared him a liar and cut the she-camel's tendons.
Therefore, God destroyed all of them and levelled their land.

29

The Figs

In the name of Allah
He is love
He gives
He forgives

1

By figs and olives.
By Mount Sinai.
And by Mecca, the city of peace.
We have created humankind in the fairest form.
Then We let them grow old and weak.
Only those who believe and perform good deeds shall be rewarded for all eternity.
You, human! What makes you judge and deny everything?
Is God not the best to judge?

30

The Quraysh Tribe

The Quraysh tribe was one of the most important Arabic tribes in the realm.
The wise men from the tribe were former keyholders of the Kaaba.
Muhammad belonged to this tribe, and in addition to him many other great caliphs emerged from the same family.

In the name of Allah
He is love

He gives
He forgives

1

For the unity of the Quraysh tribe.
And for their protection during their summer and winter travels.
Let them praise the Owner of this house.
Who provides their bread in times of famine, and ensures their safety in times of danger.

31

Al-Qari'a

In the name of Allah
He is love
He gives
He forgives

1

Al-Qari'a.
What is al-Qari'a?
How can you know what al-Qari'a is?
It is the day on which people shall be like scattered butterflies.
And the mountains like carded wool.
Those whose scales tilt far on that day shall live a happy existence.
But for those whose scales are light, hell shall be their mother.
And how do you recognise al-Qari'a?
It is like a raging fire.

Rebirth

Allah swears that the day of resurrection shall take place.
He who created humans from a falling drop is capable of reunit-
ing detached bones after death.
Woe to those who do not listen.

In the name of Allah
He is love
He gives
He forgives

1

Yes! I swear by the day of the resurrection.
I swear by the soul that accuses itself.
Humans think We cannot heal their broken bones.
Of course We can. We can remake them to the tips of their
fingers.
They ask when the day of resurrection shall take place.
Say, 'When the eyes gaze in astonishment at the moon that
darkens, and when the sun merges with the moon.'
On that day humans shall say, 'Where can we flee?'
Say, 'Nowhere! There is no place of refuge.'
Everyone shall be informed about what they did, and what
they failed to do.
Humans are their own testimony.

2

Muhammad! Do not hurry! Do not move your tongue so fast
when you pronounce the words of a revelation.
We are responsible for giving you the words. Receive Our

words in peace and quiet first, and only then, when We are finished with the proclamation, may you reveal it. Further explanation is Ours.

On that day some faces shall be bright and cheerful, and some faces shall be dark and dejected.
As the final breath reaches the throat, the question arises, 'Who can heal him? Who shall ward it off?'
The human shall know that the time for the separation has come.
And one leg rubs against the other.
Then he is carried back to his Creator.

3
He gave nothing to the needy nor did he pray.
And he called the messenger a liar and ran away.
He went to his family with pride.
Woe to that person! Woe to that person, and again, woe to that person!
Do humans think they have been left to their own devices?
Were they not once a drop that fell?
Which then became a clot of blood which He perfected.
Which He made into man and woman?
Is such a Creator perhaps unable to call the dead back to life?
It is one of the greatest events.

33

The Gossiper

In the name of Allah
He is love

He gives
He forgives

1

Be warned, every slanderous gossiper.
Everyone who gathers more and more possessions and counts
them incessantly.
They think their possessions grant them eternity.

Let them be warned! They shall be thrown into al-Hutama.
What is al-Hutama?
It is God's fire,
which consumes hearts
and shall close them in
with lofty columns.

34

Those Sent Forth

*Muhammad suggests that two angels accompany every person,
one walking in front, the other walking behind, and that they
take note of everything this person does.*
*When you die and are buried, the two angels pay a visit and ask
all sorts of questions, including, 'Where did your money come
from? Is it clean money or did you raise it illegally? Or were you
perhaps one of the deniers?'*
Woe to the deniers, the liars, on the day of judgement.

In the name of Allah
He is love
He gives
He forgives

1

By those sent out, who follow one another.

By the mighty floods.

By the winds that scatter the clouds far and wide.

By those who distinguish between good and evil.

By the angels who bring the message of warning and justification.

The punishment assigned to you shall be imposed.

2

When the stars go out.

When the heavens tear asunder.

When the mountains shatter.

When the messengers gather together.

On which day has the day of judgement been set?

And what do you know about the day of judgement?

Woe to the deniers, the liars on that day!

3

Did We not already destroy a number of peoples?

Did We not bring forth other peoples in their place?

We shall do the same with the present sinners.

Woe to the deniers, the liars on that day.

4

Did We not make you from a trivial drop? Which We set down in a reliable place? For a fixed time.

Woe to the deniers, the liars on that day.

5

Did We not make the earth spacious, for both the living and the dead?

Did We not establish lofty mountains on the earth? And did We not give you delicious water to drink?

Woe to the deniers, the liars on that day.

6

Go, and face the punishment you have always denied.

Go to the smoke that has three branches, that does not cast a shadow, and that does not offer protection against the heat.

Look! The fire throws up sparks, some the size of castles, and some the size of yellow camels.

Woe to the deniers on that day.

It is a day on which they do not speak; they are given no opportunity to show their remorse.

Woe to the deniers, the liars, on that day.

7

It is the day of judgement on which We gather you together with the former peoples.

And if you have devised another plan, then use it against Me.

Woe to the deniers, the liars on that day.

But those who fear shall find themselves surrounded by glorious shade and springs, where fruit is at their fingertips.

Eat and drink. Good health!

But woe to the deniers on that day.

35

Qaf

Q is the twenty-first letter of the Arabic alphabet and the twenty-fourth letter of the Persian alphabet. It is pronounced 'Qaf'.
Some chapters of the Qur'an begin with one, two or three letters, such as 'Alif (A) Lam (L) Mim (M), or Ha' (H) Mim (M), or Ta' (T).
Some argue that the letters have no meaning, others claim that they are very important, and others still insist that they are even the Qur'an's sacred codes.
A medieval explanation from Abulfath states, 'Q, or Qaf, is one of the keys to the secret of the creation of the earth.'

In the name of Allah
He is love
He gives
He forgives

1
Qaf.
By the magnificent Qur'an.
Truly! They are surprised that a messenger has emerged from among them.
The unbelievers say, 'It cannot be. It must be a miracle. Shall we return to life after death, although we have become dust? Such a rebirth is improbable.'

2
We know well enough what the earth does with their bodies when they are buried. Everything is in the book *In the Beginning* that is in Our possession.

But did they not look up at the heavens above them, how We made it so immense, and how We adorned it? How complete it is, without a single fissure?

3

We spread out the earth and set the mountains firmly upon it. And we caused many sorts of plants and vegetation to grow on it.
We caused healthy and delicious water to fall from the heavens, with which We brought forth gardens and grain. And tall palm trees with bunch after bunch of delectable dates.
All for the sake of humankind.

In this way We bring dead soil back to life.
And in the same way We cause you to return after death.

4

Were We perhaps weak during Our first creation? No, that is beyond question. Why, then, do they doubt Our new creation, the return from death?

5

We created humans and We are closer to them than their own arteries. We know what their bodies whisper to them.
On the day of judgement, when the two angels receive them, the one who noted their good deeds and the one who noted their bad deeds, they shall be unable to say a word.
The intoxication of death shall reveal the truth; that is precisely what humans feared.

6

On that day the trumpet shall be blown; it is the announcement of the day of the great punishment.

And everyone shall come with a guide and a witness.

And it shall be said to them, 'You did not believe this. You did not see it coming. Now We are removing the veil from your eyes. This day you shall see everything more clearly.'

7

Allah shall say, 'I have not been unjust toward you. I warned you more than once. And today the decision shall not be revised by Me.

'I shall ask hell, "Are you now filled to the brim?"

'And hell shall answer, "Are there more to come?"'

8

But for the devout, the gardens of paradise shall be brought closer. That is what We have promised them.

They shall be told, 'Salaam. Welcome. Enter. This day is the beginning of eternity.'

They shall have all they desire there. And We have even more for them.

9

We created the heavens and the earth and all that lies between in six days, and We did not tire.

Muhammad! Be patient! Tolerate what they say to you! And pray to your Creator at dawn and dusk. And the night.

And wait until the caller hails you from a nearby place. They shall hear the cry. It is the beginning of life after death.

10

The earth shall break open, and the dead shall come out of their graves. We are accustomed to this, for it is We who give life and bring death. And to Us is the return.

11

We hear everything they say.

And you, Muhammad, it is not your task to force them.

Warn them with the Qur'an.

36

The City of Mecca

God spoke to Ibrahim, 'Go and build a house for Me.'

By that time, Ibrahim had a son, Isma'il by name. Ibrahim said, 'My son. Come help me. God has given me the task of building a house for Him.'

Together they took their spades and axes and climbed Mount Safa in search of the place where God once caused a source of water to spring up for Hajar, the mother of Isma'il, but they could not find it.

A crow landed on the ground and pretended to drink water, thereby indicating the location.

Ibrahim and his son Isma'il went to work and did not stop. They built four walls with the same length, breadth and height.

When they were tired, they rested in the shadow of one of the walls.

While Ibrahim was still napping, Isma'il went for a walk in the mountains. There he found a black stone, large and extraordinary.

'Father, come!' he shouted. 'There's a stone here you have never seen before.'

God had caused the black stone to fall from the heavens for His own house.

With great effort, Father and son rolled the stone to the house and placed it in the wall on the east side.

*With the stone in place, the house looked splendid. And they
called the house 'The Kaaba'.*

In the name of Allah
He is love
He gives
He forgives

1

Muhammad!
I swear by this city.
Mecca, in which you live.
By father Ibrahim, and by the one he begot, Isma'il.
It is true, We created humankind in misery.

Does Muhammad's enemy perhaps think that no one has
power over him?
He says, 'I have given away much property to combat Muham-
mad.'
Does he think that no one has seen him ?
Did We not make two eyes for him?
And a tongue and a pair of lips?
Did we not point to the two ways for him, toward good and
evil?
But he himself did not choose himself for an Aqaba.
Do you know what an Aqaba is?
It is the freeing of a slave.
It is giving food in time of famine.
It is caring for an orphan who is kin.

Those who do good deeds shall be rewarded.
But those who deny Our signs shall be shut in and surrounded
by blazing fire.

37

The Moon

The unbelievers constantly demanded new things of Muham-mad, and they taunted him because he could not work miracles. 'Muhammad! If you're really a prophet, tear the moon into two pieces,' they said.
Muhammad turned to the moon, raised his arms, spoke under his breath to Allah, and suddenly the moon was torn into two parts.
One part of the moon rested on top of Mount Quayqian and the other part on top of Mount Abu Qubays.
Although Muhammad worked this miracle for them they said, 'It is pure sorcery. He is a conjurer. A liar.'
And they urged children to throw stones at him.
Muhammad was saddened, climbed Mount Hira, sat down in the cave, and wept.

In the name of Allah
He is love
He gives
He forgives

1
The hour is approaching; and the moon is torn into two parts. But when they see a miracle, they turn away and say, 'It is sorcery.'

2
They continue to refuse. They explain everything as lies, and they follow their own desires. But everything comes to an end. Reports about the terrible end of the other peoples have

already reached them. An instructive wisdom, but it did not help.

Muhammad!

Turn away from them, and wait for the day on which the summoner invites them to the atrocious event.

3

Then they shall come out of their graves while they look at the ground like driven locusts.

They shall hurry toward the summoner and say to one another, 'It is going to be a harsh day.'

4

Before it was their turn, the people of Nuh declared their messenger a liar. They said he was mad, and they chased him away.

He called out to God, 'Help me! I am defeated. I have lost hope.'

We opened the gates of heaven and caused water to fall. And We caused the earth to split apart so that springs started to flow.

Then We asked Nuh to get into the ship that was made of planks and pins. And the ship started to move under Our eyes.

It was a reward for the one who had been rejected.

Let this be a sign from Us. But is anyone willing to learn from it?

See how My punishment was for them.

We have sent the Qur'an in plain language as an admonition. But is anyone willing to listen to it?

5

The people of 'Ad declared Our messenger to be a liar.

See how My warning was, and My punishment.

It was an ill-fated day for them. We sent a relentlessly cold west wind that plucked them up as if they were uprooted palm trees.

We have sent the Qur'an in plain language as an admonition.
But is there anyone willing to listen to it?

6
The people of Thamud likewise declared their cautioner to be a liar.
We send that peculiar she-camel to them. Thus, We put them to the test.
They chased the she-camel and cut its tendons.
See how My punishment was for them.
We sent a death cry over them, and they became like the dry twigs used to make a fence.
We have sent the Qur'an in plain language as an admonition.
But is there anyone willing to listen to it?

7
The people of Lut declared their messenger to be a liar.
We had warned them, but they revealed their lust to the guests of Lut.
See what our punishment was for them.
We made them blind. And in the early morning a rain of stone fell on their city. We said, 'Taste the punishment!'
We have sent the Qur'an in plain language as an admonition.
But is there anyone willing to listen to it?

8
We also sent Our cautioners to the pharaohs. But they declared all Our miracles to be lies.
We struck them as a mighty conqueror would.

9
Muhammad!
We made all things according to their measure.

Our command is once-only and it is implemented in the blink of an eye.
We destroyed their like. But is there anyone willing to learn from it?
Everything they have done has been noted, from the small to the great.
But those who fear shall soon walk beside the rivers in the gardens of delight. Next to the almighty King.

38

The Letter Sad

This sura recounts excerpts from the lives of the ancient prophets.

One day a beautiful bird landed in the window of the house of the prophet Dawud. He made his way softly toward the window, intent on grabbing the bird, but the creature spread its wings. Suddenly Dawud's gaze fell on a beautiful naked woman in the lake.
'Who is that woman?' Dawud asked, impressed by what he saw. She was the wife of his enemy Oria, and she had always been beyond Dawud's reach.
When Oria died in the war, Dawud married his wife, and they were granted a child, Sulayman.
Sulayman later became a prophet, and he spoke the language of the animals.

In the name of Allah
He is love
He gives
He forgives

1

By the Qur'an, the advice-giving.

Yes, the unbelievers have false pride, and they are stubborn.

They are surprised that a messenger emerged from among them.

And the unbelievers say, 'Does he want to make all those gods into one God? Why was the Qur'an revealed to Muhammad in our midst?'

Yes, they doubt My will.

No, they have not yet tasted My punishment.

2

Muhammad, do they possess the treasuries of your Creator? Your God, the Mighty, the Formidable.

Or are they perhaps the kings of heaven and earth and what lies between?

If that is so, then let them climb up with ladders.

There they shall be defeated and humiliated.

3

The peoples of Nuh, 'Ad, and Pharaoh were all seized by a death cry. These people can expect nothing different.

Muhammad! Patiently tolerate what they say, and remember the prophet Dawud.

We tamed the mountains, made them hum in unison with him in the evening and in the morning. The birds, too, that visited him and obeyed him.

We made his kingdom strong and gave him wisdom and the power to judge.

Have you heard the story of the men who climbed over his wall, and how Dawud was taken aback?

They said, 'Fear not. We have a conflict. One of us did the other an injustice. Judge, therefore, according to the truth.

This is my brother and he has ninety-nine sheep. I have only one sheep. He wants more, he says, "Give your only sheep to me." He thus acquires power over me.'

Dawud said, 'You are right. He does you an injustice when he asks for your sheep.'

Dawud sensed We were putting him to the test. So he got to his knees and asked for forgiveness.

We forgave him and he became one near to us.

Oh, Dawud! We appointed you as Our caliph on earth. Judge, therefore, according to the truth. And do not follow your desires. Otherwise you will be severely punished.

4

Muhammad! We did not make the heavens and the earth, and all that lies between, for nothing. The Qur'an we gave to you is an extraordinary book. Let the people reflect on the verses.

5

And we gave Sulayman to Dawud. An exceptional and obedient man.

One evening, a pair of fine racehorses of the most noble pedigree was paraded in front of him.

Sulayman said, 'Oh, I was so taken by the horses that I forgot my prayer and the sun disappeared beneath the veil.'

He started to stroke the horses on their legs and neck.

We put Sulayman to the test by throwing a dead horse on his throne. He showed remorse and said, 'God, forgive me. And give me a kingdom that no one will inherit after my death.'

We commanded the wind to obey Sulayman.

We also put devils that were good at diving at his disposal. Other devils We chained as bonded labourers. And We said, 'This is Our gift. Give without hesitation to whomever you choose, or keep it for yourself.'

6

Muhammad! Recall the prophet Ayoub and how he called to His Creator, 'I am exhausted! Satan has inflicted much misery on me.'

We said, 'Stamp your foot on the ground. Now you have clean water to dip and to drink.'

We returned his family and his people to him.

And We said, 'Ayoub! Do not break your promise. Take a couple of young branches and beat your wife.'

Ayoub was an exceptional man. He was patient.

7

And recall Ibrahim, Ishaq and Yaqub, men with power and insight. We gave them a good characteristic: 'Thinking about life after death.'

For Us they were the chosen. The good people.

Recall Isma'il, Ilias, and Zulkifl.

The doors to the gardens of delight are open wide for these extraordinary people. There they shall recline on benches and ask for fruit and wine. And shy female companions shall come and sit beside them.

It is precisely what was promised you. An endless favour to those who believe. A terrible end awaits those who do not obey. The hell of fire! A terrible place of rest. There they shall drink boiling water and impure fluids.

8

Muhammad!

Say to them, 'I am merely one who warns, and there is no God besides the supreme Allah. He is One!'

Say, 'It is great news, but you do not want to hear it. I know nothing about the assembly of the exalted ones in heaven, or about what they discuss. I am only a messenger.'

9

Muhammad, say, 'I do not ask for payment. And I did not invent the Qur'an myself. It is nothing more than a warning for humankind. You shall soon find out.'

39

ﻱ

The Elevations

Musa was one of the prophets. He went into the mountains to pray with seventy wise men of his people.
He took his leave of the group and climbed higher. There he met God and spoke with Him.
When he returned, he told his story to the wise men but they said, 'Unless we hear the voice of God with our own ears, we refuse to believe you.'
Musa took them with him, and they heard the voice of God.
They said, 'We also want to see Him with our own eyes.'
Then they were struck by lightning, and all of them died.

Muhammad is sad because the people refuse to listen to him. He opens this sura with a word of comfort for himself.

In the name of Allah
He is love
He gives
He forgives

1

'Alif Lam Mim Sad.
Muhammad! The most important thing is the book that was sent to you, so do not be sad and disappointed because you warn by it.

2

When We created humankind, We asked the angels to kneel before Adam. They all obeyed, with the exception of Satan.

'Why do you not do what I command?' said God.

'I am better than Adam. You made me from fire and made him from clay,' said Satan.

'You shall descend! From paradise! You are small and trivial.'

'Now that You have humiliated me, I shall stand in the path of humans and send them in the wrong direction. I shall come to them from their left side and from their right, from the front and from behind, and You shall no longer find them grateful.'

'Go! I despise you, be gone! I shall fill hell with you and your followers! And you, Adam, stay with your wife in paradise. Eat whatever you want, but do not come too close to this tree. Otherwise you too shall be among those who do not obey,' said God.

3

Satan started his work by causing Adam and Hawwaa to be ashamed of the parts of their body that were still uncovered. And he tried to tempt them, 'God forbade that tree to you, to prevent you both from becoming angels and living for eternity.' And he swore that his intentions were all good. He continued to talk until they tasted the fruit of the tree and their shame became visible. They tried to cover themselves with leaves.

God called out, 'Did I not forbid this tree to you? Did I not tell you that Satan is your enemy? Go! Descend. To the earth! You shall stay there until your time has come and you die. Thereafter you shall be restored to life and brought here.'

4

You, children of Adam! We devised clothing for you to hide your shame, and for elegance. But the best clothing is your piety.

Children of Adam! Satan is your enemy. Do not let him mislead you as he did Adam and Hawwaa. Satan and his followers are watching you, they see you, but you do not see them.

5
Muhammad, say to them, 'Just as He made you in the beginning, so He shall call you back.
'A time has been determined for every people. When their time has come, they will not be granted a single hour more nor an hour less.'
For those who have called Our signs lies, the gates of heaven shall not be opened, and they shall not enter paradise unless a camel passes through the eye of a needle.
Their bed and their clothing shall be of fire.
But those who believe shall enter paradise and shall dwell there forever.
And those going to paradise shall say to those going to hell, 'We found the promises of God to be true. Did you also find His promises to be true?'
And a high wall shall separate them. And men who know everyone by sight shall stand on the wall. They shall call out to those going to paradise, 'Welcome! Salaam to you! Enter the gardens of delight. There is no fear and nothing to be sad about.'
The inhabitants of hell shall beg the inhabitants of paradise, 'May we have some of your water?'
They shall answer, 'God forbade it to you.'

6
Your God is the One who created the heavens and the earth in six days. Then He established Himself on His throne and started to give shape to the rest of His kingdom.
He caused the day to cover the night and the night the day, as

they pursue each other in haste. And He made the sun, the moon, and the stars that listen to Him.

Praised be God. He is the Maker of the universe.

7

He is the One who sends forth the winds to herald His rains. They drive the clouds to lands that are dead.

And We then cause water to fall. And thereby We bring forth fruit. We do the same with the dead.

8

And so it continued until we sent Nuh to his people. And he said, 'My people! Praise God. There is none other than He.

'I fear the punishment of the great day for you.'

The chiefs of his people said, 'We see clearly that you have gone astray.'

He said, 'My people, I have not gone astray, rather, I am a messenger of God, the Maker of the world.'

They branded him a liar, but We saved him and those who were with him in the ark. We let the others drown.

9

We sent Hud to the people of 'Ad.

He said, 'Praise God. There is none other than He!'

The chiefs of his clan said, 'We see clearly that you are a fool and a liar!'

Hud said, 'My people! I have no foolishness in me, rather, I am a messenger of God, the Maker of the world. Do you not remember how He made you the successors of Nuh? He gave you more. Recall God's favours. Then perhaps you shall enjoy success.'

They said, 'Is this all you came here to tell us? That we should worship God and abandon the gods our fathers worshipped?

If you speak the truth then let us see your great divine punishment.'

Then we saved Hud and all those who were with him. And we uprooted the others, to the very last of them.

10

Then We sent Saleh to the people of Thamud.

He said, 'My people! Praise God. There is none other than He! A clear sign from God came for you. This she-camel is from God, a miracle for you. Let it feed undisturbed on God's earth, and do it no harm, otherwise you shall be mercilessly punished.

'And recall how He made you the successors of the people of 'Ad. He gave you a land where you built great strongholds and made homes in the rocks of the mountains. Remember God's blessings and do not commit crimes on earth.'

The chiefs of his clan said, 'We do not believe Saleh.' Then they held God's word in contempt. They chased the she-camel, killed it and said, 'Now it is up to you, Saleh! If you are a real prophet then let us feel something of the endless punishment you spoke about.'

They were seized by an earthquake, and in the morning they were found dead in their houses. Saleh left them behind and went on his way.

11

Then it was the turn of Lut.

He said, 'My people! You are doing what no one has done before you. You sleep lustily with men instead of women. You are a shameful people.'

His people's answer was, 'Send Lut and his followers out of the city. They are men who want to retain their purity.'

We saved Lut and his family, except his wife, who remained behind.

And We caused stones to rain over them. Look, therefore, at what happened to the sinners.

12

We sent Shuayb to the people of Madyan.

He said, 'My people! Praise God. There is none other than He. And there is a clear sign for you from God. Be honest, therefore, with the scales and the weights. Do not give people less than what is theirs, and do not spread destruction on earth.'

The chiefs of his clan said, 'Shuayb! We shall drive you and your followers from the city if you do not return to the faith of our fathers.'

Shuayb said, 'If we do that, we have lied to God. We trust Him. We shall leave everything to Him. He decides. He is all-knowing.'

The chiefs of the clan said, 'Those who follow Shuayb belong among the losers.'

They were seized by an earthquake, and in the morning they were found dead in their houses. It looked as if those who had branded Shuayb a liar had never lived there.

13

Then We sent Musa with his miracles to Pharaoh.

And he said, 'Pharaoh, I am a messenger of God. And I have brought a clear message for you. Let the Israelites go with me.'

Pharaoh said, 'Let me see your sign!'

Musa threw his staff to the ground, and it became a twisting snake.

The chiefs of Pharaoh's people said, 'He is a clever magician. He wants to drive the Egyptians out of their land.' Pharaoh said, 'What then do you suggest?'

They said, 'Keep him and his brother here for a while, and summon all the skilful magicians in the land.'

The magicians came and they said, 'Musa, would you like to

throw down your staff first, or would you have us begin?'

Musa said, 'You first!'

They threw ropes to the ground, and they started to bewitch the eyes of the people so that those present found themselves in an extraordinary state of fear and amazement.

And We said to Musa, 'Now it's your turn.'

Musa threw down his staff, which changed into a huge snake and devoured what the others had conjured up.

Their fraudulence thus failed, and they were counted among the losers. They got to their knees in front of Musa and said, 'We believe in your God!'

Pharaoh said, 'How can you follow him without my permission? Did you perhaps conspire together to drive the inhabitants from this city? I shall punish you without mercy. I shall have your right hand and left foot cut off and vice versa. Then I shall have you all hung.'

The chiefs of Pharaoh's people now said, 'Would you leave Musa and his people unpunished so that they can spread destruction in this land and ignore you and your gods?'

Pharaoh answered, 'We shall kill their sons and take their women as slaves.'

Musa said to his people, 'Ask God for help and be patient, for the land belongs to God. And He shall give it to whomever He wants.'

They said, 'Musa, we have always lived in misery before you came, and also after you came.'

Musa said, 'Perhaps God shall destroy your enemy and choose you to succeed them. He shall show you what you must do.'

14

We punished Pharaoh's people with famine and drought, and blighted their fields so that they might understand the warning. But when they tasted prosperity again, they said that it was on their own account. When misery struck them anew, they put the blame on Musa and his people.

They said to Musa, 'Whatever miracles you work, we shall not follow you.'

We sent a storm to them, and locusts and lice, and frogs, and even death itself. But they still refused to obey.

Only when they were no longer able to bear the burden did they say, 'Musa! Ask your God to put an end to the punishment. If you do, we shall follow you, and we shall let the Israelites go with you.'

When We put an end to their punishments, they followed Musa for a short time, but as soon as the misery was forgotten, they resisted him anew. We took revenge, and we drowned them to the last man in the sea.

And We gave the humiliated people the east and the west of the land with our blessing. We destroyed Pharaoh and his people with all their artefacts, palaces, and glory. We let the Israelites pass through the sea to the safety of the shores. There they encountered a people who served idols.

15

They called out, 'Musa! We want a god like their gods.'

Musa said, 'What are you talking about? You are an ignorant people. God has just redeemed you from Pharaoh who killed your sons, who used your daughters as slaves.'

Musa then asked to meet Us. We promised an encounter of thirty nights, and We added a further ten nights.

And when Musa came at the agreed time he said, 'God, show Yourself! So that I can look at You.'

'Musa, you shall not see Me, but if your truly desire to see me, look toward that mountain. If you stay where you are, you shall see Me.'

Musa looked toward the mountain, and when God decided

to reveal Himself, the rocks fell to pieces. And Musa fell to the ground unconscious. When he came back to his senses he said, 'I repent. You are magnificent.'

16

In the absence of Musa, his people used their gold and jewels to make a lowing calf.

Then Musa returned with the commandments given him by God. He threw the stone tablets to the ground, and they were smashed to pieces. He grabbed his brother Harun by his head and pulled him close.

Harun pleaded, 'Musa, son of my mother. These people have ruined and almost killed me. Do not make our enemies happy. Do not hand me over to them!'

When Musa calmed down, he collected the fragments of the broken tablets. They were a guide for those who sought the right path.

And Musa selected seventy men from among his people who truly wanted to see Us. But they were seized by an earthquake.

17

Among the people of Musa was a group of righteous men. We divided them into twelve tribes. When they asked Musa for water, We said to Musa, 'Strike the rock with your staff.' He did what We asked, and twelve springs gushed forth. Each tribe knew their designated spring.

And We caused the cloud to cast a shadow over them, and We sent them manna and roasted quails.

They did not wrong Us, they wronged themselves.

And when the people had forgotten the warning, We saved the righteous and severely punished the rest.

Because they held what had been forbidden in contempt, We turned them into apes with a tail, chased them away, and humiliated them.

This continued until We caused Mount Tur to rise above their heads like a great cloud, and they thought it was going fall on them. And we said that they should pay heed to the book they had received from us. Perhaps they would thus find the right path.

18

Muhammad! Tell them the story of the man to whom We gave Our signs but who ran away. He followed Satan and went astray. If We had wanted to, We could have elevated him, but he preferred the earthly life. You can compare him to a dog that hangs its tail when you assail it, and does the same when you leave it alone.

That is the story of those who deny Our signs.

So tell them this story, perhaps it will make them think.

Muhammad, say, 'I have no control over what happens, and have no personal advantage or disadvantage, except what God plans for me. If I had known the secrets, I would have achieved much good, and I would not have suffered misery. I am no more than a messenger of Allah, and I merely do what He asks of me.'

He is the One who created Adam from clay, and his wife Hawwaa from him so that he would find rest at her side. When he slept with Hawwaa she sensed a slight burden. She made nothing of it, but when the burden grew heavy, she turned to God and asked if she and Adam might be granted a child. God gave them a child. Later, their descendants devised someone who was an equal to God.

19

My King is Allah, who sent this book. The idols you praise in His stead are not capable of helping you or even themselves.

And if you call on them for help, they do not hear you. They look at you, but they do not see you. So turn your back on the ignorant. And if Satan tempts you, seek refuge in God. He is all-hearing. All-knowing.

Muhammad, say to them, 'I only follow what has been revealed to me by God.'

Believers! Be silent and listen carefully when the Qur'an is recited. Perhaps He shall grant you His protection.

Think of God weeping and with fear in your heart, but calmly in the early morning and in the night.

40

The Jinn

The following sura tells the story of a group of jinn who set out in the middle of the night. At a given moment they hear a man with a beautiful voice reciting a text.
They stand beneath his window and listen to him in silence. They find the words exceptional and good, and they are genuinely impressed by the way the man recites them.

In the name of Allah
He is love
He gives
He forgives

1

Muhammad, say, 'It has been revealed to me that a group of jinn listened and said to one another, "We have heard wondrous words that lead to the right path, and we believe in them. We shall set no one next to our Creator.

"He has no wife and no son.
"He is Majesty and He is great.'"

2

The fools among us speak nonsense about God.

We think that neither jinn nor people should spread lies about Allah.

There are men among the people who seek refuge among the male jinn in order to commit more sins.

And they think, like others, that no one shall be reawakened after death.

3

In the past we took to the skies and sought ways to spy on the highly placed, but everywhere we encountered sturdy guards and burning stones.

We would sit down somewhere to listen in on the conversations secretly, but those who do such a thing are pelted with smouldering stones.

4

Since we heard the Qur'an, we believe.

And those who believe in their Creator no longer need to fear shame and slander.

Some of us have handed ourselves over to God, but some have lost their way.

5

Every mosque belongs to Allah. Pray, therefore, to no one other than Him.

When Muhammad turned to Allah to call upon Him, they almost attacked him.

Muhammad, say, 'I invoke only my Creator. He is One.'

Say, 'Of myself I have no power to bring you harm nor do I have power to manoeuvre you to the right path.'

Say, 'There is no one who can protect me from God, and there is no refuge besides Him.'

Say, 'I do not know if the foretold punishment is near or if God has postponed it.'

It is He who knows the secrets, who reveals His secrets to no one, except to the messenger He chooses for the purpose. And He makes a guard walk before him and a guard walk behind him. He encompasses all things. He knows the measure of all things.

41

Ya' Sin

The Qur'an appears to be a chaotic book. There is no logical sequence in the recitations, and the segments seem to have been joined together at random. As a result, it is sometimes difficult to understand what is being said.

However, a linguist by the name of al-Jahiz, from the period in which Islam was in its ascendancy, writes, 'I see no chaos in his suras. I compare his prose to bunches of dates hanging high in the trees. Muhammad recounts something, but interrupts his story midway and moves on to something else, just like a bunch of dates branches off but stays complete nonetheless, and forms a unity. Consider the chapter entitled "The Table".

He starts with livestock, then moves on to the trinity, then speaks about wine, then talks about gambling, then turns his attention to Maryam, then settles scores with the Jews, then enters paradise and makes his way into hell, only to return to the table, to Isa. Each story is a sprig of a bunch.'

Another example of this manner of recounting is sura 'Ya' Sin'.

In the name of Allah
He is love
He gives
He forgives

1
Ya' Sin.
By the Qur'an, by Wisdom.
Muhammad! You are a prophet. This is without doubt.
You follow the right path.
The Qur'an is a revelation from the beloved Forgiver.
That you may warn an ignorant people who have never before received a warning.
Most of them will be punished, for they do not believe.
We have placed heavy chains around their necks and have manacled their hands while they tried to look downward.
We have set a wall in front of them and a wall behind them, a veil over their eyes so that they can see nothing.
It does not matter to them whether you warn them or not. They shall never believe.
You can only warn those who follow the Qur'an and fear Allah in their heart.

2
We bring the dead back to life again, and We describe everything they did in life, even their footprints. Everything is written down in the book *In the Beginning*.

3
Have they not seen how many peoples We destroyed before them? That they are all brought back to Us?

Time and again We call the dead earth back to life, and We bring forth grain from it so that they may eat. That is a sign for them.

And We made date gardens and vineyards, and caused springs to gush forth. So that they might eat fruit and eat what they cultivated with their own hands. Will they not then be grateful?

4

Spotless is He who created everything in pairs. Everything that comes from the earth, man and woman, and what we do not yet know.

The night is also a sign. Look! We draw aside the day, and everything is shrouded in darkness.

And the sun goes to its resting place. It is the decree of the Almighty.

And We have determined a fixed place for the moon, until it disappears and returns to life again, like a dead date stalk that comes back to life.

It is not fitting for the sun to chase after the moon. It is also not fitting for the night to overtake the day. They each move in their own orbit across the vault of heaven.

5

It might also be a sign for them that We caused humankind to sail in a fully laden ship.

That We also created something in which they can sail.

That We, should We wish, could let them drown. No one shall be saved unless We do so out of generosity.

6

When they are told, 'Give some of what Allah has given you!'
they answer, 'Why should we give? Allah can do it Himself.'
Or they say, 'Muhammad! If you are genuine, tell us when the
day of judgement is due.'
A deadly cry shall catch them unawares while they are in the
middle of an argument. They shall not have time to make a
will or to briefly return to their families.
On the day of judgement the trumpet shall sound. They shall
stand up from their graves and walk toward their Creator,
muttering all the while, 'Woe to us. Who has awakened us?'

7

On that day, those who find themselves in paradise shall be
very happy. They shall sit with their spouses on benches in the
shade.
They shall have fruit there and be given whatever they desire.
Salaam! This is Allah's greeting of welcome to them.
A voice shall shout, 'You guilty ones! Stand to one side!'
Did I not warn you, children of Adam, that you should not
follow Satan? That he is an enemy? That you should praise Me?
This is the hell you were warned about. Go in and do penance
for what you have done.

8

Today We seal their mouth, but their hands shall tell us every-
thing, and their feet shall testify to what they have done.
If We wanted to, We could make them blind. They would hurry
to the path, but where would they go if they could not see?
And if We wanted to, We could make them powerless on the
spot, unable to move forward or backward.
Even the bodies We granted a long life, We shall cause to decay.
Will they not, then, consider?

9

We did not teach Muhammad the art of poetry nor does it
befit him. What he relates is a warning from a clearly articu-
lated Qur'an.

10

Do people not see that We also made the herd animals with
Our powerful hands?
We tamed them on their behalf so that some can be used to
ride and others used for food.
Will they not, then, be grateful?
They serve gods other than Allah in the hope that they shall
be helped. But such gods are a help to no one, even an army
of them.
Thus, Muhammad! Do not let them sadden you with their
words. We know what they hide, and what they do in public.

11

Does humankind not consider the fact that We created them
from a drop? See how they rebel, and how they behave like
Our enemy, how they forget how they were made.
They ask, 'Who can call our perished bones back to life?'
Muhammad, say to them, 'He who first made them shall call
them back to life. He knows everything of all creation.
'He made fire from a green tree so that you can make use of it.
'Is He who created the heavens and the earth not capable of
creating their like? Of course He is. He is an all-knowing Crea-
tor.
'If he desires something, all He has to say is, "Be!" And it is.
'Glory to Him from whom all things come and to whom all
things return.'

42

The Distinction

It would be an insult to Muhammad to say that the prose of the Qur'an is not from him but from Allah.
Consider the suras about the female companions in paradise, for example.
Muhammad says, 'And those who feared shall be happy on that day. They shall find themselves in gardens with grapevines and girls with young breasts, all of the same age. And cups filled to the brim.'
Compare Muhammad's prose here with the lyrical words of Sulayman in the Old Testament:
'My love.
'See, how beautiful you are.
'Your two breasts are like two fawns, twins of a gazelle, which feeds among the lilies.'

Both are instances of human speech.
(According to Ali Dashti, an admirer of Muhammad who lived in the third century AH)

In the name of Allah
He is love
He gives
He forgives

1
Blessed is He who sent down the Qur'an to His servant Muhammad so that he might warn the world.
He to whom the kingdom of heaven and the earth belong.

He who has no son and no wife.

He who made all things and gave each their precise measure.

2

But people sought refuge in other gods instead of Allah. Idols that can make nothing; that are themselves made; that have no power over themselves, and no power to kill, to create life, or to return to life.

The unbelievers say, 'The Qur'an is a lie. Muhammad devised it himself and was helped by other people.'

But these are lies.

They say, 'He had all sorts of ancient myths written down, and they are recited to him day and night.'

Muhammad, say to them, 'Allah sent it. He who knows the secrets of heaven and earth. He is kind and forgiving.'

The unbelievers say, 'What kind of a prophet is this man? He eats, and he walks around the market. Why was no angel sent with him so that they might warn us together?

'And why was he not sent with a wealth of gold, and why does he not have a garden to eat of its fruit?'

And those who refuse to believe, say, 'You follow a man who is bewitched.'

Muhammad, do not listen to them. They are lost, and they shall not find the path.

3

Blessed is He who, should He desire, shall give you something better. The gardens of happiness under which rivers flow.

For those who call Our suras lies, We have a blazing fire at the ready.

When they see this blazing fire from afar, they also hear its growls and groans. And when they are thrown into the fire in a sinister place, chained hand and foot, they begin to beg and weep.

Do not weep once today, but weep many times over.

4

Muhammad, say to them, 'What is better for you, this, or the gardens of happiness where you shall dwell for eternity, and where you shall be given what you want? This is the promise of Allah.'

Muhammad! All the prophets we sent before you ate and walked around the market just like you do.

Muhammad. Your Creator sees all things.

5

Those who do not look forward to meeting Us, say, 'Why do the angels not descend. Why can we not see our Creator?'

Such people are too proud, and they have gone too far with their questions.

The day they see the angels is not a good day for them. The angels shall say, 'Proud criminals! We shall turn you and your ugly deeds to dust, and scatter it.'

But those who are destined for paradise shall have a splendid place where tranquillity holds sway.

On that day, heaven shall be torn asunder with clouds and the angels shall descend.

On that day, Allah is the true King of the universe.

6

The unbelievers ask why the Qur'an was not sent down all at once. Why piece by piece?

Muhammad, say to them, 'It is what it is. We did it like this to gratify your heart, and to make it bearable for you.'

7

We gave Musa the book, and We appointed his brother Harun as his adviser.

Then We said, 'Go to the people that deny Our signs.'

Thereafter We destroyed that people.

And We let the people of Nuh drown after they branded the prophets as liars.

We also destroyed 'Ad, Thamud, Al Ras and many other peoples.

In spite of this, the people walk past the city on which an evil rain of fire once fell.

Do they not see? No, they do not expect to be brought back to Us.

8

Muhammad! When they meet you, they laugh at you. They call out, 'Is this the man Allah sent as a messenger?'

Later, when they face punishment, they shall know who has gone astray.

Muhammad! You cannot champion those who see their own lust as their god.

Or do you think that most of them listen or reason?

They are like animals. They have gone astray.

9

If He had desired it, He would have made the sun, the moon, and the stars incapable of moving.

After we appointed the sun as a reference point, We then draw it slowly back to Us.

It is Allah who made the night like a blanket for you, and sleep as rest, and the day for your movement.

It is He who sends the wind as herald of the rain.

10

We caused clean water to fall from heaven, to bring a dead region to life, and to allow humans and animals to drink from it in large numbers.

We have said this often, perhaps people will learn from it, but most are ungrateful.

If We had wanted to, We could have sent a prophet for every city.

Muhammad! Do not listen to the unbelievers, but strive against them with all your might.

11

Allah caused two seas to flow together. The one fresh and delightful, the other salty and bitter. And He created a separation between them.

It is He who created humankind from water, and gave them family ties and friends.

Muhammad! Your Creator knows all things.

We sent only you as messenger and cautioner.

Say to them, 'I do not ask you for payment. If someone takes the path toward Allah, that is enough for me.'

12

Muhammad! Seek support from Allah, He who does not die. And praise Him! He is aware of the sins of humankind.

It is He who made the heavens and the earth and all that exists between in six days. Thereafter, He sat down on His throne.

He forgives.

13

If you say to the unbelievers, 'Pray to the forgiving God.' They shall say, 'Who is this forgiving one?'

Blessed is He who made the high towers in heaven, and placed the lantern and a light-giving moon in them.

14

The servants of Allah are those who walk humbly upon the earth.

And if the ignorant speak to them they shall say in humility, 'Hail'. And it is they who spend the night on their knees, and rise again for Allah.

Those who say, 'Allah, avert the punishment of hell from us. It is a heavy punishment, and it is a bad place.'

Those who do not exaggerate when they give something away, but are also not miserly.

Those who praise no other God than Allah and do not kill a soul Allah has declared inviolable unless the law determines otherwise.

And those who do not commit adultery.

15

Allah is forgiving and loving.

Those who show remorse and do good deeds, who exhibit genuine repentance to God.

And those who say, 'God, let our wives and children be like light to our eyes, and make us examples for the believers.' They shall find themselves in paradise for the patience they have shown. They shall be welcomed there with 'Salaam', and they shall dwell there for eternity. What a beautiful place it is.

43

The Maker

Muhammad had sleepless nights and could not bear to watch the people around him worship idols of stone and wood in the Kaaba.
He saw it as his vocation to get rid of these idols.

The first idol was made by Jamshid, the first Persian king.
Jamshid was handsome and bore a name that means, 'the man with the beauty of the sun'.
Jamshid ruled over the east and the far west of the earth.
When he had ruled for eight hundred years, he thought, I am so great and so powerful that no one can defeat me. I can and do whatever I want. I seem to be god on earth.
He gave the command to have seven statues of himself made, one of gold, one of iron, one of copper, one of brass, one of yellow stone, one of marble, and one of red stone.
He sent these statues to the seven corners of his kingdom, intent on his people's continuing faithful service.
This tradition was later adopted by other cultures.

The statue he had ordered to be made of red stone found its way to the people of the prophet Nuh.
(From The Life of the Ancient Persian Kings*)*

In the name of Allah
He is love
He gives
He forgives

1

Praise be Allah, the maker of the heavens and the earth, who made the angels into messengers; angels with two wings, or three, or four. He adds whatever He desires to creation. He can do all things.

2

It is Allah who sends the winds to set the clouds in motion. Then they are taken to a dead place on earth to call the ground back to life.
The resurrection shall take place in the same way.
Those who desire to worship should turn to Allah. Fine words ascend to Him and He praises good deeds.
But those who devise wicked plans are severely punished and their plans fail.
Allah made you from earth, first from a drop, and then He made you male and female.
No single woman falls pregnant without Him knowing it. And no one's life is extended or shortened without it being noted in the book *In the Beginning*.

3

The two seas are not alike; one is delightfully fresh to drink from and the other is salty and bitter, and yet you eat fresh food from both, and extract jewels to wear. You see ships that cleave through the sea. This way you go looking for your share of His bounty. Perhaps you shall thus be grateful.
He hides the night during the day and the day during the night. He has tamed the sun and the moon and has determined when they appear.
Such is Allah and the kingdom is His.
Others you invoke besides Him have nothing; they do not even have power over a date skin.

When you invoke them, they do not hear you, and if they hear you, they cannot answer.

4

Oh humans! You have nothing; you need God. But God needs no one. He is wealthy.

Should He wish, He could remove everyone and make a new creation. That would not be difficult for Him.

Those who cleanse themselves do so for their own benefit.

The blind person is not equal to the seeing person; nor is the light to the dark nor the cool of the shade to the heat; those who live are not equal to the dead.

God makes whomever He wills hear, but you, Muhammad, you cannot make those who lie in their graves hear.

You are only a cautioner. We sent you as a messenger of good tidings. No people have ever been without a messenger.

If they brand you a liar, do not forget that others did the same with the ancient prophets.

Then I took hold of the unbelievers, and see what I did to them.

5

Have you not seen how I cause water to fall from the sky and thereby bring forth fruit in different sorts and colours? The mountains, too, have different layers: white and red, black and raven-black.

Likewise, the people and the birds, walking and winged, consist of different sorts and colours.

Allah is magnificent.

6

Without a doubt, those who read the Qur'an and pray, and give of what We have given them in secret and in the open, can look forward to a reward from Allah. He shall reward them

fully; and still more. He rewards and forgives. They shall find themselves in the gardens of happiness, where they shall wear bracelets of gold and pearls and clothing of silk.
They shall say, 'Praised be Allah, who has taken away sorrow from us, and given us a place for eternity, where we shall never weary.'
But those who do not believe have a place in hell, where death shall not take them and pain shall not cease.
This is how We punish the ungrateful.

7
Muhammad! Say, 'Have you looked closely at your idols? Show me something they have made. Did they perhaps participate in the creation of heaven? Did He ever give them a book? No.'
Do the people not see how it ended for those who lived before them and were stronger than they are?
There is nothing in the heavens and on earth that can subdue Allah.
He is all-powerful. He is all-knowing.
If Allah were to punish humankind for their deeds, He would not leave a single person on earth; but He gives them time until their fixed term. When their time has come, Allah knows what He must do with them.

44

Maryam

Maryam was standing naked in the river when a handsome man suddenly appeared.
Maryam was frightened and ran to the bushes to hide herself.
'Don't be afraid, Maryam,' the man called out. 'I am the angel

Jabra'il. I have come to give you a child.'
The angel persuaded Maryam, seduced her behind the palm trees, and made her pregnant.

Maryam bore a son and his name was Isa.
Isa was later chosen as a prophet by God.
He was crucified and died but came back to life.
He was the only prophet who returned to God alive.

Before his death, Isa confided in his apostles, 'I have a joyous message. After me, a prophet shall arise from an Arab clan, and his name shall be Ahmad (Muhammad). But people shall brand him a liar. They shall hurt him, and he shall suffer much sadness, but he shall fulfil his mission. And he is the last of the prophets. After him there shall be no more messengers.'
'What is his sign?' the apostles asked Isa.
'He bears a sign of the moon on his left shoulder.'
(From The Lives of the Prophets, *as recounted by Abu Ishaq Ibrahim, a medieval poet)*

In the name of Allah
He is love
He gives
He forgives

1
Kaf Ha' Ya' 'Ayn Sad.
This is the story of your God, concerning His subject Zakariya.
Zakariya spoke in secret with his God, 'God, my bones are brittle and my hair is grey, and I have never made demands in my prayers!
My wife is without child, and I want descendants when I die.
God! Grant me a successor, to be heir to my house and to that

of Yaqub. And make him a good person.'

God said, 'You, Zakariya! We announce a son to you. His name is Yahya. And no one has ever borne this name before.'

Zakariya answered, 'How can I have a son when my wife is infertile, and I have grown old and weak?'

God said, 'So shall it be. For Me it is easy. I also made you out of nothing.'

He said, 'God, give me then a sign.'

God said, 'As your sign, you shall be unable to speak for three nights.'

Zakariya hurried to his people and signed to them, 'Praise God! In the morning! And at night!'

2

God said, 'You, Yahya! Hold on firmly to the divine book! Declare the name of Maryam, and recount how she left her family and went east, and how she screened her face with a veil.'

Salaam be with Yahya on the day he was born, on the day he dies, and on the day he comes back to life.

3

We sent Jabra'il to Maryam in the form of an engaging man.

Maryam said, 'I seek my refuge in God.'

He said, 'I am Jabra'il the messenger of your God, and I have come to give you a son.'

Maryam said, 'How can I have a son, since I have never been touched by a man? I am not an immoral woman.'

He said, 'It is what it is. This is what God said, "For Me it is easy. We shall make it a miracle for the people. A gift from Us, and it has already been decided."'

4

Maryam withdrew with Jabra'il to a remote place, and she fell pregnant.

The pain of delivery drew her to the trunk of a palm tree and she said, 'Oh, would that I were dead, would that I were forgotten.'
Jabra'il called out, 'Do not be sad. Your Creator has caused a stream to flow beneath you. Shake the trunk of the tree; fresh dates shall fall upon you.
'Eat, drink, be happy, and if you meet someone, say, "I vowed to God that I would not speak to anyone today."'

5
Maryam took her child and went to her people.
They said, 'Oh, Maryam, did you do something inappropriate? You, sister of Harun, your father was not a bad man nor was your mother an unchaste woman.'
Maryam pointed in silence to her child.
They said, 'How can we speak with a child in the cradle?'
The child said, 'I am a servant of Allah. He gave me the book, and He made me a prophet.
'And He has given me His blessing for all time.
'Salaam be with me on the day I was born, on the day I die, and on the day I come back to life.'

6
Muhammad! That was the story of Isa, the son of Maryam. Without doubt, these are important words.
It is not befitting for Allah to have a son. He is above such things.
If He desires something, all He has to say is, 'Be!' and it is.

7
Muhammad, quote Ibrahim, an honest person and a prophet.
Ibrahim said to his father, 'Father! Why do you pray to something that cannot hear you, cannot see, and has nothing to offer you?

'Father, something has been revealed to me that has not been revealed to you. Follow me, therefore! I shall guide you along the right path.

'Father, do not serve Satan, for Satan rebelled against God. I fear that God shall punish you severely.'

The father of Ibrahim said, 'You, Ibrahim! Are you renouncing our gods? If you do not stop, I shall stone you. Leave me, and stay out of my sight for a long time!'

Ibrahim said, 'Salaam be with you. I shall ask my God to forgive you. He is kind to me. And I shall distance myself from you and from what you worship besides God.'

When Ibrahim separated himself from his father and from their gods, We gave him Ishaq and Yaqub. And We made them both prophets.

8

Muhammad, also mention Musa. He was a prophet and a virtuous man.

We called him to the right side of the mountain, and We allowed him to come close to talk to him. And of Our generosity, We gave him his brother Harun as a prophet.

And mention Isma'il. He was also a messenger, and he fulfilled his promises.

Mention Idris. He was sincere as a person and as a prophet, and We led him to a high place.

9

All these were prophets from the progeny of Adam, descendants of those who were in the ship with Nuh and heirs of Ibrahim and Isma'il.

When the signs of God were recited to them, they fell to their knees respectfully and they wept. Others came after them who neglected prayer and followed their desires. Depravation awaits them unless they repent and perform good deeds.

They shall enter the gardens of happiness. The place Allah has promised to his servants.

Allah fulfils his promises. They shall hear no nonsense in the gardens, only Salaam. And their food shall be ready for them, morning and evening.

10

Praised be Allah.

All things belong to Him; whatever is in front of us, and whatever is behind us, and everything in between. And He forgets nothing.

He is the Creator of the earth, the heavens, and of everything between the two.

Serve Him!

And be patient in His service.

11

And the people ask, 'Do we come back to life after we have died?'

Do the people remember that We created them when they were still nothing?

Muhammad! By your Creator! We shall bring them and the demons together. Then We shall bring them to hell on their knees.

12

Muhammad! Do not hurry on their behalf. We are counting their days.

Until the day We bring the believers to paradise as cherished guests; and the guilty to hell in a thirsty herd.

No one shall defend them if they have not received a promise from God on account of their faith.

13

They say that God has a son. It is an astonishing rumour. The heavens shall be torn asunder, the earth shall crack, and the mountains shall crumple because they invent a son for God.
It is far from Him to have a son.
Everything on earth and in the heavens serves Him.
He has counted it all, and He knows the outcome.
And on the day of judgement, they shall all pass before Him one by one.
Muhammad! We have recounted the Qur'an with simplicity in your own language so that you can bring the good news to those who believe and warn sinners.
We have destroyed many peoples. Do you still see a remnant of them? Do you still hear a footstep?

45

Taha

When Musa rebelled against Pharaoh and God destroyed the Egyptian king, Zahhak, a Persian king, was given the opportunity to conquer the world. He was a tyrant. He killed his father to claim his throne. His kingdom lasted three thousand years.
He committed crimes against his own people and put pressure on other peoples.
One night while he was sitting on his throne, two black snakes slithered from his shoulders.
Zahhak was taken aback, and he cut the snakes from his shoulders, but they grew back in the same place.
Under Zahhak, the Persians lived in fear, and they longed for deliverance.
All at once, one of the men of this people got to his feet and pro-

claimed, 'I am Zarathustra, a messenger of Ahura Mazda.'
(According to the account of Abolghasem Ferdosi, a thousand
years ago)

But the text of the sura is about Muhammad. Each time he is
sad and impatient, Allah says, 'Muhammad, do not hurry! Have
patience! Pray to Me, praise Me, and you shall be happy.'

In the name of Allah
He is love
He gives
He forgives

1

We did not reveal the Qur'an to you to make you feel miserable. It is merely a warning for those who fear.
A revelation, from He who made the lofty heavens and the earth.
The Forgiver who took His seat on the throne of the universe.
Everything is from Him; all things on earth and in the heavens, whatever lies in between, and whatever is under the ground.
And He knows what is secret, and what is hidden.
There is no god but Allah. And He has beautiful names.

2

Muhammad! Let us tell you the rest of Musa's story.
He saw fire in the mountain and said to his people, 'Stay here! I see fire. I shall go and collect some of it; perhaps I shall find a sign there.'
When he came close to the fire, he heard a voice, 'Musa! It is I. Your God. Take off your shoes. You are in the sacred valley of Tuwa. And I have chosen you. Listen, therefore, to what is revealed to you. I am Allah. And there is no other God besides

Me. Pray to Me to remember Me. Musa, what do you have in your right hand?'

'It is the staff on which I lean, and which I use to beat down leaves for my sheep.'

'Musa! Throw it to the ground,' said God.

Musa threw down his staff, and it turned into a coiling snake.

'Pick it up and do not be afraid,' said God. 'We shall restore it to its old form. Slip your hand into your collar. It shall become white without illness. This is one of Our great wonders. Go to Pharaoh; he is resisting Me.'

Musa said, 'My creator, expand my chest, and make my work easier; untie the knot in my tongue that they may better understand me. And make me strong with my brother Harun.'

God said, 'Musa! We grant you your wishes. We have also helped you before. When we revealed to your mother, "put him in a basket and throw it in the river. The current shall wash it up on the riverbank so that an enemy of Mine and of his shall find the child and take him home."'

3

Musa appeared before Pharaoh, and Pharaoh asked him, 'Musa, who is your creator?'

Musa said, 'My Creator is He who gave everything its proper form and then guided all things.'

'What happened to the peoples of the past?'

Musa said, 'Such knowledge is with my God in the book. My God does not err nor does He forget.'

4

He made the earth as a cradle for you, and the roads, and the water that falls from heaven, causing many sorts of plants to grow.

Eat and pasture your livestock.

5

We created you from earth; We shall bring you back to earth, and We shall draw you forth from it a second time.

We let Pharaoh see Our wonders, but he pronounced them lies, and he refused to believe. He said, 'Musa, you came here to drive us out of our land with your wizardry. Know this, we shall return with wizardry as great on a day yet to be determined.'

Musa said, 'Let us choose a festival for the purpose, when everyone will be present.'

6

On that appointed day, the wizards of Pharaoh threw down their ropes, which crawled over the ground like snakes. Musa's heart was stricken with fear.

We said, 'Musa, do not be afraid. Throw down your staff, and it shall devour their snakes.'

And so it happened. The wizards fell to their knees and said, 'We praise the God of Musa and Harun.'

7

And We revealed to Musa, 'Take my servants with you in the middle of the night, and clear a dry path for them through the sea. Do not fear the enemy or the sea.'

Pharaoh pursued Musa and his people, but the sea washed over him and his army.

8

The people continued on their way. When Musa returned after a period in isolation, God said, 'In your absence We put your people to the test, and Samiri has misled them.'

Samiri made golden adornments for them and a lowing calf. He said, 'This is your God and the God of Musa.'

Musa was angry at what had happened, and spoke harsh words against his brother, 'Harun! Why did you do nothing when you saw them go astray? Have you ignored my command?'

Harun said, 'You, son of my mother, do not pull so at my beard and the hair on my head. I feared you would say, "Harun has sewn division among the people of Israel because he did not listen to me."'

Musa asked, 'And what do you have to say, Samiri?'

He said, 'I saw something no one else could see. I then took a handful of earth from the footprint left behind by Jabra'il and I added it to the image of the calf.'

Musa said, 'Go away, Samiri! Do not come near me! That is your punishment.'

9

Muhammad! We tell you about the peoples of times gone by, and We gave you the Qur'an as a reminder.

If the people ask you about the mountains, say to them, 'My Creator shall destroy them all and scatter them, and He shall leave the ground as a barren surface; neither hollow nor slope shall be visible on it.'

On that day, everyone shall follow the sound of the trumpet of Israfel, the summoner. Every voice shall be subdued in the presence of God, and all you shall hear is the sound of muffled footsteps.

Heads shall bow before the Living One and the Existing One.

We have sent down the Qur'an in the form of an Arabic book, and We have given warning in it, many times over so that they might fear.

Great is Allah. He is the true King.

10

Muhammad! Do not rush to recite the Qur'an before its revelation is complete.

And say repeatedly, 'God, give me more knowledge.'

We had warned Adam in advance, but he turned a deaf ear.

We considered him weak and commanded the angels, 'Kneel before Adam!'

Everyone obeyed, except Satan. He refused.

We said to Adam, 'This is an enemy to you and your wife. Resist his temptations, otherwise you shall be unhappy.'

Yet Satan whispered, 'You, Adam! Shall I show you the tree of life, and the kingdom that does not perish?'

Thus, Adam and Hawwaa both ate of the forbidden fruit. And their shame became apparent to them, and they covered themselves with leaves.

11

Muhammad!

Stay calm, regardless of what they say! And pray to your Creator before sunrise and sunset. Praise Him in the portions of the night and in the two portions of the day.

Muhammad! Invite your family to prayer, and persevere.

We ask nothing of you. It is We who provide for you.

Say, 'Each of us is waiting; you too should wait. Later, you shall see which people followed the right path.'

46

The Resurrection

Muhammad speaks of the resurrection repeatedly, throughout his recitations, 'We shall all return.'

But his opponents harass him, 'Shall our forebears also return, those who are now dust and bones?'

In this sura, Muhammad introduces something new. Allah says, 'We shall bring you back in new forms, but you shall be unaware of it.'

So we shall all return in a different form, but we shall not recognise ourselves.

Muhammad is surprised that people find this simple matter so difficult to understand, 'Look at the drops that fall from your bodies. Why do you refuse to think? You are concealed in those drops, and it is thus that you shall return to life.'

In the name of Allah
He is love
He gives
He forgives

1
When the great event takes place, no one shall be able to dismiss it as a lie anymore.
It shall be a humiliation for some and glorious for others.

2
When the earth is shaken to its foundations, and the mountains crumble and are scattered like dust, you shall be divided into three groups.

3
The group on the right; who shall they be, and how shall they feel?
The group on the left; who shall they be, and how shall they feel?
The third group are the forerunners, the loved ones, who shall come close to God.

They shall be brought to the gardens of happiness, where they shall sit opposite one another on couches encrusted with jewels.

Young men who never age shall go around with jugs and cups of wine drawn from a flowing spring.

This wine shall not pain their heads or intoxicate them.

And fruit shall be brought, from which they are free to choose what they desire.

And the flesh of birds, whatever their desire.

And wholesome maidens with beautiful, dark, and expressive eyes like well-preserved pearls.

As reward for their good deeds.

No gossip shall they hear there nor sinful words, but instead, 'Salaam! Salaam!'

4

How shall the group on the right feel?

They shall be brought to thornless lotus trees and banana trees, in the extended shade by flowing water, and they shall be provided with an abundance of fruit. Everything in ample measure, everything in freedom.

And there shall be sweet maidens. We have formed these tender female companions into a wonderful creation. They are faithful beloved virgins of the same age.

All intended for the group on the right, which consists of those who came first and those who came later.

5

How shall the group on the left feel?

They shall find themselves in a scorching storm and in boiling water, in the shadow of a cloud of black smoke, neither refreshing nor pleasant.

These people once lived in prosperity, and persisted in great sin.

They asked, 'When we are dead and have turned to dust, and our bones are rotten, shall we then return to life? We and our forebears?'

Muhammad, say, 'Yes, those who came early and those who came late shall be gathered together on an appointed day.'

Thereafter, you sinners, you who declared everything a lie, shall eat from the Zaqqum tree. Then you shall drink boiling water like thirsty camels.

This shall be your reward on the day of judgement.

6

We have created you, but why did you not want to admit it?
Have you considered the seed that falls from your body?
Did you create those drops or did We?
We have fixed the time of your death.
And it is in Our power to bring forth others instead of you, and bring you back in new forms.

7

You know the first creation.
Why do you refuse to learn from it?
What do you think when you sow?
Is it you who makes it germinate or do We make it germinate?
If We desire, We could mow it to chaff. And then you would be left groaning and say, 'We are afflicted. We are powerless. We have nothing left.'

8

Have you considered the water you drink?
Do you make it fall from the clouds or do We?
If We desire, We could make it bitter and cold.
Why are you ungrateful?

9

And have you considered the fire that you make?
Did you make the tree used for it grow or did We?
We made fire as a sign, and to benefit those who dwell in the desert.
Praise your God. Exalted is His name.

10

I swear by the stars at the moment they disappear, and this oath is a weighty oath when you realize how precious this Qur'an is.
A book under Allah's protection.
No one is allowed to touch it, except those who have washed their hands.
This is a proclamation of the Maker of the universe.
Do you despise the revelation?
Do you deny the bread We have given you, instead of being grateful?

11

When death takes hold of you, and the last breath reaches your throat, and you look on powerless; at that moment We are closer to death than you, but you do not see it.
I shall bring back that breath should you finally speak the truth.

12

Salaam to those on the right side.
But if you are among the deniers, boiling water shall be your reward.
This is the truth about which there is no doubt.
Praise then your God.
He is great.

47

The Poets

While this sura bears the title 'The Poets', it is only the final passage that alludes to poets as such.
Muhammad admired the poets as a young man, but now he hates them. They menaced him incessantly with their derisive poems, which people could easily remember and pass on to one another.

This sura also continues the account of the ancient prophets.
When prophets such as Lut, Hud, Ibrahim, Isma'il, and Musa tried to guide people onto the right path in Egypt, Palestine, Lebanon, Habasha, Medin, and Jerusalem, Persian history also had a prophet: Zarathustra.
And this Persian prophet had a book that bore the name Avesta.

The following words can be found in the Avesta:
In the beginning was Ahura Mazda.
He lived in a boundless universe of light.
Ahura Mazda possessed all knowledge.
To create his world, he transformed the immaterial into material.
He made fire from light, wind from fire, water from wind, and the earth from water.
In the heart of all this he placed water, but also fire.

He first made the sky, great and limitless, in the form of an egg.
He made joy with the help of the sky, because he considered joy a necessary component of the mixture he planned to use to create human beings.
Ahura devised the cow. The cow was large, white in colour, and radiant as the moon.

Ahura Mazda created grass for the cow, and it was long, without branches, without a protective layer, without thorns, but crisp, sweet, and green.
Finally he made Keyumars.
Keyumars means 'the dying life', and it is the name of the first human being.

Keyumars later died a natural death, after which his body brought forth eight elements: gold, silver, iron, copper, zinc, lead, mercury, and diamond.
The gold remained under the ground for forty years, after which a plant with immense branches grew from it. The branches detached themselves from the stem and started to move, changing into human beings. It was not clear who was a man and who was a woman, and who bore the spirit of Ahura Mazda.

In the name of Allah
He is love
He gives
He forgives

1
Ta' Sin Mim.
These are the signs of the clear speaking book.
Muhammad, perhaps you are tormenting yourself because they refuse to believe.
Should We desire, We could send a miracle from heaven that would make them bend their necks in humility.
Yet they turn away and call the texts of the Qur'an lies.
Do they want to see a sign from Allah?
Do they not see how many excellent species We have caused to grow on earth?
Surely this is a sign, but most of them refuse to believe.

Without doubt, your Creator is powerful and forgiving.
You want more signs? Then listen.

2

God said to Musa, 'Go to that criminal Pharaoh and say, "Do you refuse to fear God?"'

Musa said, 'God! They shall accuse me of lies. Then I shall become anxious, and my tongue will refuse to work. Ask Harun to go with me. Pharaoh has charged me with a crime. I fear they might kill me.'

God said, 'It is not so. Go, both of you, with Our miracles. We are with you, and We are listening. So go to Pharaoh, and say that you are the messenger of the Maker of the world. Insist that the people of Israel go with you.'

3

Musa did what God asked. Pharaoh answered, 'Did we not raise you as one of us? Did you not spend many years of your life in our midst? You are ungrateful, Musa.'

Musa said, 'I was still misguided then, and I fled from you because I was afraid. But my God, the Creator of the world, granted me insight and chose me as one of the prophets.'

Pharaoh said, 'The Creator of the world? Who is that?'

Musa answered, 'He is the Maker of the heavens and the earth and everything between the two.'

Pharaoh said to his people, 'Do you hear what he is saying?'

Musa said calmly, 'He is your Creator and the Creator of your forebears!'

'The prophet sent to you is truly mad,' Pharaoh shouted.

But Musa was imperturbable, 'He is the Creator of the east and the west and everything between the two.'

Pharaoh lost his patience, 'If you serve another god, I shall have you imprisoned.'

'Even if I give you a clear sign?' asked Musa.

'Do it, then, if you speak the truth!'

At that, Musa threw his staff to the ground, and it changed into an enormous snake.

Then he held out his hand to those present, and it was suddenly white!

Pharaoh shouted, 'He is nothing more than a skilful magician.'

4

When Musa fled Egypt with his people, Pharaoh and his soldiers gave chase. They arrived at the sea, and We revealed to Musa, 'Strike the sea with your staff!'

The sea immediately divided, and each side was like a great wall of rock. We allowed Pharaoh and his army to come close. We saved Musa and the people who were with him, and We let the pursuers drown.

5

That was a clear sign, but most refused to believe.

Your Creator is powerful and forgiving.

Muhammad! Tell them about the life of Ibrahim.

Ibrahim said to his father and his people, 'To what do you pray?'

They said, 'We pray to the idols, and we shall be their subjects.'

Ibrahim said, 'Do those idols hear you, when you give praise? Do they benefit you, or harm you?'

They said, 'No, but we observed that our fathers did the same.'

Ibrahim said, 'Did you and your fathers never think about what you worship? Know this! Those idols are enemies to me, but the Creator of the world is not an enemy. It is He who created me, who leads me, who will cause me to die, and will restore me to life.'

Truly, this is a sign, but most of them refused to believe.
Your Creator is powerful and forgiving.

6
The people of Nuh branded the prophets liars.
It continued thus, until their brother Nuh said to them, 'Do you refuse to fear? I am a genuine prophet. Fear God, and follow me. I am merely a messenger.'
They said, 'Nuh, if you do not desist, you shall be stoned.'
We saved Nuh and those who were with him in that fully-laden ship. Then we let those who remained drown.
Truly, this is a sign, but most of them refused to believe.
Your Creator is powerful and forgiving.

7
The people of 'Ad branded the prophets liars.
Their brother Hud said to them, 'Do you refuse to fear? I am a genuine prophet. Fear God, and follow me.
'Do you build a building on every high place for your own ease?
'Do you build castles in the hope of living forever? When you lay hands on people, you do so with violence. Fear God, and follow me. Fear Him, for all that you have, He has given you. He has helped you with livestock, sons, gardens, and springs. I warn you of the punishment on a dreadful day.'
They said, 'It makes no difference to us whether you preach to us or not. We have heard this before, and we were not punished.'
They branded him a liar, and We destroyed them.
Truly, this is a sign, but most of them refused to believe.
Your Creator is powerful and forgiving.

8

The people of Thamud branded the prophets liars.

Their brother Saleh said to them, 'Do you refuse to fear? I am a genuine prophet. Fear God, and follow me!

'Do you think you shall live here forever amidst the gardens, springs, meadows, date palms replete with delightful blossoms, and in the houses you built with such skill in the mountains? Fear God, and follow me.'

They said, 'Saleh! You are under a spell! You are an ordinary person just like us. Show us a miracle, if you speak the truth.'

Saleh said, 'Here! This she-camel is my miracle. It drinks at fixed times and you drink at fixed times. Do it no pain, otherwise you will be punished on the Great Day.'

But they pursued the she-camel nonetheless and cut its tendons. Later they regretted it, but they were seized by the punishment.

God is powerful and forgiving.

9

The people of Lut branded the prophets liars.

Their brother Lut said to them, 'Do you refuse to fear? I am a genuine prophet. Fear God, therefore, and follow me!

Do you take men and leave behind the women God made for you? No, you are a sinful people.'

They said, 'Lut! If you do not desist, we shall expel you.'

Lut said, 'I despise what you do. God! Save me and my family from what they want to do with us.'

We saved Lut and his family, all except Lut's elderly wife; she stayed. Then We destroyed the others, and We caused a rain of stones to fall. It was a terrible punishment.

Truly this is a sign, but most of them refused to believe.

God is powerful and forgiving.

10

The people of al-Aykah branded the prophets liars.

Their brother Shuayb said to them, 'Give the full measure and no less; weigh equitably with the scales. Do not bring misery on earth, and fear Him. He who created you and your forebears.'

They said, 'Shuayb! You are under a spell. You are an ordinary person just like us, and, above all, you are a liar. Cause a piece of the sky to fall on us, if you speak the truth.'

Shuayb said, 'My Creator knows what you are doing.'

And they made him out to be a liar. They were seized by the punishment of the shadow of a cloud that fell upon them. Truly, this is a sign, but most of them refused to believe.

God is powerful and forgiving.

11

Muhammad! The trustworthy angel Jabra'il brought the Qur'an down to you in portions, and placed it in your spirit so that you would be one who warns. In beautiful Arabic. It is mentioned in the ancient sacred scriptures of other peoples. Is it not enough for the unbelievers that the scholars of Israel knew about it long before now?

12

Muhammad! We have never destroyed a people that did not have someone who warned them.

Say to them, 'Take no other God besides Allah, otherwise you shall be punished.'

Muhammad! Warn your family! Be kind to those who follow you. And if they still refuse to listen, say, 'I distance myself from what you are doing.' And place your trust in the great Forgiver. He who sees you when you rise, and when you walk around between those who pray. He hears all things. He knows all things.

13
Shall I tell you upon whom the devil descends?
He descends upon everyone who spreads lies, and upon everyone who lends an ear to sinful rumours, for many of them are liars.
Those who have gone astray follow the poets. Have you not seen how they wander around in desperation? That they say what they should not say?
Those who sin shall soon perceive the consequences.

48

The Ants

Muhammad's followers asked him questions, 'Who invented the mirror?'
'The mirror is an art work from Allah. He loves the mirror, and looks at Himself in it. Allah taught the prophet Sulayman how to make a mirror.'
And they also asked him, 'What is love?'
'When Allah formed human beings from clay, He added something of His own soul. I believe that was love,' said Muhammad.
'What did Sulayman write to the queen of Sheba?' his followers asked.
'Sulayman had not yet seen the queen, and could not thus have been impressed by her beauty. He wrote a noble letter, in a somewhat abrupt tone: "Either the queen accepts my faith or I shall come with my army."'

Later, when the queen of Sheba received his message, she sent a reply, 'I shall come to you and listen to you.'

Sulayman said to the jinn, 'Accompany her; I intend to welcome her warmly.'

But the jinn had their doubts. They feared that Sulayman would lose his heart to her from the moment he saw her. In an attempt to avert her arrival they said, 'We are concerned. She is a strange creature. Her legs are like those of a donkey.'

Sulayman said, 'I shall find a way to avoid having to look at her legs.'

He asked the jinn to cover the corridor of his palace with reflective plates of glass, and to arrange for flowing water underneath, filled with aquatic plants and little fish.

The queen of Sheba announced her arrival and Sulayman called out, 'Come inside!'

She thought that Sulayman's palace was under water so she took off her shoes and uncovered her legs.

Sulayman looked, and saw that the jinn had been right.

Sulayman said to the jinn, 'Think of something. Help her remove the hair from her legs.'

The jinn deliberated against their better judgement. They made a lotion and offered it to the queen when she was taking a bath. She took the lotion and removed the hair from her legs.

When Sulayman saw the queen after that, he could no longer resist her.

(This story is related in the Tafsir, *Tabari's explanation of the* Qur'an)

In the name of Allah
He is love
He gives
He forgives

1

Ta' Sin.

These are the signs of the Qur'an, a book that speaks clear language.

A guide with a beautiful message.

And you, Muhammad! The Qur'an is given to you by the Most Wise and All-Knowing One.

2

Musa said to his people, 'I see a fire. Let me go and see what it is, and I shall bring back some fire to warm you.'

When he came close to the fire, a voice called to him, 'Beautiful is He who is in the fire, and he who stands close by. Pure is God, the Maker of worlds. Musa! It is I, God, the Wise, the Almighty.'

3

We granted knowledge to Dawud and Sulayman and they both said, 'Praised be God who has exalted us above others.'

Sulayman succeeded Dawud and reigned over a vast land. Jinn, people, the wind, and the birds were his servants. He understood the language of the birds, spoke to the wind, and wore a magic ring on his finger. God had granted him all these things.

When Sulayman arrived in the valley of the ants with his army of jinn, people, and birds, an ant said, 'Oh ants, go into your dwellings lest Sulayman and his army trample you carelessly underfoot.'

Sulayman heard it and smiled. He turned to the birds and said, 'Why don't I see my messenger, the bird Hudhud? Is he perhaps absent? I shall punish him severely; slaughter him unless he can clearly explain where he was.'

It did not take long before Hudhud appeared and spoke to

Sulayman, 'I know something you do not yet know. I have just come back from the land of Sheba. I saw the queen, and she had everything, including a majestic throne. And I saw that she and her people bowed down before the sun instead of God.'

Sulayman said, 'We shall see if you speak the truth or if you are lying. Take this letter, and drop it beside her. Then pull back, and observe her reaction.'

The queen of Sheba said to the wise men who gave her advice, 'Counsellors, a noble letter has reached me. It is from Sulayman, and its salutation reads, "In the name of God the Loving One, the Forgiving One."

'He asks me to obey him.

'Wise ones! I need your counsel. I shall make no decision without your approval.'

They answered, 'We are strong and capable of considerable violent resistance against this Sulayman, but the decision is yours. Speak your mind.'

She said, 'The kings destroy everything when they conquer a land, they humiliate the beloved of the people. They shall certainly do the same with us, but I plan to send Sulayman a gift. And we shall see what our messengers bring back in reply.'

4

When the messengers came to Sulayman, and Sulayman saw the gift, he said, 'Are you planning to bother me with this? Know that what God has given me is better than what you intend to give me. I see that you are happy with this gift. Turn and go back! We shall come with an army that no one can resist. We shall humiliate your nation, and we shall belittle it.'

When the queen of Sheba heard Sulayman's harsh words, she sent him a letter. 'I shall come to you, to hear what you have to say.'

5

Sulayman turned to his advisors, 'Which one of you can bring me her throne before she gets here?'

An elderly jinn said, 'I can do it before you get the chance to stand up.'

One of them, a well-read man, said, 'I shall bring you her throne in the blink of an eye.'

Sulayman agreed, and the queen of Sheba's throne appeared in front of him in an instant.

He said, 'Disguise her throne. We shall see if she recognises it.'

6

When the queen of Sheba arrived, she was asked, 'Is this throne perhaps similar to your own?'

She said, 'This bears a striking resemblance to our throne.'

She was invited to enter the palace.

When the queen saw the floor she thought it was a puddle of water, and she uncovered her legs.

Sulayman said, 'It is not water. The floor is made of glass and mirrors.'

The queen replied in admiration, 'We were informed in advance about your power. We place our fate in your hands.'

49　　　　ﻯ

The Stories

After Ibrahim came Lut.
Lut was a nephew of Ibrahim. After Lut came Shuayb, a distant descendant of Lut's eldest daughter.
Shuayb became the prophet of the people of Madyan.

The merchants of Madyan traded with merchants from Palestine and Lebanon.
The merchants who rescued Yusuf from the well were also from Madyan. Musa, moreover, sought refuge among the people of Madyan.
The elderly Shuayb lived for ten more years after Musa came to live in his house, and seven more years after Musa left his house because God had given him the task of warning the pharaohs.

In the name of Allah
He is love
He gives
He forgives

1
Ta' Sin Mim.
We recount once again the story of Musa and Pharaoh.
Pharaoh committed crimes in his land. He divided the population into different groups and oppressed the Israelites. He killed their sons and left only the women alive. Musa belonged to the Israelite people.

2
We said to the mother of Musa, 'Suckle him, and if you fear for your life, place him in a basket, and let the river carry him off. Do not be afraid, and do not be sad. We shall bring him back to you, and We shall make him a prophet.'
The mother of Musa followed My advice. Musa was found and taken to the court of Pharaoh. Pharaoh gave Musa a place in his home, not knowing that the child would later become his enemy.

3
The woman said to Pharaoh, 'He is as light to my eyes and also to yours. Do not kill him; perhaps he will be useful to us. We can adopt him as a son.'

4
The heart of Musa's mother lost all hope after she let the river carry him off. She heard nothing more about her son and out of impatience almost gave away her secret.
She said to her daughter, 'Go and see what has become of him.'
Musa's sister kept a close eye on everything without causing suspicion.
As a precaution, We had taught the child to refuse the breast of others.
When his sister saw this, she went to the wife of Pharaoh and said, 'I know a family who can feed him and take care of him.'
We thus sent little Musa back to his mother to make her eyes sparkle with happiness and take away her sadness.
And so that God's promise would come true.

5
When Musa grew into adulthood and became strong, We gave him wisdom and knowledge. One day he saw two men fighting with each other in the city. One of them belonged to his own people, the other to the people of Pharaoh. The man who belonged to his own people called for his help. On the spur of the moment, Musa struck the other man with his fist, and he fell to the ground dead.

6
Shortly after this incident, a man from the other side of the city ran to Musa and called out, 'Oh, Musa, the leaders have decided to kill you. Flee!'

Musa fled the city in fear and took refuge in Madyan. He said to himself, perhaps God will lead me in the right direction.

7

When he arrived at the well in Madyan, he found a group of men watering their flocks. Two women waited behind them with their flocks. He said, 'Why are you standing here?'
They said, 'We must wait until the shepherds have departed. Our father is old.'
Musa watered their flocks, stood in the shadow, and said to himself, God, whatever You give me, I am in need of it.

8

Then one of the women came back and said, coyly, 'My father Shuayb has invited you to receive your reward for watering our flocks.'
When Musa came to Shuayb and told him his story, Shuayb said, 'Fear not, Musa! You have escaped an oppressed people.'
And one of his daughters said, 'Father, ask him to work for us. He is the best you can find. He is strong and reliable.'
Shuayb said to Musa, 'I shall give you one of my daughters, on the condition that you work eight years for me, and perhaps it will become ten.'

9

At the end of the agreed term, Musa departed with his family. During their journey he saw fire in the mountain.
He said to his family, 'Stay here and wait. I see a fire in the distance. Let me go and see what it is, perhaps I can fetch some fire for you to warm you.'
When he came close to the fire he heard a voice coming from a tree standing on a blessed spot, 'Musa, it is I, God, the Maker of the world. Throw your staff to the ground!'

Musa did what he was asked, but when he saw the staff writhing like a snake, he turned on his heels to flee.

The voice called out, 'Musa! Turn back! And fear not, you are safe. Put your hand inside your collar, and it shall turn white without being sick. Your hand and your staff are two signs from your God for Pharaoh and his advisors. They are oppressors.'

10

When Musa presented Our clear signs, Pharaoh said, 'My advisors. I know no other God than myself. Haman, shovel clay into the fire. Bake bricks and make a high tower for me so that I can see the God of Musa. He is a liar.'

11

Long after Musa, We sent Muhammad.

And the unbelievers said, 'Why was he not given the same as was given to Musa?'

They said, 'The Torah and the Qur'an are two works of magic, the one following the other. We do not believe in these writings.'

Muhammad, say to them, 'Then bring me a book that gives better guidance than those two books, and I shall follow it.' But if they do not respond to your question, know that they follow their own desires.

12

No, they did not listen, and We destroyed many cities in which the inhabitants were drunk with prosperity. Look, their houses are still there, but almost no one lives in them. We inherited all of it.

Muhammad! Surely your Creator would not destroy a city without first sending a messenger to it with a document to warn the people?

And We only destroyed those cities whose inhabitants had committed crimes.

13

Muhammad, say, 'Consider this! If Allah were to allow the night to continue until the end of time, which God would then be able to bring you light? Do you refuse to listen?'

Say, 'If Allah were to allow the day to continue until the end of time, which God is there who would be able to bring a night to you, for you to rest in it? Do you refuse to see?'

Allah forgives, and it is because of his lenience that He made the night and the day for you, to rest in and to search for your bread from His abundance. You should thus be grateful.

14

Qarun belonged to the people of Musa, and he oppressed them. We had given him so many treasures that he needed a group of strong men to carry his keys.

His people said to him, 'Do not be so cheerful! God does not like people who are needlessly cheerful. Seek rather the life to come with the wealth that God has given you. Also, do not forget your part in this world, and give as God has given you. And do not sow corruption on earth.'

15

Qarun said, 'My knowledge has brought me everything I have.' Did he not know that God had destroyed many peoples before him that were stronger and wealthier than he?

Qarun came out to his people in all his pomp and finery. Those who love the life of this world said, 'Ah! Would that we had been given what Qarun has been given. He is overloaded with good fortune.'

We buried Qarun and his house deep under the ground. And there was no one to help him.

Those who do good deeds shall be rewarded, and those who commit crimes shall be punished like Qarun.

50

The Night Journey

This sura makes reference to Muhammad's remarkable journey, an amazing fantasy journey from Mecca via Jerusalem to the seventh level of heaven, where Allah dwells.
Allah invites Muhammad to pay Him a visit, and He shows him around His house and His inner court. Muhammad thus takes a walk with his Master through His kingdom.
This sura only mentions the journey; Muhammad discloses no further details.
He recounts that he met the prophets Nuh, Ibrahim, Sulayman, Musa, Yaqub, and Isa in one of the gardens of paradise and that he spoke with them.

In the name of Allah
He is love
He gives
He forgives

1
Pure is He who transported His messenger in the night, from the Sacred Mosque in Mecca to the Distant Mosque in Jerusalem. We have given glory to that place to reveal a few of Our signs to the messenger.

2

If you do good you do it for yourself, and if you do evil you also do it for yourself.

Humans seek the bad and the good alike. Humans act with haste. We made the night and the day as two signs. We wipe out the night to let the day come so that you can earn your bread and that you may count and number the years. We have created all things with clarity.

And We have hung the fate of every human around their necks, and on the day of judgement We shall present them with an overview of their deeds, 'Read it!'

3

Your Creator has commanded you, 'Serve no one but Him! And treat your parents well. And if one of them grows old with you, or both, do not complain. Embrace them with the wings of humility, and ask your God to take care of them, just as they took care of you when you were young.

'And give your kin their right, including the poor and travellers. 'Do not rest your hand on your neck in miserliness, but open your hand. Not too wide, otherwise you will regret it.'

4

'Do not kill your children for fear of poverty. It is We who feed them. To kill them is a great crime. And do not commit sexual offences; it is shameful, an evil deed.

'Do not touch the possessions of an orphan. Be honest with the scales, and give the full measure when you weigh. Weigh with pure scales; that is better for you.

'Do not follow what you do not know, for your eyes and your ears are responsible. Do not strut around the earth with arrogance, for you cannot cleave the earth nor can you reach higher than the mountains.'

In this Qur'an We have spoken about various life issues so that unbelievers might learn a lesson, but it does not work. Their aversion simply grows.

5

Muhammad, say to them, 'The seven heavens and the earth and everything between praise Allah. And there is nothing that does not praise Him. He is forgiving and patient.'

Muhammad! When you recite the Qur'an, We draw a curtain between you and those who do not believe. We draw a veil over their heart and over their ears so that they cannot understand it. When you call the God of the Qur'an the Only One, they turn their backs to you in abhorrence.

We know well enough how they listen to you when they listen to you, and We know when they talk with one another in secret. They say, 'Look! You follow a man bewitched.'

6

Muhammad! Do you see what they compare you with? They have gone astray and cannot find the path.

They say, 'Shall we really be resurrected as new humans after we have turned to bones and dust?'

Muhammad, say to them, 'It makes no difference, even if you had turned to stone or iron.'

They shall say, 'Who shall bring us back?'

Say, 'He who created you at the outset.'

And then they shall shake their heads and ask, 'When shall it be?'

Say, 'Perhaps soon.'

Muhammad, say to my servants, 'Speak clear language, for Satan is stirring strife among them. Satan is humankind's greatest enemy.'

No city exists that We shall not destroy or punish on the day of judgement. This is written in the book *In the Beginning*.

7

And thus it continued until We said to the angels, 'Kneel before Adam.' All of them did, except Satan who said, 'Me? Kneel? Before someone You created from clay?'

Your Creator is He who makes ships sail across the sea for you so that you can seek your living in His bounty, for He is caring. And when you encounter danger at sea, you hear nothing from the idols. He is the One who brings you safely to the shore. But you turn away after being rescued. Humans are ungrateful.
Do you really think you are safe when He makes a portion of the land on which you stand cave in? Or when He sends a violent sandstorm over your heads?
Or do you really think you are safe when He sends you back to sea and causes a powerful storm to rage in which you drown?

8

We have separated the children of Adam from the others and carried them to the land and across the sea. We have given them good fruit to eat and chosen them above everything We created.

Muhammad! Perform your prayer at the setting of the sun until the dark of night. And read the Qur'an at dawn. And stay awake part of the night as an obligation. Perhaps God shall grant you a worthy place.
And say, 'God, let me go in with sincerity, and let me go out with sincerity, and sustain me with something of your own power.'

9

And they ask you about the spirit.
Say to them, 'The spirit is something that belongs to the

knowledge of my Creator, little of which has been granted you.'
Say, 'When humans and jinn come together to write a book like this Qur'an, they fail, even if they support one another. We have given repeated examples in this Qur'an, but most people are ungrateful.'

Muhammad! They say to you, 'We shall not believe you until you make a spring come forth from the ground, or until you make a garden with palm trees and vines and cause water to flow between them, or until you cause the sky, as you describe it, to fall on us in pieces, or until you come together with Allah and the angels, or until you have a house and jewels from God, or until you climb to the heavens.'

They say, 'We shall not believe in your journey to heaven unless you send a book to us from heaven that we can read.'

Muhammad, say, 'Great is my Creator. I am a mere human, an ordinary messenger.'

Say, 'Call upon Allah, or call upon Rahman. It does not matter how you call upon Him, He still has the most beautiful names.'

Muhammad, do not pray too loud or too soft, but choose a middle course.

And say, 'Praise be to Allah, who has no child. He is the Only One in His kingdom, and He has no need of a companion.'

Say, 'Allah is great!'

51

Yunus

There has never been a prophet in the history of the world who abandoned his people, except Yunus.
Yunus was a descendant of Hud, and his mother was a daughter of the people of Israel.

Yunus talked to his people for forty years to help them onto the right path. But they said, 'We shall not follow you under any circumstances.'

They insulted him and pained him. Yunus was impatient. He gave up and asked God several times to punish his people.

'Be patient, Yunus. Everything has its time,' said God.

But Yunus could not bear it any longer, and he left his people in anger.

He had no idea where to go, until he found himself by the sea and saw a group of people about to sail off on a ship. He decided to go with them.

The ship sailed three days and three nights. On the fourth day the sky grew dark unexpectedly. A giant fish came to the surface and held the ship back. No one knew what to do. One wise man said, 'There is someone on this ship who has committed a sin. We must throw him overboard or the fish shall destroy the ship.' Yunus knew that the fish had come for him. He jumped into the water and the fish swallowed him up.

Yunus was imprisoned for thirty-nine days in the belly of the fish. On the fortieth day, the fish swam to land and gave Yunus his freedom. A voice said to him, 'Go back to your people, Yunus; they are sad without you. And learn to be patient.'

In the name of Allah
He is love
He gives
He forgives

1
'Alif Lam Ra'.
These are the verses of the Book of Wisdom.

Is it astonishing that we chose a man from their midst as our emissary to warn them?

A man of whom unbelievers said, 'He is a conjurer.'

2

It was Allah who created the earth and the heavens in six days.

He then took His place on His throne to regulate the affairs of the universe.

You shall all return to Him to give account; such is His promise.

This is Allah. Praise Him.

He is the One who gave light to the sun, caused the moon to shine, and established its different phases, so that you would be able to count the years and calculate with them.

God did all this in righteousness.

In the difference between day and night, and in all that God created in the air and on the earth, there are clear signs for those who reflect.

3

God shall lead those who believe and do good deeds to paradise, where rivers flow beneath the gardens, and where people shall dwell in happiness.

There, their call shall be, 'We praise you.'

And their greeting, 'Salaam!'

And they shall conclude with, 'Praise be to the King of the worlds!'

4

When people have problems they call upon Us, whether lying on their side, sitting or standing.

And if We take away their pain, they continue on their way as if they had never called upon Us.

And when Our clear verses are proclaimed they say, 'Bring us a different Qur'an. Or change the texts.'

Muhammad, say to them, 'It is not up to me to recount something from myself. I follow only what has been revealed to me. I fear the punishment.'

Say, 'If God did not will it, I would not recite the verses to you. Have I not lived my entire life among you? Why do you refuse to think?'

5

They say, 'Why did his Allah not reveal a miracle to Muhammad as a sign?'

Muhammad, say to them, 'Only Allah knows the secret. Wait, therefore, and I shall wait with you.'

Say, 'Our angels note down all you devise.'

Allah allows you to travel on land and sea.

When they are in their ships, and a pleasant wind carries them, and they take pleasure in it, they forget God. But as soon as a strong wind blows, and the waves hit them from every side, and they are staring death in the face, they cry out to God, 'Save us! We shall show our gratitude!'

When they have been saved, and set foot on dry land, they start with their vile plans anew.

6

Know this, Oh, people! Your wicked deeds shall only be to your detriment. The joy of life is short; you shall all return.

Life's narrative is like the water We cause to fall from the sky. It makes vegetation grow for people and animals to eat. The earth is adorned with flowers, blossoms and plants. And people think they are masters over it all.

On a given night or a given day, We make our decision, and

We transform the earth into a field of stubble, as if nothing had ever adorned it.

This is how we reveal Our signs to those who reflect.

7

Those who do good deeds can expect fine things and more. Their faces shall not be covered with a layer of pain and humiliation. Such are the ones who shall dwell in the gardens of paradise.

But a layer of humiliation shall cling to the faces of those who do bad deeds. No one can protect them against God. It shall be as if their faces are covered with pieces of the night. They are the inhabitants of the fire.

8

Muhammad, ask, 'Who gives you bread from heaven and earth? Who has control over your ears and eyes? Who causes the living to come forth from the dead, and the dead from the living? And who regulates the affairs of the universe?'

They shall say, 'Allah.'

Say, 'Why, then, do you refuse to listen!'

Muhammad, ask them, 'Is there one among your idols who can create and cause to come back?'

Say, 'Only Allah can do this! Why, then, do you choose the wrong path nonetheless?'

9

It is not true that this Qur'an is not from Allah; that someone else has devised it.

This book is a confirmation of the other ancient, divine books. That is beyond any doubt.

But the unbelievers say, 'Muhammad made it up himself.'

Muhammad, say to them, 'Show me a text like the Qur'an, if you speak the truth!'

When they are unable to comprehend something, they call it lies.

If they call you a liar, say, 'My deeds are my deeds, and your deeds are your deeds. You are unconnected to what I do, and I am unconnected to what you do.'

Some among them pretend to listen to you, but how can you make the deaf hear?

And some among them pretend to look at you, but how can you make the blind see?

Know this, however, they shall all be brought back to Us.

10

For every people there is a messenger.

The unbelievers say, 'If you speak the truth, tell us when the day of judgement is due.'

Muhammad, say to them, 'I do not know. I have no words of my own, I only say what Allah desires. All peoples have their ascribed end. When their time has come, it shall not be postponed or advanced, not even by an hour.'

Ask them, 'How can you run away if you are stricken by His punishment at night in your sleep, or during the day when you are working?'

11

Muhammad, say to them, 'Whatever preoccupies you, whatever engrosses you, and whatever you do, We see all of it.'

Not even the tiniest thing on the earth or in heaven is hidden from Allah. Everything, small and great, is in the book of creation, the book *In the Beginning*.

Say, 'Without doubt! Everything and everyone in the heavens and on the earth is from Allah.'

But what they follow as God, is an illusion.

God made the night for rest, and the day for sight.

It contains signs for those who reflect.

12

The unbelievers say, 'God has a child.'

God is pure. He needs no one. Everything in the heavens and on the earth is from Him.

They do not understand what they say, and have no reason for it.

Why do you attach something to God of which you know nothing?

You shall all return to Him.

And you shall be punished severely for the lies you spread.

Muhammad! Tell them the story of the prophet Nuh, when he said to his people, 'Oh, my people, if you continue to deny my words and God's signs, and continue to afflict me, I shall seek refuge in God.'

And they accused him of lies!

We saved him together with those who were with him in the ship. And We allowed those who ignored our signs to drown. Behold, thus, how those who have been warned come to their end.

13

After Nuh We sent others as emissaries to their people with Our signs. But those peoples did not want to know.

Then We sent Musa and Harun with their miracles to Pharaoh and his chiefs, but they ignored everything. They were a criminal people.

When they saw Our clear signs they said, 'This is pure sorcery.'

But We let the Israelites pass through the sea.

Pharaoh and his army pursued them in hostility. When Pharaoh was surprised by the water he said, 'I believe in God, in whom the Israelites believe. And I surrender.'

Now? While you resisted everything thus far?

Today We shall save you, and cast your body on the rocks as a warning for those who come after you.

14

Why have no other people come to faith, except the people of the prophet Yunus?

When the people of Yunus came to faith, We ended their punishment and We allowed them to enjoy life until their time came.

Muhammad, say, 'Look at Our signs in the heavens and on the earth!'

But these signs mean nothing to those who do not believe.

Do they expect something other than the punishment of the people who died before them?

Say, 'Just wait! I shall wait with you.'

Then We shall save Our messengers together with those who believed. It is Our duty to save them.

Say, 'People! If you doubt my faith, know at least that I do not serve your idols. I pray to Allah, who causes you to die when your time has come. I have been asked to be one of the believers.

'Accept, therefore, this pure faith, and distance yourself from the unbelievers.

'Do not be a worshipper of something that neither helps nor hinders you. If you do so nonetheless, then you are cruel.'

Muhammad, say, 'People! The truth of God has come to you. Those who chose the right path, do so to their own advantage. And those who go astray, do so to their own disadvantage. I am not your guard.'

Muhammad! Follow what has been revealed to you. And wait with patience until Allah gives His judgement.
He is the greatest of those who judge.

52

Hud

After Yunus came Ayoub, the paragon of patience.
God liked Ayoub, and he achieved a great deal on account of his ability to wait. His people loved him, and he was able to lead many to the right path.

After Ayoub came al-Khidr.
Al-Khidr was not his real name.
The people named him al-Khidr, which means, 'He who makes all things green.'
When al-Khidr walked over dry ground it became green.
He had imbibed water from the eternal spring. Thus, he became immortal and shall live until the end of time.
Al-Khidr fulfilled people's dreams.
If they desired something, al-Khidr made it possible.
In particular those who wanted to travel to Mecca, but did not have any money, would ask al-Khidr for help, and he would arrange it.

After al-Khidr came Nuh.
After Nuh came Hud, the prophet of the people of 'Ad.
Hud was a direct descendant of Zina, the daughter of Nuh.
The people of 'Ad were tall and strong, and they lived in a place in the mountains between Yaman and Sham, with their houses carved into the rock face.

The people of 'Ad worshipped idols, and had carved giant images of them in the mountains.

Hud warned his people for forty-seven years but they did not listen.

Hud said, 'My people, follow me, otherwise a harsh punishment shall afflict you.'

They answered, 'We live in indestructible houses. Nothing can touch us.'

God caused the mountains to shake so that the people were forced to flee.

When they arrived on the plain, God caused a hard and cold wind to blow for eight days and seven nights. The people fell to the ground like uprooted trees, and their sturdy dwellings in the mountains were left empty.

Two hundred years later, God chose Saleh and sent him to his people with an exceptional she-camel. But no one would listen to him either, and they killed his she-camel.

In the name of Allah
He is love
He gives
He forgives

1

'Alif Lam Ra'.

This is a book of the All-Knowing, the signs of whom are clear and irrevocable.

Serve none but Allah. I am a proclaimer of good tidings, and a cautioner sent by Him.

You shall all return to God. And He is able to do all things.

Yet the unbelievers try to conceal their secrets from Him. They pull their garments over their heads.

To no avail! Allah knows everything they conceal and reveal. He knows what a heart contains.

2

There is no creature on earth whose life does not depend on Allah. He provides for everything.

He knows where you stand and where you rest.

Everything is in the book *In the Beginning*.

It was He who made the heavens and the earth in six days while His throne stood on the water.

Muhammad, under pressure you shall sometimes be tempted to leave out some of the suras.

Your heart grows anxious when they say, 'If only a treasure had come down for him. Or if only an angel had accompanied him.'

Muhammad! You are only a cautioner.

God concerns Himself with all things.

3

Or they say, 'Muhammad made up the Qur'an.'

Say to them, 'Bring ten forged suras that are equal to those of the Qur'an. And call out for help to everyone except Allah, if you speak the truth.

But if you cannot do it, know, then, that Allah sent down this text with His knowledge. And there is no other God than He.'

Therefore, do not doubt! It is God's truth, but most people refuse to believe it.

And who is more depraved than the person who associates God with a lie?

They have brought this injury on themselves. They are the losers.

4

But those who believe and surrender themselves to God, they are the future inhabitants of paradise, where they shall dwell for eternity.

These two groups can be compared to the blind and deaf on one hand and the sighted and hearing on the other.

Are they thus equal?

Why, then, do they not want to know?

5

We sent the prophet Nuh to his people. He said, 'I am a cautioner! Pray to none other than God!'

He said to his people, 'I ask nothing from you. My reward is with God. And I shall not abandon those who have accepted the faith. They shall meet God. But I see that you are an ignorant people.

I do not say that I have God's treasures with me nor do I know anything about the secrets. And I do not say that I am an angel. No, I know nothing, but God knows everything.'

They said, 'You, Nuh, have always disputed with us, and it has been a very prolonged dispute. Now, if you speak the truth, bring upon us the punishment with which you have threatened us so often.'

He answered, 'Only Allah shall bring it upon you if He sees fit, and you shall be unable to escape it. He is your God, and you shall be sent back to Him.'

They said, 'Do you see, he has invented something else.'

He answered, 'If I invented it, the sin is mine, and I shall be punished for it. But I am innocent of your sins.'

The following was revealed to him, 'Nuh! None of your people shall accept the faith, except those who already believe. So do not be sad about what they have done. Build the ship according to Our revelation and under Our eyes. And no longer speak to Me about those who refuse to listen. They shall drown.'

Nuh built the ship. Each time the leaders of the people passed by, they laughed at him.
Nuh said, 'We shall mock you later, as you mock us now. You shall soon know who will be punished, who will be humiliated, and who will suffer a lasting punishment.'
When We made our decision, and the water started to rise We said, 'Load two of every species of animals, and take your family and the believers with you in the boat.' But the believers were few.
And Nuh said to his people, 'Embark. The ship shall sail and cast anchor in the name of God.'

6

The ship carried them over waves as high as mountains. And Nuh called out to his son, 'Oh, my son, come, go with us. Do no stay with the unbelievers!'
He answered, 'I shall seek swift refuge on a mountain to protect me from the water.'
Nuh said, 'Today nothing can stand its ground against God's command.'
A towering wave came between them and his son drowned, like all the others.

7

And a voice said, 'Earth, draw back your water! Sky, withhold your rain!'
The command was followed. The ship came to rest on Mount Judi.

And Nuh turned to God and said, 'God! My son is part of my family. And your promise is also true. You are the best of judges.'

A voice answered, 'Nuh, your son is not part of your family. His deeds were not good. Do not ask about something of which you do not know the truth. I caution you, do not side with the ignorant.'

Nuh said, 'God! I seek refuge in You when I am burdened with something I do not understand.'

A voice answered, 'Descend from the ship with Our Salaam and blessing for you and for the nations these people shall produce. They may enjoy my lenience now, but later they shall face harsh punishment. This is a secret that we share with you.'

8

To the Thamud We sent their brother Saleh.

He said, 'My people! Worship God! There is no other God than He. He brought you forth from the earth and let you dwell on it. Repent to Him. Ask Him for forgiveness. My God is close to you, He hears you.'

They said, 'Oh, Saleh! You were one of us until today. We had placed our hope in you. Do you now forbid us to serve what our fathers served? Your appeal leaves us in doubt!'

Saleh said, 'My people! This is the she-camel of God. A marvel to you. Let it wander free on earth, and do not harm it. Otherwise a severe punishment shall soon come upon you.'

But they did not listen; they pursued the she-camel and killed it.

Saleh said, 'You have three days to live and enjoy life.'

We made Our decision, and We saved Saleh and his followers from humiliation.

And a deathly shriek overtook those who had done wrong in their houses.

When the day dawned, they were dead. As if they had never existed.
Cursed be the Thamud!

9

Our angels brought Ibrahim glad tidings.
They said, 'Salaam!'
Ibrahim greeted them, 'Salaam!'
And without delay he served them a roasted calf. But when he noticed that they did not reach for the meat, he found it strange. He was afraid.
They said, 'Do not be afraid! We have been sent to the people of Lut.'
Sarah, Ibrahim's wife, who was standing at his side, laughed with delight when We brought her the good news that she would fall pregnant and give birth to Ishaq, and that Yaqub would come after Ishaq.

10

Sarah said, 'It is a miracle. How can I bear a child? I am an old woman, and my husband is also old. It is astonishing.'
The angels said, 'Are you surprised at God's decision? His blessings be upon the inhabitants of this house.
'He is magnificent. Praised be He.'

11

When Ibrahim's fear left him, and he perceived the good news, he started to argue with Us about the people of Lut.
Ibrahim, of course, was gentle and kind.
We said, 'Ibrahim! Stop! God has made His decision. That people's punishment cannot be repealed.'

12

To the people of Madyan We sent their brother Shuayb.

He said, 'My people! Worship God! There is no other God than He. And do not use a dishonest measure in the scales. I see you in prosperity. I fear for your punishment on the great day.

'My people! Deal honestly with weights and measures; give the people no less than their due, and do not spread destruction in this land.

'My people! Do not let your quarrel with me take you so far that something befalls you similar to what befell the people of Nuh, and the people of Hud, and the people of Saleh. The people of Lut are not far from you.

'Ask Him thus for forgiveness. He is kind and forgiving.'

13

They said, 'Shuayb! We do not understand much of what you say. We see you as the weakest among us. If it were not for your clan, we would have stoned you already. You do not deserve our respect.'

Shuayb said, 'My people! Is my clan more important to you than God? Have you cast Him aside as something worthless?

'Know this! My God is aware of all that you do.

'My people! Do what you will, and I shall do the same. We shall see soon enough which of us is stricken by a humiliating punishment, and which of us is a liar.

'Just wait, and I shall wait with you.'

When we made Our decision, We saved Shuayb and his followers, but those who did wrong were seized by a deathly shriek. In the morning they lay motionless in their houses. As if they had never existed.

Cursed be the people of Madyan!

14

Muhammad! Stand firm! Perform prayer at both ends of the day and in the portions of the night. And be patient, for Allah shall not allow your reward to be lost.

Muhammad!

All the life stories of the prophets We recount to you are intended to give you courage.

Say to those who do not believe, 'Do what you will. We shall do the same. And wait! We too shall wait.'

The secrets of the earth and the heavens belong to Allah. Everything returns to Him. Praise Him, and place your trust in Him. He is not heedless of what you do.

53

Yusuf

In many respects, this sura is a love story. It is a Jewish-Christian text that has acquired an Arabic guise.

Ibrahim had grown old and so had his wife Sarah.

One day, a couple of handsome strangers appeared at their door unannounced.

Ibrahim welcomed them while Sarah made something to eat and set it before them. But they did not touch it.

The guests were strange, and their behaviour unusual.

Ibrahim was worried and thought to himself, they don't eat, they don't drink, and they don't have a lot to say. Who are these men?

'We are angels, Ibrahim,' said one of them. 'We have good tidings for you. Your wife Sarah shall bear a son.'

When Sarah heard this, she cried out in surprise, 'Me? But I'm too old.'

Sarah gave birth to Ishaq.

He succeeded Ibrahim, lived one hundred and eighty years, and had many children.

After Ishaq came his son Yaqub.

When he was still young, Yaqub dreamt that he was married to his niece Rahil, that she gave him many children, and that he was wealthy.

When he reached adulthood, he took his staff and travelled to the house of his uncle near Iraq.

He worked for his uncle for seven years, but was not granted Rahil. Instead he had to marry her older sister Laya.

Only after fourteen years was he able to marry Rahil. She bore him Yusuf.

One day, young Yusuf said to his father Yaqub, 'Father, I dreamt about eleven stars. And about the moon. And the sun. They bowed down before me.'

Yaqub said, 'You did not dream this without reason. Tell it to no one! Be silent about it!'

Yusuf's brothers were standing behind the door, and they heard what he said.

They said, 'Yusuf, the son of our father, wants to be our king.'

They decided to prevent it. They took him away and threw him into a well.

The angel Jabra'il came to the boy in the well and said, 'Yusuf, do not be sad. Later they shall save you, and you shall become king of Egypt.'

Yusuf is saved, and he finds himself in the house of the most powerful man in Egypt. He grows up into a handsome young man, and Zulayka falls in love with him.

The sura is about Zulayka's love for Yusuf.

In the name of Allah
He is love
He gives
He forgives

1

'Alif Lam Ra'.

These are signs of the book *In the Beginning*. We sent it in Arabic so that you might reflect on it.

We tell the most beautiful stories in this Qur'an, whereas until now you knew nothing.

One day Yusuf said to his father, 'Oh, father! I dreamt about eleven stars, and about the sun and the moon, and I saw them bow down before me.'

Yaqub said, 'Oh, my son! Do not tell your brothers about the dream. If you do, they will devise malicious plans. Satan is clearly the enemy of humankind.

'I see that God intends to choose you, and He shall teach you how to interpret dreams. Your God is all-knowing and wise.'

2

Yusuf's brothers said, 'It seems that Yusuf and our youngest brother Binyamin are our father's favourites, while we are all brothers. Our father is in error.'

'Kill Yusuf and abandon him in some remote plot of land. Then our father shall be for us alone,' said one of them.

'Do not kill Yusuf,' said another, 'but throw him into a well. If a caravan passes, they shall find him.'

3

They said, 'Father, why do you not trust us with Yusuf, when we clearly love him? Let him go with us tomorrow. He can play and enjoy himself, and we shall keep an eye on him.'

Yaqub said, 'It saddens me to let him go with you. I fear a wolf shall devour him if you do not keep a good eye on him.'

They said, 'We are a strong group. If a wolf were to devour him, we would indeed be unworthy losers.'

4

When Yusuf finally went with them, they carried out their plan to throw him into a well. We revealed to him, 'Yusuf! Do not be sad! In a number of years, you shall tell your brothers about this affair without them comprehending it.'

At night, they visited Yaqub in tears and said, 'Father, we went racing, and left Yusuf with our things, and a wolf devoured him. Yet, even though we tell the truth, you will not believe us.' And unbeknown to their father, they had smeared blood on Yusuf's clothes.

Yaqub said, 'Your own desire brought you to this deed. Now I must be very patient!'

5

This is what happened. A caravan was passing, and a servant was despatched to fetch water. The servant lowered his bucket into the well and shouted, 'Good news! There's a boy in the well.'

Like a piece of merchandise, they hid Yusuf among their goods. And God saw everything.

The brothers sold Yusuf for a couple of silver coins, for they attached little value to him.

The Egyptian who had bought him, said to his wife Zulayka, 'Give him a decent lodging. He might be useful to us. Or perhaps we can adopt him as our own child.'

Thus, We established Yusuf in that land, and We taught him how to explain dreams.

God knows what He is doing, but people are unaware of it.

When Yusuf was a young man, We granted him knowledge and a capacity to judge.

6

Zulayka, the woman of the house where Yusuf lived, asked him for his love. She locked the doors and said, 'Come!'

Yusuf answered, 'Seek your refuge in God. Your husband is my master, and he has sheltered me well.'

But she was determined to have him, and he would have desired her also, had he not seen God's signs.

Thus, We turned evil away from him, for he was a chosen one.

7

When Zulayka heard someone fumbling with the lock, she ran to the door. She tore open the back of Yusuf's shirt when she realized that it was her husband on the other side of the door.

She said baselessly, 'The punishment for someone who has bad intentions toward your wife is nothing other than imprisonment or painful retribution.'

Yusuf said, 'She wanted to seduce me!'

A witness said, 'If his shirt is torn at the front, she speaks the truth, and he is lying. But if his shirt is torn at the back, she is lying, and he is telling the truth.'

When her husband saw the shirt was torn at the back he said, 'This is female cunning. And the cunning of women is astonishing. Yusuf! Put this out of your mind. And you, woman, ask forgiveness!'

8

There were women in the city who said, 'The wife of Aziz asked her servant for love. She is in love.'

When Zulayka heard the gossip, she invited the women to join her for a meal. She gave each of them a knife and said to Yusuf, 'Show yourself.'

When the women saw him, they found him incredible. They cut their hands mindlessly and said, 'By God. This is not a human being but a precious angel.'

Zulayka said, 'This is the one about whom you made accusations. I did indeed ask him for love, but he refused. And if he does not give me what I ask, he shall be thrown into prison and humiliated.'

Yusuf said, 'God! I prefer prison to what she asks of me. If You do not foil her plot, I shall submit.'

God heard him, and He foiled her plot.

9

Thus, Yusuf was thrown into prison together with two young slaves. One of them said, 'I saw myself in a dream pressing wine from grapes.'

The other said, 'I saw myself carrying bread on my head with birds pecking at it. Yusuf, explain it to us!'

Yusuf said, 'No food shall come to you before I have revealed the explanation of your dreams. This is what my God taught me.

'Oh, my fellow prisoners. One of you shall pour wine for his master, but the other shall be crucified, and the birds shall eat from his head.'

And he said to the one he knew would be set free, 'Mention my name to your master.'

But Satan made him forget it. Yusuf thus remained in prison a number of years.

10

One day, the king of Egypt declared, 'I dreamt about seven fat cows that were devoured by seven lean cows. I also dreamt of seven green ears of grain and seven dry ears. Oh, counsellors! Explain my dream!'

They said, 'These dreams are foolish, we cannot explain them.'

One of those present was the slave who had spent time in prison with Yusuf. He said, 'I can provide you with an explanation.'

Pharaoh agreed, and the slave visited Yusuf in prison.

He said to Yusuf, 'Explain the significance of the seven fat cows being eaten by the seven lean cows, and the seven green ears of corn, and the seven that were dry. I shall pass on your explanation to those who are waiting for me.'

Yusuf said, 'Continue to sow for seven years as usual, and store away your abundant harvest, except for a small portion that you may eat.

Seven difficult years shall come in which you shall eat what you stored away.

'Thereafter, a year shall come in which it shall rain, and the people shall be able to press olives once again.'

11

Pharaoh heard Yusuf's explanation and said, 'Bring that man here!'

And when he had spoken to Yusuf he said, 'From today, you are granted a place with us. You have our confidence.'

Yusuf said, 'Appoint me as supervisor of the storehouses, for I am a skilled guard.'

We thus established Yusuf in the land so that he could do what he wanted.

12

Yusuf's brothers came to the storehouses. He recognised them, but they did not recognise him. When he gave them their portion he said, 'Bring me your youngest brother. Do you not see that I gave you the complete portion and that I am the best of hosts? But if you do not bring him, you shall receive nothing more from me.'

They answered, 'We shall try to persuade our father to let him come with us. We are sure to succeed.'

Yusuf said to his servants, 'Hide their money among their possessions. They shall see it when they arrive home, and they shall surely return.'

13

When the brothers arrived at their father's house they said, 'Father! They gave us a measure too little. Send our youngest brother with us so that we might fetch it. We shall take good care of him.'

Yaqub said, 'I do not trust you. I did so once before. God is the best guard.'

As they were unpacking their things, they found their money. They said, 'Oh, father! What more could we want? Our money has been returned to us. We can buy corn for our family once more. We shall keep a good eye on our brother, and we shall be granted an extra camel load.'

Yaqub said, 'I shall not let him go with you unless you swear by God that you shall bring him back to me.'

They swore by God and Yaqub said, 'God knows what we have agreed.'

And he added, 'My sons. Do not enter through a single gate. Enter through several gates, although there is nothing I can do that is against God's will. I have placed my trust in Him. Those who trust Him must continue to trust Him.'

They entered the city as their father had asked them, but this changed nothing of God's will.

When they came to Yusuf, he received his youngest brother Binyamin separately and said, 'I am your brother Yusuf. Do not be sad.'

After he had given the others their portion, he hid a drinking cup among Binyamin's belongings.

A servant cried out, 'Hey, you, people of that caravan, you are thieves!'

Yusuf's brothers said, 'What do you mean?! Is something missing?'

'We cannot find Pharaoh's drinking cup.'

Yusuf's brothers said, 'By God! We did not come to do evil in this land. We are not thieves.'

Passers-by asked themselves what the punishment would be for such a theft.

Yusuf's brothers said, 'If you find the drinking cup with one of us, he is a thief, and you may punish him for it.'

The servant started to search their bags. When he came to the last, to Binyamin's bag, he pulled out the drinking cup.

We suggested this trap to Yusuf, otherwise he would not have been able to detain his brother according to the law of the king.

14

The brothers said, 'As Binyamin steals, so did his brother steal in the past.'

But Yusuf pretended not to hear them. He said to himself, you are still preoccupied with that error, and God knows it.

They said, 'Oh, lord, he has an elderly father. Take one of us instead of him. You are a fair-minded man.'

Yusuf said, 'By God, we shall lock up no one but the person who was found with the drinking cup.'

The brothers withdrew disappointed to confer among themselves.

The eldest said to the others, 'I shall not leave this land until I have permission from my father. Return to our father and say, "Father, your son is guilty of theft. And we have only said what we knew. In all honesty we could not have known this secret. Ask the people in the city and the people of the caravan. We are telling the truth."'

So they went home without Binyamin and told their father what had happened.

15

Saddened, Yaqub said, 'Your greed led you to this deed. Now I am in need of much patience. Perhaps God shall bring back my sons to me. He is almighty.'

And he turned away from them and said, 'I am sad on account of Yusuf.' His eyes were blinded with grief.

They said, 'Your pain shall be the death of you, father.'

He said, 'I lament my sadness before God alone. Go in search of Yusuf and his brother, my sons, for I have heard something from God that you do not know.'

16

When they came to Yusuf they said 'Oh, lord! We and our family have suffered much adversity. We have a small amount of money with us, but give us back our brother.'

Yusuf said, 'Do you still remember what you did with your brother Yusuf when you were still ignorant?'

Only then did they recognise him. 'Are you Yusuf?'

He said, 'Yes, I am Yusuf. And this is my brother.'

They said, 'God has chosen you over us. We were at fault.'

Yusuf said, 'This day you shall not be reproached. May God forgive you. Take this shirt of mine and pull it over my father's eyes. Then he shall be able to see again. And bring all your family to me!'

17

Later, when the caravan had arrived in Egypt, their father said to his fellow travellers, 'Do not think me insane, but I smell the smell of Yusuf.'

They said, 'By God! Your old thoughts still lead you astray.'

When the proclaimer of good tidings arrived, he pulled the shirt over Yaqub's eyes, and he was able to see again.

He said, 'Did I not say to you that God had told me something you did not know?'

18

When they were reunited, Yusuf embraced his parents and said, 'Welcome to Egypt. By the will of God, here you are safe!'

54

The City of al-Hijr

Allah had a fondness for the devil because he continued to worship God, and his praise was so exaggerated that the angels looked at him disapprovingly. But Allah found it amusing. The devil was dear to Him.

When Allah created humankind, He fell in love with His own creation. That made the devil jealous.

The devil had expected Allah to give the earth to him and his descendants, but Allah apportioned it to Adam instead. He even created a woman from Adam's side to make life more pleasant for him. The devil was almost blind with hatred.

But because Allah had a soft spot for the devil, He gave him permission to join Adam on earth.

(According to Sheig Ahmad Gazaie Razi)

In the name of Allah
He is love
He gives
He forgives

1

'Alif Lam Ra'.
These are the signs of the Qur'an.
We have never destroyed a city outside its established hour.
The hour of a people does not come too early nor does it come too late.
The unbelievers said, 'Oh, you to whom the Qur'an was sent, you are mad. Why did you not come with angels, if you speak the truth?'
We only send the angels if it is necessary, but when the angels come, the time of those people is past.

2

Muhammad! We sent the Qur'an, and We shall be its guard.
Long before your time, We sent prophets to the ancient peoples.
But there was not a single prophet they did not humiliate.
Even if We had opened a door in the sky through which they could have ascended to heaven, their response would have been, 'Our eyes are clouded. We are under a spell.'

3

We made high towers of the stars in the heavens, and We adorned them finely for those who behold them. And We protected them against the accursed Satan. Every Satan who approached the heavens to eavesdrop was pursued by a burning meteorite.

4

And We spread out the earth and placed the mountain ranges on it.

We caused all sort of important things to grow in the correct form.

We provide the necessary nourishment, and We provide for those you do not maintain.

And there is nothing that does not have its treasury with Us.

We send nourishment in the required amounts.

5

We send fertilizing winds, and We cause water to fall from the sky, with which We quench your thirst, for you cannot store it yourselves.

It is We who give life and bring death, and We are the heirs of it all.

And We know the ones who came before you and the ones who shall come after you.

Muhammad! Your creator shall bring them all together.

He is all-wise! He is all-knowing!

6

We made humankind from a lump of clay, old, dry and stinking.

Before that, we made the jinn from pure fire without smoke.

Muhammad! Thus it was, until your Creator said to the angels, 'I intend to create Adam from stinking clay. When I am done and have breathed something of My spirit into him, you must kneel before him!'

The angels knelt as one before Adam, but Satan refused.

God said, 'Oh, Satan! What is wrong with you? Why do you refuse to kneel?'

Satan said, 'I am not one to kneel before a human You made from stinking clay.'

God said, 'Get out of here, you outcast. A curse be upon you, until the day of Judgement.'

Satan said, 'My Creator! Give me time, until the day on which the humans are raised after death.'

God said, 'The time is granted you.'

Satan said, 'My Lord! Now that You have misled me, I shall mislead the people on earth.'

God said, 'Know that you cannot reach my true servants, except those who have gone astray. And hell is the place where they shall be reunited. Know this! Hell has seven gates, and each gate is destined for a specific group.

'But the believers shall find themselves in the gardens of happiness where springs well up.

'A voice shall say to them, "Enter in health and peace."

'We shall remove whatever resentment is in their hearts. They shall lie down opposite one another on couches. No tiredness shall overcome them, and they shall not be sent away.'

7

Muhammad, say to My servants that I am a loving God, but that My punishment is merciless.

Muhammad, tell them about Ibrahim's guests when they entered his presence as angels.

The angels said, 'Salaam!'

Ibrahim said, 'I am afraid. Who are you?'

They said, 'Do not be afraid. We bring good tidings. You are granted a wise son.'

Ibrahim was on his guard, 'Do you announce such good tidings to an old man? What does this mean?'

They said, 'Do not despair. Our message is genuine.'

'What further business do you have here?' asked Ibrahim.

They said, 'We have come for the people of Lut.'

8

When the angels entered Lut's presence, Lut said, 'I do not know you.'

They said, 'We have brought something for you about which your people doubted. We have brought the truth for you. And we are sincere.'

The men of the city entered the house of Lut.

Lut said, 'Men! These are my guests. Do not embarrass me! Fear God, and do not humiliate me. Here are my daughters.'

9

Muhammad! Those people were blind and had gone astray.

At dawn they were seized by a deathly shriek. And We turned the city upside down. And we caused blocks of clay to rain down on them. The ruins of that city are still clearly visible at the side of the road.

10

The people of the city al-Hijr were also unjust. They called the prophets liars. We also took revenge on them. They had built houses in the mountains for safety, yet they were seized by a deathly shriek in the early morning.

Muhammad! Your Creator is the All-Knowing One.

And We gave you the great Qur'an.

Muhammad, say to them, 'I am a clear speaking cautioner.'

Proclaim aloud what was revealed to you, and turn aside from those who do not believe.

We know that you are saddened by what they say, but persevere until death comes to you.

55

The Cattle

Namrood was king of a country located in what is now Egypt.
He reigned as a tyrant and served idols. Azar, Namrood's sculptor, made idols for him.
The astronomers warned the king, 'A child is to be born who shall later destroy the idols. And he shall take your life.'
Namrood ordered the death of every newborn son.
The wife of Azar was pregnant. She bore a son and called him Ibrahim. To protect her son from Namrood's men, she took him with her to the mountains.
One night, when young Ibrahim left the mountain cave for the first time in his life, he was taken by the beauty of the star-filled sky.
What is this? he asked himself in amazement. Who is responsible for this?
A clear star appeared and a voice was heard in the distance, 'Hadha Rabbi, from Him, from your Creator.'
The star disappeared and Ibrahim said, 'I don't like things that disappear.'
Then the moon appeared and that brought Ibrahim comfort.

When Ibrahim grew up he left the mountains, and when he had grown sturdy and strong he smashed the idols to pieces.
King Namrood had a fire set, the flames of which blazed as high as the lofty mountains. And he gave orders for Ibrahim to be thrown into the fire.
God said to the fire, 'Be cold!'
The fire became cold, and later, trees, plants, and flowers grew on that very spot.

In the name of Allah
He is love
He gives
He forgives

1

Praise be to Allah who made the earth and the heavens, and gave existence to darkness and light.
Yet there are people who devise other gods besides Him.
It is He who made you from clay, and has determined the length of your life, and when you shall die. Yet you still have doubts.
But He is God, and He knows all your secrets.

2

Have they never considered how many peoples We destroyed?
The peoples to whom We gave power that We did not give to you.
And We caused much rain to fall upon them, and made rivers flow for them.
But nonetheless, We punished them with death for their sins, and We caused new peoples to come forth.

3

Muhammad! Even if We had sent a book made of paper to descend on you, which they could have touched with their own hands, they would still have said, it is sorcery.
And they would say, 'Why, then, does no angel come down to him?'
But if We had sent an angel, that would have been the end. They would have been given no more chances.
Muhammad, say to them, 'Travel over the earth and witness the ultimate fate of such liars.'

Ask them, 'Who has possession of all that is on earth and in the heavens?'

And explain, 'Everything is from God, who ascribes mercy to Himself. All that moves and rests by night and by day belongs to Him.

And He hears all things.'

Say, 'How can you choose another protector than God? He who is the Maker of the heavens and the earth? He who gives everyone substance, but gives nothing to Himself?'

Say, 'He has ordered me to praise Him above all, and not be among those who worship idols.'

Explain, 'You should be afraid to disobey Him.'

Ask, 'Whose testimony is the best?'

Say, 'God, who is witness between you and me, revealed this Qur'an to me so that I could warn you and everyone it reaches.'

Ask, 'Do you really testify that there are other gods besides God?'

Say, 'I bear no such testimony.'

Explain, 'He is One, and I want nothing to do with what you are doing.'

4

The unjust shall find happiness nowhere. They are liars.

They say that there is no life after death, and they cannot be called back to life once they are dead.

Life on earth is nothing more than a game, but life after death is better by far for those who believe.

Muhammad, We know that their lies sadden you. They know that you are not lying, but they are determined to reject God's word.

It was no different in the past. They accused the ancient prophets of lies. But the prophets continued their mission with patient perseverance, and they put up with their suffering until Our help came to them.

Muhammad! We have told you about the lives of the other prophets. There is no one who can change God's word. But if you still cannot bear their loathing, then dig a tunnel in the ground, or make a tall ladder reaching to the sky to fetch a miracle for them.

Do so if you are able. But you are not, so do not be one of the fools!

5

Only those who truly listen, hear the message.

God shall raise the dead, and they shall all return to Him.

And they said, 'Is it not possible for God to send a sign to Muhammad?'

Muhammad, say, 'God is capable of sending down a sign, but most of them do not know it.'

There is no creature on earth nor any bird that has a community like yours.

We did not omit anything in the book.

They shall all return to God.

Those who say Our words are lies, are dead and stupid, and wander astray in the darkness.

6

Muhammad, say, 'Reflect! Which deity can help you when God takes the light from your eyes, makes you deaf, and seals your heart?'

See how We explain the signs with clarity and cohesion. Yet, they still turn away.

Say, 'Reflect! Who shall be destroyed if not the unjust, when God's punishment comes to you, plainly and unexpectedly?'

Explain to them, 'I am not saying that God's treasures are at

my disposal, or that I know what is hidden, or that I am an angel. All I do is fulfil the task given to me from above. Are the blind equal to those who see? Why do you refuse to think?'
Say, 'I am forbidden to serve those you serve instead of God. I do not follow your desires. And if I did, I would stray from the right path.'
Tell them, 'I have a clear sign from my God, although you call it lies. I am unable to give you what you ask of me with such force. If I had power, I would have settled matters between us long ago. It is up to God alone to judge. He knows the unrighteous better than any.'

7
Say, 'The keys to what is hidden are with Him. He alone knows it. And He knows what is on the land and what is in the sea. Not a single leaf falls from a tree that He does not know of. And there is not a single grain under the layers of the earth, nothing moist and nothing dry, that is not inscribed in the book *In the Beginning*.

'And it is He who takes away your spirit in the night and who knows what you have done in the day. Then He awakens you again, and so it continues until your time has come and you are informed of what you did in life.'

Say, 'He has power over His servants. And He sends guards for you to register your deeds. And if death comes to one of you, he is taken away.
'God makes the decision and His reckoning is swift.'
Ask them, 'Who shall save you from the darkness, from the menaces of land and sea?'

8

And so it continued until Ibrahim said to his father Azar, 'Do you consider your idols to be God? I see that you and your people have clearly lost their way.'

We let Ibrahim see the kingdom of heaven and the earth so that he would be among those who did not doubt.

When night covered him, he saw a star. He said, 'This is my God.' But when the star set he said, 'I do not like the ones that disappear.'

When he saw the moon rising he said, 'This is my God.' But when it set he said, 'If God does not lead me, I shall become one of those who go astray.'

And when he saw the sun rise he said, 'This is my God. He is greater.' But when it set again, Ibrahim said, 'My people, I have nothing to do with your idols. I turn to Him who made the heavens and the earth.'

Muhammad, ask them, 'Who sent down the book that revealed Musa as light and guide, parts of which you hide?'

Say, 'God!' Then leave them alone with their word games.

We sent a blessed book, testimony to what came before it.

9

It is God who makes kernels and seeds split. He brings forth the living from the dead, and the dead from the living.

Such is God. How can you turn down the wrong path?

It is He who makes a breach in the night to bring forth morning, and He who made the night restful. He made the sun and the moon to calculate time.

Such is the demarcation of power. He is all-knowing.

It is He who made the stars so that you can find your way in the dark by sea and on land. Our signs are clearly visible for those who have insight.

And it is He who brought you into existence from a single body, after which an abode was made in your father's back, and an abode in the belly of your mother.

It is He who causes water to fall from the air.

With it, We bring forth every kind of vegetation. And We made leaves sprout from green branches in which We brought forth sheathed seed kernels. And from the palm trees we made blossoms grow and hanging date clusters. And vineyards, olive trees, and pomegranate trees, some alike some not.

Look at their fruit when it is ripe; it contains signs for those who believe.

10

They considered God to be equal to the jinn, whereas He created the jinn.

And out of ignorance, they devised daughters and sons for Him.

Allah is holy and He is above all that they ascribe to Him.

How can He have a son, when He has no wife?

Allah is the cause of all things. The eyes do not see Him, but He sees the eyes.

11

Should I thus call upon someone other than God to testify, whereas it was He who sent the book to you, unrivalled and clear? So do not be one of the doubters.

And if you believe in His signs, eat only of that over which God's name has been pronounced.

And do not eat of that over which God's name has not been uttered, for that is clear disobedience.

Muhammad, say, 'My people, do what you want. Then we shall see who is granted the reward of the final dwelling place.'

12

And they set aside part of the produce of their fields and of their cattle for God. And they say, 'This is for God. And this is for our idols.'

No part of the idol portion finds its way to God. On the contrary, they give of God's portion to their idols.

They think that the idols will thus forgive them for killing their children.

Muhammad, leave them alone with their lies.

They say, 'What is in the wombs of these cattle, is exclusively for the men. But if it is dead, it is for everyone.'

They shall soon be punished for their behaviour, for God is full of wisdom.

Those who kill their children, they are the losers. They go astray and do not find the right path.

It is God who brought forth gardens with trellised and untrellised trees, palm trees, plants with different fruits, olive trees, and pomegranate trees, some alike and some not.

Eat the fruit thereof at the appropriate time, but do not forget the poor during the harvest.

Eat, but do not be wasteful, for God does not love those who are wasteful.

And among the animals, He created beasts of burden and livestock for slaughter. Eat what God has given you and do not follow Satan. He is clearly your enemy.

13

Muhammad, explain to them, 'Eight animals in pairs are permitted to you: two sheep, two goats.'

Say, 'Did He forbid the two male or the two female, or what the female has in her womb?'

Tell me, then, if you know better.

'Two camels, two cows.'
Why do you lie to put people on the wrong path?
Explain, 'In everything that has been revealed to me, I see nothing that you cannot use. Except the meat of a dead animal, and flowing blood. Or the flesh of swine—for that is abhorrent. Or the meat of a sacrifice whereby the name of one other than God was invoked intentionally during the slaughter. But if you find yourself in need, it is permitted. God is forgiving.'

14

And to the Jews we forbade the following:
'Every sort of creature that has claws.
'For them the fat of a cow, sheep, or goat is also forbidden, except the fat on the back of such animals, and the fat attached to their intestines or attached to their bones.'
We imposed this as a punishment on them because they are so greedy.

15

Muhammad, say, 'Come close so that I can tell you what God has forbidden you:
'It is forbidden to identify anything with God.
'It is forbidden to treat your parents badly.
'It is forbidden to kill your child because of poverty. It is We who provide you with bread and bread for your children.
'It is forbidden to perform unfitting acts, be it in public or in secret.
'It is forbidden to kill a person declared inviolable by God unless the law determines otherwise.
'It is forbidden to lay a hand on the property of an orphan. Be honest with the scales. And be without bias when you testify or when you give judgement, even in the case of your own kin.

'We ask no one to do what they are unable to do. This is the right path. My path!'

16

Those who do good, shall be rewarded tenfold. And those who do evil shall only be punished according to their deed.
Muhammad, tell them, 'My God set me on the right path toward the faith of Ibrahim.'
Say, 'My prayer, my life, and my death are for God, the Maker of the universe.'

56

Row after Row

Of all the thousands of prophets, Muhammad felt most at home with the prophet Ibrahim.
Musa belonged to the Jews, Isa to the Christians, Dawud and Sulayman to almost everyone, but Ibrahim was special; he had built the Kaaba.
He had always loved Mecca, and Mecca had offered Ibrahim safety. The city gave lodging to Ibrahim's young wife Hajar and her son Isma'il.
The mountains of Mecca provided Hajar and her son with water when they almost died of thirst.

Ibrahim set out to sacrifice his favourite son Isma'il in the mountains of Mecca. But Allah sent a sheep to Ibrahim so that he did not have to give up his son.
Ibrahim was a part of Mecca, a part of the Kaaba, and Muhammad took him as his example.
Ibrahim, Mecca, the Kaaba, and the mountains served Allah as one.

Muhammad, Mecca, the Kaaba, and the mountains likewise
served Allah as one. Muhammad was intent on finishing some-
thing Ibrahim had been incapable of finishing.

In the name of Allah
He is love
He gives
He forgives

1
By the angels lined up row after row.
And by those who reprimand.
And by those who recite the Qur'an.
It is true. Your Creator is one.
The Maker of the heavens and the earth, and everything in
between.
And the Maker of the place where the sun rises.
We decorated the lowest level of heaven with stars and shielded
it against the rebellious satans, to prevent them from eaves-
dropping on the assembly of the most exalted on the upper
level.
They are fended off on every side, driven away and punished.
If one of them still secretly listens in, a fiery falling star shall
pursue him.

2
Muhammad! Ask those who do not believe, what is more dif-
ficult, to create them, or to create the greater things We have
made?
We made humans out of clay.
Truly you are amazed, Muhammad, but they laugh at you.
When they are warned, they pay no attention.
And if they see something miraculous, they laugh even louder

and say, 'It is sorcery. When we are dead and have been reduced to dust and bones, shall we be raised to life again? And our forebears with us?'

Muhammad, say, 'Yes!'

3

Bring those who commit injustice, and their friends, together with all they serve other than God, and lead them to hell.

This is how We deal with criminals.

When they were told, 'There is no God but Allah,' they responded with arrogance and said, 'Must we give up our gods for the sake of a mad poet like Muhammad?'

You shall taste immense pain.

But the following awaits the righteous servants of Allah: fruit of every sort. And they shall be welcomed in gardens of happiness with couches facing each other.

Cups with flowing wine, crystal clear and delicious, shall be handed round among them.

They shall not be left with a headache from it nor shall they get drunk.

Beautiful, obedient virgins with eyes the size of eggs shall be at their disposal.

4

Is this a more appropriate reception than the Zaqqum tree, the tree that grows in the depths of hell? Its fruits are like the heads of satans. The unbelievers must eat from it and fill their bellies. Then they receive a brew of boiling water, after which they are ready to be brought to hell. They saw their forebears go astray, although We had sent cautioners among them. Still, they hurried after their forebears.

Look how those who did not listen met their end.

5

Nuh cried out to Us for help, and We saved him and his people from great danger. Thereafter, We drowned those who remained.

Salaam be with Nuh and all the inhabitants of the world.

Ibrahim was one of his followers.

He said to his father and his people, 'What do you serve?! Do you prefer false gods above Allah? What do you think, then, of the Creator of the World?'

He glanced up toward the stars and said, 'I feel far from what you are doing.'

They turned their backs on him, and left him alone.

He turned to the idols and said, 'Why do you not eat? Why do you not speak?'

And he started to strike them with his right hand.

The people ran to him.

Ibrahim said, 'Do you prefer to serve your own inventions, whereas God created you and everything around you?'

They said, 'We shall build a soaring fire, and we shall throw you into it!'

Ibrahim said, 'I shall go to my God.'

They hatched a plot against him, but We thwarted it and humiliated them.

6

Then We proclaimed good news to them, the arrival of a son.

When the child grew up, Ibrahim said to him, 'Oh, my son, I had a dream in which I sacrificed you. Tell me! What should I do?'

His son said, 'Oh, Father! Do what you have been commanded. You shall find me patient.'

When they submitted to the will of God, and Ibrahim placed his sleeping son on the ground, We called to him, 'Ibrahim!

You have made your dream a reality. We shall reward you. This was a terrible ordeal. Instead of him, We shall accept another sacrifice.'

Salaam be with Ibrahim!

And we announced good news to him of Ishaq, a messenger. We lauded him and Ishaq.

7

Ilias was also one of the messengers.

He said to his people, 'Have you no fear? Do you prefer to serve Baal and forget the Creator? God, your Maker and the Maker of your forebears?'

They branded him a liar.

Salaam be with Ilias. He was one of Our best followers.

Lut was also one of the messengers.

We saved him and his family, except his wife, who remained behind. And we destroyed the others.

You pass the ruins morning and evening. Do you still refuse to show sense?

8

Yunus was also among the messengers. He fled with a fully laden ship. A great fish swallowed him up, a humiliation he deserved. If he had not shown remorse he would have remained in the belly of the fish until the day when all are raised to life. We threw him onto an empty beach, and he was ill. We caused a pumpkin plant to grow above him. Then We sent him as a messenger to his people.

9

Muhammad, ask them if your Creator has daughters, while they have sons. Did we create the angels as female in their presence?

They say in a spiteful tone, 'Did Allah beget children?'
They are liars.
Did God perhaps choose daughters over sons? Where do you get such things? Do you have evidence? Let it be seen, if you speak the truth.
They presume a similarity between Allah and the jinn.
But Allah stands above everything they ascribe to Him.
Do they want to witness Our punishment as quickly as possible?
When it descends upon their house, it shall be a bad day for them.
Muhammad, repeat what the angels say, 'Each one of us has an appointed place. We stand row after row. And we praise Him.'
Muhammad! Turn away from them for a while.
Pure is your Creator, the Victor.
And Salaam be with the messengers.
And praise to Allah, the Maker of the world.

57

Luqman

Luqman was an elderly philosopher who had bought his freedom from slavery with his wisdom.
God offered him the choice between prophethood and learning. He chose learning, and he earned an excellent reputation.
People asked him questions, 'What is most bitter for humans?'
'Poverty,' said Luqman.
'What is most delightful for humans?'
'Wealth.'
'What is the worst for humans?'
'A wicked woman.'

'What is the saddest for humans?'
'The moment of death.'
'What is greater than the sea?'
'A big heart.'
'What burns more painfully than fire?'
'Jealousy,' Luqman answered.

In the name of Allah
He is love
He gives
He forgives

1
'Alif Lam Mim.
These are the signs of the book filled with wisdom.
There are people who set out to lead others astray with fancy words. They shall be shamefully punished.
And when Our texts are recited to them, they turn away in arrogance as if they do not hear, as if they are deaf.
Muhammad! Proclaim a painful punishment for them.
Allah is almighty. Allah is all-wise.

2
He made the heavens with invisible pillars.
He attached the mountains firmly to the ground so that the earth would not cause you to sway.
He distributed animals of every kind across the earth. He caused water to fall from the sky, and He made an abundance of excellent varieties grow.
This is the world of Allah. So show Me what the other gods have done.

3

We granted wisdom to Luqman, and Luqman gave advice to his son.

Luqman said, 'My son, do not consider anything to be part of Allah, for that is a great injustice!'

We advised humans to take care of their parents.

Your mothers carried you as they grew weaker and weaker, and they weaned you for two years.

Be grateful to Me and your parents!

But if your parents urge you to append something or someone to Me, you must not listen to them. Stay with them in this life, but opt for the path of those who follow Me, for you shall all return to Me.

Luqman said, 'My son! Know this! Even if your deed is as small as a mustard seed, and even if it is in a rock, or in the heavens, or on earth, Allah shall find it. He sees all things.'

Luqman said, 'My son! Praise Allah! And give. And bear what befalls you with patience. Patience is a great virtue.'

Luqman said, 'Do not turn your face from the people and strut around with arrogance on earth, for Allah does not love the arrogant.'

Luqman said, 'My son! Be moderate! And soften your voice, for the ugliest voice is like the noisy braying of an ass.'

4

Muhammad, do not be sad on account of those who wish to remain without belief. They shall all be returned to Us. Then We shall show them what they have done. Allah knows what is in their hearts. We shall grant them enjoyment for a while, but thereafter we shall seize them, and their retribution shall be severe.

If you ask them who made the heavens and the earth they shall say, 'Allah.'

Say, 'Praise be to Allah!'

5

Everything in the heavens and on earth belongs to Allah. He is the Prosperous One; He lacks nothing. But many do not know this.

If all the trees on earth were pens and the sea ink, and seven more seas came to replenish it, there still would not be enough to describe Allah.

Your creation and your return form a unity. Allah is all-wise.

6

Muhammad! Have you not seen how Allah makes the night flow into the day and the day flow into the night? How He has tamed the sun and the moon so that they each have their appointed time, and how He is aware of everything you are doing?

Are you not aware that the ships move across the sea on Allah's command to reveal something of His signs to you?

Without doubt, there is a lesson in this for those who are patient and grateful.

When they are struck by waves high as mountains, they call out to Allah, but when He saves them and brings them safely to shore, only a few follow the right path. Others deny Our signs.

7

People, fear your Creator! And fear the day on which a father can no longer help his son, or a son his father. God's warning is resolute.

Do not let everyday life mislead you, and do not let Satan deceive you.

Only Allah has knowledge of life hereafter, and it is He who causes the rain to fall. He knows what is in the belly of a mother, and no one knows what tomorrow shall bring.

Allah knows all things.

58

The People of Saba

Talut was a righteous king. When his death was near, he appointed his courageous and wise son-in-law Dawud as his successor.
The Israelites were also happy with his choice.
Dawud was a descendant of Yaqub, of Ishaq, and of Ibrahim. He was later chosen as a prophet.
Dawud had red hair and green eyes that sometimes sparkled blue. He also had a beautiful voice. God had not given such a magnificent voice to anyone before Dawud.
When he sang, the people, the birds, and the animals held their breath to listen to him.

Dawud was the first person to wear a suit of armour.
The angel Jabra'il taught him to smelt iron and cast it. He wore his armour under his clothes in battle, and no one was aware of his secret.
He became the strongest and most mysterious king in the world.
God granted him a son who acquired the name Sulayman.

The present sura returns to the life of Sulayman.
When Sulayman died, no one realized it because he remained standing.
A woodworm was the first to notice.

In the name of Allah
He is love
He gives
He forgives

1

Praise be to Allah. Everything on earth and in the heavens belongs to Him.

Praise to Him also in the life hereafter.

He knows what goes into the earth and what comes out of it, what falls from the heavens and what ascends thereto. He is kind and forgiving.

2

The unbelievers say that the day of judgement shall not come upon them.

Say to them, 'It shall certainly come! By Allah who knows what is hidden, it shall come upon you.'

There is nothing in the heavens or on earth that escapes Him.

And there is nothing too small or too great that it is not clearly mentioned in the book *In the Beginning*.

3

The unbelievers say, 'Shall we take you to a man who claims that you shall come back to life after death, when you are decayed?

'Is he lying about his God or has he gone mad?'

Muhammad! Do they not look on occasion to the sky and to the earth in front of them and behind them?

Should We so desire, We could drag them into the earth, or cause part of the sky to fall on them.

This contains a lesson for those who turn to God.

4

We gave something of Ourself to the prophet Dawud. And We said, 'Mountains, sing praise with him! Birds, join in!'

We made iron pliable for him.

And We said, 'Make long coats of mail; measure each interwoven link with care, and be precise, for We see all things.'

We tamed the wind for Sulayman so that he could make a lunar journey in the morning and in the evening.

We also helped him to melt copper, and he had a group of jinn who worked for him. If one of them refused Our command, We gave him a taste of fire.

They made everything he desired: houses of prayer, statues, immense basins that served as reservoirs, and massive standing pots. And We said, 'People of Dawud, be grateful.' But few were grateful.

5

When we allowed Sulayman to die, only a woodworm noticed it. It was not until he fell to the ground that the jinn realized he was dead. If they had known what is hidden, they would not have continued to work in such humiliating circumstances for such a long time.

6

The people of Saba had a marvel in the midst of their houses: two gardens, one on the left and one on the right. We said to them, 'Eat what your Creator has provided for you. And be grateful. You have a fine city and a forgiving Creator.'

But they turned away, so We sent a devastating flood over them, and we transformed those two magnificent gardens into two barren planes with tasteless fruit, tamarisks, and a couple of lotus shrubs. They were punished because they were ungrateful.

And between them and the cities in which We had brought them happiness, We located beautiful villages a short distance apart and We said, 'Travel safely, day and night.'

But they said, 'God! Make the roads long and the journeys distant.'

They did themselves an injustice. We turned them into people from folk tales, and We turned them to dust. This contains a lesson for those who are patient.

7

Muhammad, ask them, 'Who gives you what you need from the heavens and the earth?'

Answer, 'Allah!'

Say, 'You shall not be asked about the bad things others have done nor shall they be asked about what you have done.'

Say, 'Our Creator shall assemble everyone. Then, He shall give judgement. He is the all-knowing Judge.'

We sent you alone, as a cautioner and proclaimer of good tidings, but most do not understand. They say, 'Tell us when to expect your day of judgement, if you speak the truth.'

Say to them, 'It shall come. Neither an hour earlier nor an hour later.'

And when they see the punishment, they shall no longer be able to contain their remorse. We shall hang heavy chains around their necks.

8

It has always been like this. We sent a cautioner to the cities, and the wealthy among them said, 'We do not believe in you.'

And they said, 'We are wealthy. We have many offspring, and we shall not be punished.'

Muhammad, say, 'My Creator provides with generosity for whomever He pleases, but He also restricts His provision. However, most do not understand.'

Your wealth and your children cannot bring you close to Us.

9

When Our clear signs are recited to them, they say, 'This man only wants to prevent you from serving what your forebears were accustomed to serving.'

They say, 'This is nothing more than trickery.'

And, 'Obvious sorcery.'

Did We not already give them books to study? Did We not send prophets to them before you?

But they branded Our other prophets liars.

And you know what My punishment was for them.

10

Say, 'I advise you to do one thing. Go before Allah in pairs, or one by one, and reflect! Muhammad is not a fool. He only warns you of a severe punishment.'

Say, 'I have not asked you for a wage. My wage is with Allah. He knows all things. He knows every secret!'

Say, 'If I go astray, I go astray on my own account. But if I follow the right path, it is because of what Allah has revealed to me. He listens and He is near.'

59

Group after Group

From time immemorial, Arabs have cast their love and their hatred in poetic form. A poem could always be wielded as a sword. Muhammad knows how sensitive the Arab tribes are when it comes to their language and traditions. It is for this reason that he states repeatedly that the Qur'an is an Arabic book.

He knew that the tribal chiefs would only be persuaded with powerful poetry.

*But how could he create poetry if he was unable to read or write?
And more importantly, how could he create poetry that was
more powerful than that of the Arabic master poets?*

*Muhammad knew well enough that he was incapable of produc-
ing such poetry. But when he finally appeared with his masterful
verses, everyone said, 'Muhammad, where did you find such
language?'*

'It is not my own,' he said, 'it is from the book In the Beginning,
*which is with Allah. The verses are passed on to me, and I relate
them in beautiful Arabic.'*

*The Qur'an was thus especially for the Arabs, to safeguard their
honour and pride.*

In the name of Allah
He is love
He gives
He forgives

1

This book was sent by Allah. He is wise!
Muhammad! We have revealed this book to you in truth. Serve
Allah, therefore, and keep your faith pure for Him.

2

Allah does not guide liars.
If Allah had wanted a son, He would have chosen one from
His creation.
Give praise to Him. He is one, He is almighty.
He created the heavens and the earth in truth. He covers the
night with the day, and He covers the day with the night.
He tamed the sun and the moon, each of which follows its
appointed time.

3

He made you from one soul. Then He created its wife. And He created eight species of animals for you. And He made you in your mothers' bellies, creation after creation, in three phases of darkness. Such is Allah, your Maker. And the kingdom belongs to Him.

What, then, makes you go astray?

Are those who worship God in the deep of night, sometimes kneeling, sometimes standing; those who concern themselves with the life hereafter and hope for forgiveness from their God; are such people equal to those who do not?

Say, 'Are those who know the same as those who do not?'

Only the wise can learn a lesson from this.

Muhammad, say, 'People! Fear Allah. Those who do good in this life shall receive goodness in return. The earth is spacious.'

Say, 'I have been commanded to serve Him. I fear the great punishment.'

4

Say, 'Serve whatever you want to serve besides Him. The real losers will be those who bring injury on themselves and their family on the day of judgement.

'Layers of fire shall overshadow them, and layers of fire shall appear under their feet. This is precisely what Allah is warning people against.

'Fear Allah!'

For those who fear their Creator, there are rooms with other rooms built on top, under which rivers flow. Allah keeps His promises.

5

Do you not see that He causes water to fall from the sky and penetrate the earth? That he causes vegetation of every sort to germinate in various colours. Then He dries them, and you see them turn yellow, and then He breaks them into pieces. Herein lies a lesson for those who reflect.

6
Allah has sent down beautiful texts in the form of a book, texts that are often similar and are often repeated, making the skin of those who fear God, shiver. They shall experience rest in their skin and in their hearts when they think of Him.
We have given every kind of example in this Qur'an so that people may learn from it. It is a clear document in the Arabic language so that people might come to God.

7
God gives the example of a slave with two owners who constantly argue with each other, and a slave with only one owner. Are these two slaves alike?
Praise be to Allah. But most do not understand.
Muhammad! You shall die! They shall also die. And then you can continue your dispute in the presence of Allah.

8
Muhammad, say, 'Allah is enough for me!'
Say, 'My people! Do what you want. I shall also do what I want. Then we shall see who is humiliated, and who is faced with enduring punishment.'
Muhammad! Those who follow the good path do so to their own advantage. And those who go astray, go astray to their own disadvantage. You are not their keeper.
Allah takes the soul of those who die, and also of those who sleep and are not yet dead. Then He retains those who are dead, and sends the rest away until their appointed time.
There is a lesson herein for those who reflect.

9

Say! 'Oh, Allah! You, Maker of the heavens and the earth.
'You, Knower of the hidden and the visible.
'You judge between people when they are unable to agree.'
Do they perhaps not know that Allah gives generously when He sees fit, and gives less when He sees fit? This is a sign for those who want to believe.
Muhammad, say, 'People! If you have been lawless, you should not lose hope, for Allah forgives sins. He is kind, He forgives. Turn back to Allah, therefore, and surrender, before it is too late and great punishment confronts you!'

10

'On the day of judgement you shall see people whose faces have turned black. These are the ones who lied about God.
'And is hell not the right place for those who commit violence?'

11

Allah is the Maker of all and He is guardian over all. He possesses the keys to the heavens and the earth. Those who have ignored our signs belong with the losers.
Say to them, 'Oh, ignorant ones! Do you instruct me to serve someone other than Allah?'
Muhammad! It was revealed to you and to the ancient prophets that if you serve another God instead of Allah, your deeds shall be fruitless. And you shall be a loser.
So serve Him, and be grateful!

12

The day of judgement shall come. The trumpet shall be blown, the heavens shall be rolled up by His hand, and everyone in the heavens and on earth shall fall to the ground in a faint unless God desires it otherwise. Then the trumpet shall be blown for a second time, and they shall get to their feet. They shall wait and look. The earth shall shine in the light of its Creator. And the book shall be brought forth, the prophets shall appear, and judgement shall be passed on the people according to the truth. No one shall be treated unjustly.

Thereafter, the unbelievers shall be led to hell, group after group, and when they arrive, the gates shall be opened, and the guardians shall say to them, 'Did no messengers come to you? Did no one warn you? Come forward! And dwell here for eternity. What a miserable dwelling it is.'

And those who feared Allah shall be led to paradise, group after group. And when they arrive, the gates shall be opened, and the guardians shall say to them, 'Salaam! Welcome! Come forward and stay here for eternity!'

And you shall see the angels moving in unison to the throne to revere Allah. They say, 'Praise be to You, the Maker of worlds.'

60

He Who Forgives

When Allah desires something he simply says, 'Be!' and it is.
It is he who created the four-footed animals for us.
It is he who created the roads for us.
But why? For what reason?
Muhammad has an exceptional perspective on the world.
He sees the four-footed animals as a means of transport on which we travel to our dreams.
He does not see the roads as made by human beings, but as paths cleared by Allah.
And a road is not simply a path to follow; it is a means to achieve our dreams.

*Muhammad travels on a camel along a road, and he knows why
he is on this particular camel and this particular road.
Everything is focused on giving Muhammad the possibility of
conquering Mecca.
Every camel and every road leads to the Kaaba.*

In the name of Allah
He is love
He gives
He forgives

1
Ha' Mim.
This book was sent by Allah, the Beloved, the Beautiful.
Each people that decided to seize its messenger was seized by
Me. And see how terrible My punishment was for them.

2
Allah reveals His signs to you. He sends bread from heaven.
He stands higher than every rank, the Maker of the universe.
He reveals His word to whomever He desires, to warn of the
day of the encounter.
On that day, nothing shall remain hidden from Him.
A voice shall shout, 'This day! To whom does the Kingdom
belong?'
And a voice shall say, 'To Allah. The One. The Almighty.'

3
God sees the perfidy of the eyes, and what hearts conceal.
He judges according to the truth, but the idols are incapable of
deciding. He sees, He hears all things.

4

Without doubt, the creation of the heavens and the earth is greater than the creation of humankind, but most people do not know it.

A sighted person and a blind person are not alike, in the same way as a believer and an unbeliever are not alike.

Your Creator says, 'Call upon Me, and I shall hear you.'

But most people do not believe it.

The hour shall come, there is no possible doubt. And those who have held the prayer in disdain shall soon be brought to hell in humiliation.

5

Allah made the night for you to rest in it, and the day as an illuminated panorama.

He gives, but most are ungrateful.

He is the Maker of all things. How is it possible that you choose the wrong path?

It is Allah who made the earth as a place of rest for you, and the sky as a roof.

He formed you, and gave you fine faces.

Muhammad, say, 'I am forbidden to serve those you serve. I have been commanded to bow before the Maker of the universe.'

It is He who made you from soil, thereafter from a droplet, thereafter from a clot of blood. You come into the world as an infant, and you grow until you are old. Some of you die young, and others live to their appointed time. Perhaps there is a lesson here for you.

6

It is He who gives life and brings death. If He desires something He simply says, 'Be!' And it is.

Those who show disdain for the Book shall experience the consequences.

They shall be dragged toward boiling water with iron chains around their necks. Then they shall be tossed into the fire of hell. Then they shall be asked, 'Where are your idols to help you?'

7

Muhammad! Before your time We sent other messengers. We have told you about some of them, but not about others. No messenger was capable of performing a miracle without it being the will of Allah. What Allah wills, becomes.

And the liars shall be lost.

It is He who created four-footed animals for you. Some can be used for riding, others serve as food. This is of great benefit to you. When you ride such animals, you achieve your dreams. Likewise with the ships.

Allah has revealed His signs to you. Which of these signs can you deny?

61

Beautifully Written

At first, the sky was a mass of smoke.
Allah said to the smoke, 'Obey Me! Either willingly or unwillingly!'
The smoke listened willingly.

In the name of Allah
He is love
He gives
He forgives

1

Ha' Mim.

This book was sent by Allah.

A book recounted in a beautiful language.

An Arabic text for those who know.

As a bearer of good tidings and a warning. But most people ignore the book; they do not hear the text. They say, 'Our hearts are bolted and or ears are deaf; a curtain hangs between us and you. Do whatever you want, therefore, and we shall do the same.'

2

Muhammad, say to them, 'Do you deny Him? He who made the earth in two days? And do you really invent someone who would be a part of Him? Is He not the maker of the universe? 'He anchored the mountains firmly in the ground and blessed the earth. He covered it with water, food, and vegetation in four days. Then He started on the sky, which was first a mass of smoke, and He said to the sky and the earth, "This day! Obey me! Willingly or unwillingly!" And they said, "We shall listen willingly."'

3

In two days He made a heaven with seven levels from the mass of smoke. And He caused His command to prevail on every level.

He adorned the lowest floor with lanterns, and also gave them protection. Such was Allah's decree. He is mighty.'

But, Muhammad! If the people still turn away, say to them, 'I warn you for a flash of lightning like that which struck the people of 'Ad and Thamud.'

4

The people of 'Ad revolted and said, 'No one is mightier than we.'

Were they not aware that Allah, who made them, is mightier? We sent them a cold wind, to let them feel the punishment of this life. But the punishment that follows death is a great humiliation.

We guided the people of Thamud to the right path, but they preferred to go astray. They were struck by lightning for their deeds.

A day shall come on which the enemies of Allah shall be brought to hell in groups. There, their ears, their eyes, and their skin shall testify to what they have done.

They shall say to their skin, 'Why do you testify against me?'

Their skin shall reply, 'Allah made us speak. He can make anything speak. It is He who made you, and now He has called all of you back. You did not expect that we, your eyes, your ears, and your skin, would speak out against you. You thought that Allah did not know what you were doing.'

5

Good and evil are not alike. Fend off evil with something good. Then you shall see that your enemy will become your friend.

If Satan desires to tempt you, ask Allah for help. He hears all things.

The night, the day, the sun, and the moon are among His signs. Therefore, do not kneel before the sun and the moon, but kneel before He who made them.

And among His signs is your observation of a lifeless earth that stirs back to life and grows when He sends water. The One who calls the earth back to life, also calls the dead back to life. He can do all things.

6

Those who deny the Qur'an are not unknown to Us. It is a precious book in which nothing false is present, neither now nor later. It is a revelation of lauded wisdom.

7

Muhammad! Nothing has been said to you that has not already been said to the ancient prophets. If we had made the Qur'an in an unfamiliar and ugly language, they would certainly have said, 'Were they unable to write this book with greater clarity? A book in a foreign language from an Arab?'
Muhammad, say, 'The Qur'an is a guide for believers, and a healing, but those who do not believe have blocked ears. It is they who are called upon from a distant place.'

8

Those who do good, do it for themselves, and those who do evil, turn against themselves. Allah does no injustice to His own people. Knowledge of the hereafter is with Him. Not a single grain breaks free of its husk without His decree. And no woman falls pregnant and gives birth without His knowledge.

9

People never tire of praying for the good, but as soon as something bad happens to them, they lose hope and are inclined to doubt.
If We give people a great deal, they turn away in arrogance and follow their own path. But as soon as they are stricken with something evil, they resume their lengthy prayers.
Muhammad, say, 'Observe! The Qur'an is from Allah. And if you deny it, is there anyone who strays more than you?
He encompasses all things.

62

Deliberation!

In the name of Allah
He is love
He gives
He forgives

1

Ha' Mim.
'Ayn! Sin! Qaf!
Muhammad! In this way He reveals Himself to you and to the other prophets before you.
Allah guards those who worship idols as God, but you are not their guardian.
We revealed the Qur'an in Arabic to you, that you might warn Mecca, the Mother of cities.

2

They have adopted idols as protectors, while Allah is the true protector; He who brings the dead back to life. He has power over all things.
And where there is a matter of dispute between you, the verdict belongs to Allah.
Muhammad, say, 'Thus is Allah; I have placed my trust in Him, and I turn to Him. He is the Maker of the heavens and the earth. To meet your needs, He made pairs according to your kind. And for the four-footed animals, likewise, pairs according to their kind. He sees all things. He hears all things. There is nothing with which He can be compared.
'He has the keys to the heavens and the earth. He gives with

generosity to whomever He pleases and gives less to whomever He pleases. He can do all things.'

3

So, Muhammad, invoke Me and persevere as you have been commanded. And instead of following their desires, say, 'I believe in every book that Allah has sent. And I have been commanded to be just. Allah is our Creator and your Creator. Our deeds are ours, and your deeds are yours. Beyond this, there is no dispute between you and us. Allah shall call us together and give His judgement. We shall all return to Him.'

4

God is meticulous with His people. He gives to whomever He pleases. He is splendid and loved.
Muhammad, say, 'Whoever desires the harvest of the hereafter, we shall increase their harvest. And whoever desires the harvest of this life, We shall also give to them, but in the hereafter they shall receive nothing.
But those who believe and do good deeds shall enter the gardens of paradise, where everything shall be ready for them. This is the great gift.'

5

Muhammad, say, 'I do not ask for payment, other than love for my kin. For those who do good, we shall increase goodness.'
They say that Muhammad has invented all sorts of things about Allah in a deceitful manner.
Know this! Should Allah so desire, He could put a seal on your heart, but He shall destroy falsehood, and uphold the truth with His own words.
He knows what lives in human hearts.

6

It is He who accepts the repentance of His people, forgives sins and knows what they are doing.

It is He who sends rain after you have lost hope.

And He unfolds His clemency. He is the lauded Protector.

The creation of the heavens and the earth, and the animals He distributed over both, are among His signs.

And He has the power to bring them all together again, should He so desire.

7

Every misery that confronts you, is the work of your own hands. Yet he forgives many things. And you have no escape on earth and no refuge other than Allah.

8

And among His signs are the ships, like moving mountains in the sea.

Should He desire, He could still the wind so that they are unable to move. There is a lesson in this for those who reflect.

Or He could destroy the people on the ship for what they have done, but no, He forgives.

He also forgives those who avoid serious sin and debauchery.

Also those who forgive when they are furious.

Also those who listen to their Creator and perform the prayer.

Also those who consult with one another.

Also those who give of what We have given them.

Also those who resist when injustice is done to them.

Retribution for a bad deed is equal to the deed itself. But those who forgive shall be rewarded by Allah. He does not love cruel people.

Yet those who seek revenge should not be reproached.

Make them reproach those who are cruel and commit injustice on earth.
A severe punishment awaits them.
You shall witness them being brought to the fire in humiliation while they peer out of the corners of their eyes.
Muhammad! You are not their guardian if they turn away.
Simply pass on the message.

9
The kingdom of the heavens and the earth belong to Allah.
He creates what He desires.
He gives a daughter to whomever He pleases.
He gives a son to whomever He pleases.
Or grants a daughter and a son to whomever He pleases.
Or makes infertile whomever He pleases.
He can do all things.
It is not fitting for human beings that Allah should speak to them, except through a revelation, or from behind a curtain, or through an angel. And He sends whatever He pleases. He is great. He is wise.

10
Muhammad!
We have revealed a book to you from Our own spirit. You did not know what a scripture signified, or what a faith was. But We made it as light with which We guide whomever We please. There is no doubt that you lead the people along the right path, the path of Allah.
Everything returns to Allah.

63

Ornament and Splendour

The unbelievers say that Allah has daughters. He grows angry with them. How dare they attribute daughters to God, whereas they prefer sons to daughters?
Moreover, why would God want daughters, creatures who love ornament and cannot fight when it is necessary?

In the name of Allah
He is love
He gives
He forgives

1
Ha' Mim.
By the clear book. We composed it in Arabic so that you might learn from it.
It is a great book, full of wisdom, and it has its roots in the book *In the Beginning*, which is with Us.
Should we keep this book from you because you are a wasteful people?

2
Muhammad! If you ask them who made the heavens and the earth they shall say, 'The Mighty, the Formidable created all things.'
Yes, it is He who fashioned the earth as a cradle for you; who created paths on earth so that you might find your own way.
And it is He who causes water to fall from the sky, with which He calls arid ground back to life. Thus, you shall also be called back.

And it is He who made the different species in pairs; He who made ships and four-footed animals to ride.

When you mount them, say, 'Glory to Him who did this for us. We were not capable of taming them on our own. We shall all return to Him!'

3

But humans are ungrateful.

They equate some of His servants with Him, and they have invented daughters for Him.

Why must He take daughters, while they are allowed to have sons?

When they receive the good news that they have been granted a daughter, their faces turn grey with shame. Thus is their dejection.

Angels? Daughters for God? Daughters accustomed to ornament and splendour, and unable to fight?

4

They say that the angels are female creatures. How do they know this? Were they perhaps present when the angels were created?

And they say, 'Why was the Qur'an not revealed to an important man from the city, rather than Muhammad?'

What have they to do with it? Do they perhaps dispense the clemency of God? No! It is We who distribute bread among them, and We choose some above others so that one can make use of the power of the other.

5

If there had been no danger that believers and unbelievers might form a union, We would have made the roofs of the unbelievers' houses of silver, together with their ladders and their doors. And We would have adorned their couches with jewels on which they could recline in splendour.

But all this is nothing more than the pleasure of this life. The hereafter is for those who fear.

Muhammad! Hold fast to what has been revealed to you. It is a warning for you and your people. You shall soon be called to account.

6

We sent Musa with Our miracles to Pharaoh and his advisors. He said, 'I am the messenger of the Maker of the universe.' But they laughed at him.

Pharaoh turned to his people, 'Oh, my people! Do I not hold dominion over Egypt? Do I perhaps have no power over the river Nile, which flows beneath my palace? Who is better? Me, or this man who cannot even speak properly? Why was he not sent golden bracelets? Why were no angels sent to accompany him?'

Pharaoh thus misled his people, and We caused them all to drown.

7

Muhammad!

When the son of Maryam was named as an example, your people immediately started to laugh out loud. They said, 'Are our gods not better than him?'

The son of Maryam was an ordinary person upon whom We bestowed a blessing.

And We made him an example for the Israelites.

He is a sign of the hereafter. You should never call this into question.

8

Oh, my servants! On the day of judgement there will be no fear for you, and no sadness.

You who believed in Our signs shall enter paradise with joy, in the company of your wives.

Golden bowls shall be brought on trays for you, and you shall be granted whatever you desire and whatever you see, and there shall be an abundance of fruit for you to eat.

But the guilty shall remain in hell for eternity. We have not done them an injustice; they have done themselves an injustice.

They think that We cannot hear their secrets.

We certainly can; We hear all things. Our angels walk with them and take note of everything.

9

Muhammad, say, 'If God had a child, I would be the first to serve him.'

But Allah stands above their allegations.

He is the God of the heavens and the God of the earth.

Muhammad, if you cry out, 'Allah! These people refuse to believe.'

Then say 'Salaam' to them. And leave them be!

64

The Smoke

In the name of Allah
He is love
He gives
He forgives

1

Ha' Mim.

By the clearly enunciated book. We revealed it on a blessed night.

It is a book, a gift from your God.

We have sent it. It is a command from Us. We are the Cautioner.

2

There is no God but He. He gives life. He brings death. He is your God and the God of your forebears.

He is the Hearing One, the Knowing One.

3

No! They do not listen; they amuse themselves with their indecision.

But wait for the day on which thick smoke appears from the sky and envelops the people. It shall be a painful punishment. They shall say, 'God, take this punishment away from us. Now we believe.'

4

How can this lesson be of use to those who have heard a prophet with a clear book? They turned away from him and said, 'He is possessed. He learned it from other people.'

5

Before their time, we put Pharaoh's people to the test. We sent Musa, a beloved prophet.

Then We said to Musa, 'Depart with My servants at night. You shall be pursued. Pass through the sea and remain calm. We shall drown Pharaoh and his army.'

6

Pharaoh's people left behind many gardens and springs, together with fields and fine houses; all the things that made them happy. We handed everything over to another people. Thus it was, and neither heaven nor earth wept for them.

7

We saved the Israelites from a humiliating punishment, from that lawless Pharaoh.
And We chose them deliberately above the other peoples.

8

The day of judgement is the appointed day for everyone; the day on which friends shall not help one another. No one shall extend a helping hand to you, except Allah. He is a loving victor.
On that day, sinners must eat from the Zaqqum tree. And it shall boil in their bellies like molten iron.

9

A voice shall cry out, 'Seize the criminals, and drag them to the flaming fire.'
Boiled water shall be thrown over their heads, and it shall be said, 'Taste this! You who thought that you were mighty and precious. This is precisely what you called into question.'

10

But those who believed shall be led to gardens where they shall wear fine shirts made of silk.
Thus it shall be, and they shall be joined by beautiful female companions with wide eyes. And they shall eat whatever kind of fruit they desire, and they shall be united with beautiful

girls with beautiful wide eyes. And they shall no longer experience death.
This is a gift from Us.

11

Muhammad! We have made the Qur'an easy to understand, in your language. Perhaps they shall learn from it.
Wait, then! They too are waiting.

65

Those Who Knelt

Muhammad repeatedly mentions the ships as a sign of Allah.
He sees three miracles Allah performed to set the ships in motion.
He tamed the winds.
He tamed water and made it fluid.
He tamed wood in such a way that it stays afloat in water.

Someone who can devise such magical things is almighty.

In the name of Allah
He is love
He gives
He forgives

1

Ha' Mim.
This is a book sent by the All-Knowing, the victor Allah.
For those who believe, there are unmistakable signs in the heavens and on the earth.

In you yourselves and in the animals He has dispersed across the earth.

Likewise, in the night and the day, which follow one another.

And in the water He causes to fall with which He brings the dead earth back to life.

And in the steering of the winds there are signs for those who reflect.

2

Muhammad! What else do they wish to know before they believe?

When you tell them about Our signs they mock them. Wait! Hell awaits them.

3

It is Allah who tamed the sea for you so that ships might sail at His command, and so that you might seek His abundance. Perhaps you shall be grateful.

4

Muhammad! We put you on the original path, the true path. Follow it and do not listen to the lust of the ignorant.

They say, 'There is nothing more than the present life. We live and we die, and life itself obliterates us.'

But they are without knowledge, they contrive and invent.

And when Our clear signs are recited to them, all they have to say is this, 'Call our forebears back to life, if you speak the truth.'

Say to them, 'It is Allah who brings you life and death. Thereafter, He shall assemble you on the day of judgement, about which there is no doubt.'

But most people do not understand it.

5

On the day of judgement every people shall be called to the book, and they shall kneel. And the following shall be said to them, 'Today you shall be rewarded for what you have done. This is Our book, in which your deeds are recorded.'

6

Then the following shall be said to the unbelievers, 'Today there is no escape for you, and no one can help you, because you mocked the words of God, and because this present life misled you.'
Praise be to Allah. He is the Maker of all things.
He is the Almighty.
The Wise.

66

The Sand Dunes

In the name of Allah
He is love
He gives
He forgives

1
Ha' Mim.
This book comes from Allah, the Wise.
Say, 'Have you looked carefully at the idols you worship instead of God?
'Can you tell me what they have created on earth? Did they share in the creation of the heavens? Bring me a book from before this or a sign of knowledge, if you speak the truth.

'Is there anyone who has gone further astray than the one who worships something that is incapable of responding to his call?'

2

When Our clear texts are recited to them, they say, 'Muhammad devised it himself. It is sorcery.'
Say, 'If I invented it, God knows it. He is a true witness for you and for me. He is the Forgiving One.'
Say, 'I am not an exceptional messenger among the prophets. And I do not know what will happen to me or to you. I follow only what has been revealed to me. I am merely a plain-speaking cautioner.'

3

And We advised humans to treat their parents well. Their mothers carried them with hardship during pregnancy. They bore their children in pain. Gestation and weaning took thirty months.
It is only when they reach the age of forty that they say, 'God, grant that I should express my gratitude for the generosity You have shown to me and to my parents. And grant that I should do good deeds. I turn to you and I surrender.'
We forgive the sins of such people, and they are granted a place in paradise.

4

But those who say to their parents, 'Both of you! How can you say to me that I shall return to life after I die, while so many people have died before me and no one has returned?'
Both parents shall say, 'Woe to you! Believe in God. His promise is true.'
They say, 'These are nothing but ancient fables from long ago.'

Such people shall be severely punished together with the jinn for treating their parents badly. They are the losers.

5

Muhammad!

We sent a group of jinn to listen to you when you recited the Qur'an.

When they were with you they said to one another, 'Be silent!' And they listened closely. When it was over and they had returned to their own people they said, 'Oh, people! We heard texts being recited from a book that was revealed after the book of Musa. It is an imitation of the ancient books, and it leads to the right path.

Oh, people. Follow the way of Allah and believe in Him so that your sins may be forgiven, and you may be spared a severe punishment.'

6

Muhammad, say, 'Have you never thought that the Maker of the heavens and the earth is also able to bring the dead back to life?'

Indeed! He can do all things.

7

Have patience, Muhammad, like the ancient prophets who stood firm!

Bide your time, Muhammad!

67

The Winds

Humans swear by God or by the saints.
But if Allah desires to swear, He swears by:
The pen
The figs
The olives
The clouds
The night
The wind
And by the light
And by the ships that sail the sea with ease.
He swears by the things He Himself has made.

But by what does Muhammad swear?
He swears by Allah, and by the marvellous things that preoccupy
him:
By the honey!
By the numbers, even and uneven.
And by pregnant clouds filled with rain.

In this sura, Allah swears by the fierce driving winds that the day
of judgement is true.

In the name of Allah
He is love
He gives
He forgives

1

By the winds that fan out,
By the pregnant clouds,
And by the ships that move forward with ease,
And by the angels who share out the commands,
What has been proclaimed to you is true.
And the day of judgement is a fact.

2

And by the sky with its many levels, your opinions are diverse.
Be gone, liars engulfed in ignorance and oblivion!
Each time they ask, 'When is the day of judgement?'
Say to them, 'On the day you are punished by fire.'
Taste the punishment for which you were so impatient.

3

There are signs on the earth for those who genuinely desire to
know. Even in your own body, if you look closely.
Likewise in the heavens, the source of your bread.
Yes! By the Maker of the heavens and the earth, the return is
just as real as your speech.

4

We made the heavens with Our power. We are mighty.
And We spread out the earth. Look, how excellent Our work is.
And We made everything in pairs. Perhaps you can learn from
it.

5

Muhammad, say to them, 'Hurry to Allah. And take no other
god besides Him!'
And say, 'I am only a plain-speaking messenger.'
No messenger ever came whose people did not say, 'He is a

man possessed. He is a conjurer.'
Muhammad! Turn your face away from them. You are not responsible for them.
But continue to warn. It shall be beneficial.

6

I only made the jinn and the humans to praise Me.
I did not ask anything of them, not even that they should sustain Me.
I give them their bread.

68

The All-Consuming Day

In the name of Allah
He is love
He gives
He forgives

1

Have you heard the story of the all-consuming day?
On that day, heads shall be bowed to the ground in humiliation; broken, suffering pain, and moaning.
Their destination is the fire.

2

Do they never look at a camel, and see how exceptional an animal it is?
And at the sky, and see how high it is?
And at the mountains, and wonder how they came to be?
And at the earth, and how vast it is?

3
Muhammad! Give warning!
You are not their guardian.
You are a cautioner.
It is We who settle scores.

69

ﻱ

Kahf

A couple of men facing persecution on account of their faith seek refuge in a cave—Kahf. They have a dog with them.
They are tired and fall asleep, but the dog guards them.
When they wake up, they see that they have grown old, and their beards are long and grey.
One of them takes a coin and goes off in secret to the city where he sees that everything has changed.
They have been asleep for three hundred years.

Muhammad himself tells this story along with many others.

In the name of Allah
He is love
He gives
He forgives

1
Praise be to Allah who has revealed the book to his servant, a book that is without error.
A solid book to warn people against a severe punishment, and to inform believers of an excellent reward; that a place has been set aside for them, in which they shall dwell forever.

And to warn those who say, 'Allah begot a child.'
They do not understand what they are saying nor did their fathers.
They utter big words, but they are lies.

2

Muhammad, perhaps you shall die of grief because they do not believe in this book.
We created everything on earth to put people to the test, and We shall transform everything into arid dust.
Muhammad! Do you think that the story of the men of Kahf is a strange story in comparison with our miracles?

3

When the men of Kahf took refuge in the cave they said, 'God, grant us Your mercy!'
We covered their eyes and ears for years with a curtain.
Then We woke them to see which of them was best able to calculate the time. This is their story:
'When the sun came up, you saw it continue to the right of the cave; and when the sun went down, you saw it on the left side while the men of Kahf lay in the space between.
'It was as if they were awake while they were asleep; and we turned them over to the left and to the right while their dog stretched its legs at the entrance to the cave.
'If you had seen them, you would have turned your face and fled in fear.
'We woke them up that they might ask one another questions. One of them said, "How long were we in the cave?"
'The response came, "A day or part of a day."
'Others said, "God knows best how long we were here. Let us send one of our number in secret to the city, with a silver coin, to see what the purest food is."'

4

We thus let the people discover themselves, and they started to debate with one another.

Some said, 'Build something over them. Their God knows what is best for them.'

Those who knew who they were said, 'We shall build a tomb over them.'

Some shall say, 'There were three men and the fourth was their dog.'

Others shall say, 'There were five men, the sixth was their dog.'

Everyone guessed at the secret. 'There were seven men and the eighth was their dog.'

Muhammad, say, 'My God knows how many there were, and a limited number of others. End your discussion, therefore, and do not ask any more questions about it!'

5

Muhammad! Never say, 'I shall do it tomorrow', without also saying, *"in sha' Allah*. If it is God's will!' and always think about God!

The men remained in their cave for three hundred years, and they added another nine years.

Say, 'Allah knows best how long they stayed there. He knows the secrets of the heavens and the earth. He is the Seeing One and the Hearing One.'

Muhammad, 'Read aloud from the text that has been revealed to you. There is no one who can change His word.'

6

Muhammad, say to them, 'This truth comes from your God. Those who want to are free to believe, those who do not are free to remain unbelievers, but for those who commit evil deeds We have readied a fire that shall surround them. If they beg for a sip of water, they shall be given molten metal as water, which shall burn their faces. It is a dire drink and a dire place. 'We shall not forget the reward due to those who believe and do good deeds. They shall enter the gardens of happiness under which rivers flow. They shall wear garments of green silk and fine bracelets of gold, and they shall recline on couches. It is a fine reward and a fine place.'

7

Muhammad! Offer them a comparison, say, 'Life is like water, which We cause to fall from the sky; it mingles with plants and flowers, and thereafter they become dry stalks and are carried away one morning by the wind.'

8

On the day We set the mountains in motion and you see the earth swell, We shall cause the people to come out of their graves. And We shall leave no one behind.
They shall be lined up in front of Us.
And the book shall be placed in front of them. The guilty shall be startled by it, 'Oh! What kind of book is this?
'Look! Everything we have done is inscribed in it. All things, great and small.'

9

In this Qur'an, We have given examples of what has happened to ancient peoples. Humans are extremely quarrelsome beings. We destroyed all the cities in which the inhabitants were violent.
And so it continued until Musa said to his servant, 'I shall not rest until I have reached the place where the two seas meet, even if I have to walk an endless distance.'
When they reached the place where the two seas came

together, they forgot their fish, which found its way to the sea and swam away.

After they had walked a little further, Musa said to his servant, 'We are tired of this journey. Bring us dinner.'

The servant said, 'Did you not notice? When we were resting by the rock I forgot about the fish. It found its way to the sea in an astonishing manner. This was Satan's doing.'

Musa said, 'This is the place we were looking for.'

Then they turned around and retraced their footsteps.

10

Muhammad! They shall ask you about Dhul-Qarnayn, the ruler with two horns on his helmet.

Say to them, 'Let me tell you his story.

'We had granted Dhul-Qarnayn prosperity, power on earth, and access to everything.

'He followed his way until he reached the sun in the west, and he saw the sun set as if into a spring of mud. And he encountered a people there.

'We said, "Dhul-Qarnayn! Punish them or treat them well."

'He said, "Those who commit injustice shall be punished. Those who believe and do good deeds shall be rewarded."

'And he continued until he had reached the place of the sunrise; there he encountered a people for whom We had not provided protection from the sun. Thus it was, and We were aware of what he was doing.

'He continued on his way once again until he found himself between two mountains. There he encountered a people that barely understood language. They said, "You, Dhul-Qarnayn, listen. The people of Yajuj and Majuj use violence and bring misery to the earth. Will you build a wall between us and them if we pay the costs?"

'He said, "The prosperity that God has granted me is better.

Rather, help me with manpower, I shall erect a wall between you and them. Bring me chunks of iron." And he filled the space between the two mountains with iron. Then he said, "Blow!"

'And when the iron turned to fire he said, "Bring me molten copper to throw over it."

'The people of Yajuj and Majuj were unable to climb the wall nor could they punch a hole in it.

'He said, "It is a gift from my God!"'

11
Muhammad, say to them, 'If the sea were ink for the words of Allah it would run out before His words came to an end.'

Say, 'I am a human being just like you. But it has been revealed to me that your God is one God.

'Those who desire to meet their Creator should not devise anything or anyone besides Him.'

70

The Bees

Muhammad had a poetic view of the world and his fantasy was unlimited.

Sunrise made an indelible impression on him, and he almost set with the setting sun.

He saw everything differently. He saw the shadows on the right and the left praise God.

He looked in amazement at all things, and saw the traces of Allah everywhere.

But why did others not see these signs, Muhammad asked himself.

In the name of Allah
He is love
He gives
He forgives

1

Allah's ordinance is coming; there is no need to hurry toward it. So fear Me!

He created the heavens and the earth in sincerity. He stands above whatever they devise in addition to Him.

He created humankind from a droplet, but humans bring disaster on themselves.

He created livestock, which provides you with warmth and other benefits, and from which you eat.

It is a thing of beauty for you when you bring your livestock home at night after grazing, and when you lead them to pasture early in the morning.

They carry your burdens to destinations you can only reach with great difficulty.

He also created horses, mules and donkeys on which you can ride and with which you can strut.

2

It is He who sends water from the sky to drink; it makes the vegetation grow that you use to feed your livestock.

He thus ensures that your olives, dates, grapes, and various other fruits grow.

And He tames the night, the day, the sun, the moon, and the stars for you. These contain unambiguous signs for those who reflect.

It is He who tamed the sea so that you might eat fresh fish and wear the ornaments you take from it. And you see the ships that sail across the sea, allowing you to share in His abundance. Perhaps you will be grateful.

3

He stationed the mountains on the earth to prevent tremors; and rivers and roads to help you find your way. And you use the stars to determine the right direction.
Is He who creates the same as the one who does not create? Why do you not learn a lesson from this?
Because what they see as gods cannot create; these gods are themselves created. They are lifeless and have no bond with life. They do not know when they shall be raised up. Your God is one.

4

Muhammad! Before your time We sent men to whom We had granted a revelation. We sent them with miracles and books.
Ask those who have the writings in their possession if you do not know.
We revealed the Qur'an to you so that you might explain to the people what has been sent down to them. Perhaps then they will reflect.

5

Muhammad! Do the people who do evil deeds consider themselves secure when God unexpectedly sinks them into the ground? Or when punishment strikes them from an unexpected corner? Or when He seizes them while they are travelling for trade, without them being able to prevent it? Or when He visits them in their fears? Surely your Lord is compassionate and kind?
Do they perhaps not see that the shadows bow to the left and to the right before Allah?

6

Allah has said, 'Do not take two gods. There is only one God!' They give away a portion of what We have given them to ignorant idols.

And they devise daughters for Allah, praised be He. And they keep their sons, whom they prefer, for themselves.

When one of them hears that his wife has given birth to a daughter, his face darkens with rage and he hides himself from his people on account of the bad news. Shall he keep the girl in humility? Or shall he bury her alive? Of course not, their judgement is bad.

Those who do not believe in the day of judgement offer a poor description of judgement.

God's description thereof is beautiful.

If God were to punish people for all their sins, there would be no one left on the earth. But Allah allots them a period of time, and when it runs out, it is neither postponed nor advanced, not by a single hour. Allah is all-wise!

7

God caused water to fall from the sky, and thus He revived the earth when it was dead. There is a sign in this for those who see.

And there is a lesson in the herd animals; in their bellies we produce pure milk from the mixture of excrement and blood.

You make wine and delicious dishes from grapes and dates. There is a sign in this for those who reflect.

And your God inspired the bees to build a hive for themselves in the mountains, in the trees, and in tall houses.

And He said, 'Eat, then, of every sort of fruit, and follow the way of your Creator!'

Their bellies produce medicinal juices in different colours. There is a sign in this for those who reflect.

8

So do not compare Allah with idols. God knows and you do not know.

Allah makes a comparison: is a slave without power equal to someone to whom We have given much power?

Allah makes a comparison between two men, one of them is dumb. He is unable to do anything and is a burden to his master. Wherever he sends him, he brings nothing good. Is he equal to someone who follows the right path?

Allah knows the secret of the sky and the earth. And the day of judgement can be arranged in an instant, or even less. Allah can do all things.

9

God took you from the belly of your mother when you were ignorant. He also granted you ears, eyes, and a heart. Perhaps you might be grateful.

Do you see how the birds fly in the air? Only Allah can keep them in flight. There is a sign in this for those who believe.

10

And Allah made your houses a place to rest. He made tents for you from the hide of cattle. You can carry them when you travel.

From animal hair, wool, and fur He made household goods for you, for a certain time.

Of all that He created, Allah made shade for you. And He made caves in the mountains for you. He made clothing for you, to protect you from the heat and from the cold, and clothing that protects you from one another's violence.

Thus, He makes His gifts complete for you. Perhaps you will now surrender to God.

11

Keep your word if you enter into an agreement with Allah. And do not break your promises.

And do not be like the woman who spun and unravelled her thread fibre by fibre when it was strong.

Do not squander your treaty with Allah. That which is with God is better for you.

That which is with you perishes. But that which is with Allah remains.

12

And when you read the Qur'an, seek your protection with God against the accursed Satan. He has no power over those who believe. Satan can only reach those who befriend him, and those who devise anything equal to God.

13

Eat what Allah has given you for food, but eat pure and be grateful.

Dead animals, blood, and pork are forbidden. Likewise, the flesh of any animal over which a name other than Allah has been uttered.

But if it is essential, it is permitted. Allah is forgiving.

And for the Jews, what We related earlier remains forbidden. We do not do them an injustice. They do themselves an injustice.

14

Ibrahim was an example; he followed the pure faith and did not count among the followers of idols.

He was grateful for the gift of God, and God chose him and guided him along the right path.

We gave him everything that was good in this life, and he remained a chosen one in life and in death.

Muhammad! Then We asked you to follow the way of Ibrahim. Be patient, not sad!

71

Nuh

Jamshid, the first Persian king, had seven statues made of himself, and sent them to the seven corners of his great kingdom.
The statue of red stone found its way to the people of Nuh, a people that had made many other idolatrous images.
Nuh was a skilful speaker, able to engage effectively in debates.
For nine hundred years, he warned his people, but no one would listen to him.
In the end, the people said to him, 'Nuh, you are possessed!'
Fathers took their sons by the hand, walked up to him, pointed at him and said to their sons, 'Look! He is mad and he is talking nonsense. When I die you must not listen to him.'
It even went so far that they decided to kill Nuh.
But in spite of everything, Nuh managed to rally a group of people behind him. Eighty people joined him on his ship when the storms came.
(From The Lives of the Prophets*)*

In the name of Allah
He is love
He gives
He forgives

1
We sent Nuh to his people and We said to him, 'Warn them before they are seized by the great punishment.'
Nuh said, 'Oh, my people. I am a genuine messenger. Fear God, worship Him, and follow me. He shall forgive your sins.'

2

After a while, he said to God, 'Oh, my Creator. I cautioned my people day and night, but my warnings only drove them away. 'When I talked to them, they put their fingers in their ears, hid behind their clothes, and obstinately refused everything. Yet I continued to warn them, talking with them in public and in private.

'I said to them, "Ask your Creator's forgiveness.

"Then He shall cause the sky to rain on you in abundance.

"He shall give you property and sons.

"He shall make gardens grow for you, and rivers flow.

"What has happened to you that you do not fear His glory? He made you in different stages.

"Have you never reflected on how He created the heavens in seven levels?

"And how He caused the moon to shine therein, and how He located the sun as a radiant lantern?

"And how He caused you to grow like a plant from the ground?

"And how He makes you return to the ground? And how He brings you out from the ground anew?

"He rolled out the earth for you as a carpet so that you might follow His broad paths."'

3

Nuh said, 'God! They refuse to listen to me. All they do is follow the idols that bring shame to their property and their children. They have devised a malicious plan, and do nothing but call out the names of their idols: Wadd! Suwa'! Yaguth! Ya'uq! And Nasr!'

4

For this reason, We let them drown. And they shall be brought to a fire where no one can help them.

And Nuh said, 'God, do not leave a trace of the unbelievers behind on earth.

'God, forgive me and my parents, and everyone who enters my house.'

72

Ibrahim

King Namrood considered himself god on earth. He commanded that Ibrahim be thrown into the fire, but the fire became cold, and trees, plants, and flowers grew in its place.
Namrood decided to engage in battle with the God of the sky.
He had a tall ladder built, took his sword, and climbed the ladder. But the God of the heavens did not allow Himself to be seen. Namrood decided to go in search of God deep into the sky. He ordered the scholars to create a vehicle for him in which he could fly.
Their invention was something spectacular; a primal airplane, or rather an extraordinary sort of carriage. Four mighty eagles were attached to the four corners of a special regal wicker chair with long sturdy ropes. Namrood took his sword and settled into the chair while four chunks of raw meat were hung just above the eagles' heads. The eagles unfolded their wings and tried to get hold of the chunks of meat. They thus pulled the carriage deep into the sky. But God was nowhere to be found.
(According to the account of the great Persian poet Ferdowsi)

In the name of Allah
He is love
He gives
He forgives

1

'Alif Lam Ra.'

We revealed a book to you.

And We sent no prophets to you who did not speak the language of their own people.

We sent Musa Our miracles.

Have you never heard of the people of Nuh, 'Ad and Thamud? Or of the people only known to Allah?

Their prophets came with clear signs, but the people placed their hands over the prophets' mouths and said, 'Be silent! We do not believe in your mission. And we have serious doubts about your words.'

Their prophets said, 'Do you doubt God, the Maker of the heavens and the earth? Do you doubt Him who shall bring you back after a fixed time?'

They said, 'You are ordinary people like us, and you want to prevent us from serving what our forebears served. If that is not so, bring us clear evidence.'

Their prophets said, 'It is true. We are ordinary people just like you. And we shall bear what you inflict on us.'

And those who did not believe, said, 'We shall surely expel you from the land unless you return to our faith.'

But God revealed to His prophets that He would destroy those who committed injustice.

2

Every aggressive enemy shall thus meet the same fate.

Hell awaits them, and yellowish water shall be given to them, which they shall be forced to drink sip by sip until they are no longer able to swallow. Death shall come to them from every side, but they shall not die. A further severe punishment awaits them. The story of those who do not believe God is that their deeds shall be like ash on a stormy day: nothing shall remain.

3

But those who believe and have done good deeds shall find themselves in gardens of happiness under which rivers flow, where they shall be free to dwell forever. Their greeting there shall be, 'Salaam!'

Muhammad! Have you not heard Allah compare a beautiful word with a beautiful tree, its roots deep in the ground and its branches high in the air, bearing fruit periodically, with Allah's permission?

And an ugly word is like an ugly uprooted tree.

Allah makes such comparisons for humans; perhaps they shall learn a lesson from them.

4

Muhammad, say to them, 'Those who devise something or someone besides Allah shall find themselves in hell. And hell is a bad place.'

It is Allah who made the heavens and the earth, and causes water to fall, thereby bringing forth grains and fruit. And He tamed the sea for you to sail it with ships, according to His command; and He tamed the rivers for you and He forced the sun and the moon to follow their fixed course for you. And He tamed the night and the day.

If you attempt to number Allah's favours, you will be unable to sum them up; but humans are unjust and ungrateful.

5

And thus it continued until Ibrahim said, 'My God, make this place safe, and restrain me and my children from serving idols. 'These gods have indeed misled many people. Oh, my Lord! Whoever follows me is mine, and You decide what happens to those who do not obey me. You are full of compassion and mercy. Oh, my Lord! I settled some of my loved ones in a valley without water or vegetation. I ask you, let people treat them kindly and give them food to eat.'

Ibrahim said, 'Our Lord! You know what we do in private, and what we do in public.
'Nothing in heaven or earth is hidden from God.
'Praise be to God who granted me Isma'il and Ishaq in spite of my old age. Truly, You hear prayers.'

6
People! On the day the heavens and the earth look different than at this moment, and the dead rise, you shall see the guilty, fettered with chains. Their clothing shall be of tar, and fire shall lick their faces.
This is a proclamation for you, that you may know that He is one.

73

The Prophets

Muhammad repeatedly mentioned the names of many ancient prophets, both familiar and unfamiliar, including Lut, Hud, Idris, Uzayr, Yunus, Dawud, Musa, and Isa. But he never mentions the Persian prophet Zarathustra in his accounts.

The name Zarathustra consists of two parts:
'Zaratha', meaning 'gold'; and 'ustra' meaning 'light of'.
Zarathustra thus means 'the light that comes from gold'.
Gold symbolises the Persian god Ahura Mazda, the god of virtue.
Zarathustra's teaching has three pillars:

Good words.
Good deeds.
Good thoughts.
The Avesta, Zarathustra's holy book, was one of the books of the
ancient Persian Empire.
The Persians followed the teachings of Zarathustra until Muham-
mad came with the Qur'an.
The followers of Muhammad invaded the Persian Empire, oblit-
erated the temples of Zarathustra, and destroyed the Avestas.
They forced the Persians to accept Islam as their faith and the
Qur'an as their book.
The Persians resisted vigorously for two hundred years, but they
finally relented and accepted the Qur'an. The faith of Zarathu-
stra was thus expelled by Islam.
(*From* Two Centuries of Silence *by Sharog Mesqub*)

In the name of Allah
He is love
He gives
He forgives

1

The day of judgement is approaching, but the people still live
without care.

They talk in secret with one another, 'Is this Muhammad not
just a human being like you? Why, then, do you follow his
sorcery?'

Muhammad, say to them, 'My God knows every word spoken
in heaven and on earth. He is all-hearing. All-knowing.'

'No,' they say, 'his accounts are foolish dreams. He made it
up. No, he is a poet. Let him work a miracle, like the ancient
prophets.'

2

Muhammad! We did not make heaven and earth for Our own entertainment.

If We had wanted to make a game, We would have done so.

But We strike the false with the true, and thus We wreck the false. Woe to you for your false claims.

And We did not send a prophet before your time, without revealing to him that there is no other God but Me. So worship Me.

3

The unbelievers considered heaven and earth to be a single closed mass. We separated heaven and earth at that juncture. We made everything that lives from water.

Do they still refuse to believe?

We established solid mountains on earth that would not totter. And We made broad roads therein. Perhaps they shall find the right road.

And We provided the heavens as a protective roof, but they turned away from this sign.

Night, day, sun, and moon are from Us, each moving in an appointed course.

Every living creature shall return to Us.

4

Muhammad! When unbelievers see you, they mock you. They say, 'Is this the man who says those ugly things about your gods?'

Humankind was made in haste. I shall soon reveal My signs, but do not ask Me to hurry.

They ask, 'When is the day of the last judgement? If you are honest?'

No! The day of judgement shall come upon them suddenly and surprise them. They shall look around in astonishment;

they cannot avert it, and there is no respite for them. And they cannot keep the fire away from their backs or their faces.

5

Muhammad! Say to them, 'I warn you with revelations, but the deaf do not hear when they are warned.'

We shall ready the scales on the day of judgement. And no one shall be treated unjustly. Even if it concerns the weight of a mustard seed, We shall weigh correctly.

6

This Qur'an is a blessed warning, which We have revealed.

In the past we have already granted Ibrahim an inner maturity. Until he said to his father and his people, 'What are these stones that you worship?'

They said, 'We saw that our fathers also worshipped them.'

He said, 'You and your fathers have acted wrongly.'

They said, 'Did you bring us the truth, or are you jesting with us?'

He said, 'Your Creator is the Maker of heaven and earth. And I am a witness.'

And he said to himself, by God, I shall devise a plan against your gods.

He smashed all their idols to pieces, except the largest.

They said, 'Who did this to our idols?

'Ibrahim, was it you?'

He said mockingly, 'No, I did not do it. The largest god is to blame.'

They said, 'Burn him.'

We said, 'Oh, fire, be cold! And give happiness to Ibrahim!'

7

We saved him and Lut, and We sent them to the land We had blessed for all the world.

We granted him Ishaq as a son and Yaqub as a grandson.

Remember the prophet Nuh when he called out, and We saved him and his family from the great disaster.

8

Remember the prophet Dawud and the prophet Sulayman, when they offered judgement concerning the field in which someone's sheep had grazed through the night. We were witness to their judgement.

We gifted them both with knowledge and understanding.

We even coaxed the mountains and the birds to praise Us together with Dawud. We were responsible for this.

We taught Dawud to make armour to protect himself.

Are you still not grateful?

9

And We persuaded the wild wind to go to the blessed land on Sulayman's command, and the jinn dived out of its way.

We can do all things. We know all things.

Remember the prophet Ayoub. When We heard his prayer, We gave him back his family and took his pain away.

Remember the prophets Isma'il, Idris and Zulkifl, all of whom were patient.

Remember the prophet Yunus in the belly of the fish, after he stormed off in anger, thinking he could evade Us. He called out from the darkness of the belly, 'There is but one God and that is You! I praise You!'

Remember the prophet Zakariya. When We heard his prayer, We gave him Yahya.

Remember also Maryam, the woman who remained chaste. We blew something of Our spirit into her, and we created her and her son as two wonders for the world.
So worship Me.

10

Muhammad! The day on which We shall roll up the heavens like a written sheet of paper is coming; just as We started creation, We shall cause it all to return again. This is a promise We shall keep.
We sent you, out of clemency for the world.
Muhammad, say to them, 'It has been revealed to me that your God is one!' But if they turn away nevertheless, say, 'I spoke to you with clarity. And I do not know whether the day of judgement shall come soon or not.
'Only He knows all things.'

74

The Believers

In the name of Allah
He is love
He gives
He forgives

1

It is true, the believers shall be happy.
Those who were humble in prayer.
Those who want nothing to do with chatter and nonsense.
Those who are able to cede a portion of their income to God.
Those who safeguard what is entrusted to them. Those who

only love their own wives and their female slaves. But those who want more than this are transgressors.

2

It is true! We created humankind from a lump of clay. We placed it in a reliable place in the form of a drop. Then We transformed the drop into a clot of blood. Then We changed the blood into tissue. Then We formed bones from this lump of flesh. Thus, We brought forth a new creation.

3

You shall die, and on the day of judgement you shall be raised up.
We created the heavens above your head with seven levels, and We have never been heedless of creation.

4

We caused water to fall from the sky in modest amounts, and let it rest upon the earth. We are also able to make it disappear. With the water We brought forth gardens with date trees and grapevines on which you find much fruit.
Also a sort of tree that grows on Mount Sinai, which provides oil and a sauce for those who eat.
The herd animals also contain a sign of Our power, for you to see. We give you to drink what is in their bellies, you eat their meat, and you ride on them.

5

And We sent Nuh to his people. He said 'My people! Serve God! There is no God besides Him.'
The chiefs of his people said, 'He is only a human being like you. But he wants to stand out. If God had so desired, He would have sent angels to you. What he has to say, we did not

hear from our forebears. Wait, then! He is mad.'

Nuh said, 'God, help me, now that they are ignoring me.'

We revealed to him, 'Build the ship under Our supervision! When Our decision is made and the churning water gushes forth, bring a pair of each species of animal on board. Bring your family too. But do not speak to Me about those who do injustice.

'When you and your family are on board, say, "God! Bring me to a place of blessing. He who does this is almighty."'

6

After that, We brought forth another people for whom We also appointed a prophet.

The chiefs of his people said, 'This man is just a human being like you. He eats what you eat and drinks what you drink. If you listen to him, you will be losers. He says that after you die and your bones have been reduced to dust, you will be raised to life again. Impossible, what he says is impossible. There is no other life than the present life. We live, we die, but we are not raised up. This man invents lies. We do not believe him.'

He said, 'God, help me! They have declared me a liar!'

God said, 'They shall soon regret what they say.'

Then the shriek of death seized them.

7

We brought forth other generations thereafter.

No people die prematurely and none die too late.

Each time a prophet came to his people, they declared him a liar.

Cursed be the people that refused to believe the prophets.

Then we sent Musa and his brother Harun.

And We brought forth Maryam and her son as two marvels, and We placed them on a tranquil hill under which water flowed. You, messengers! Eat what is pure and do good deeds. I know what you do.

Know this! Your peoples together form one people. And I am your God. Fear Me!

8

We do not burden anyone beyond their capacity, and We have a book that speaks the truth.

They are not treated unjustly, but their heart is negligent toward this book. They are preoccupied with other things, but as soon as We punish the wealthy among them, they weep for help.

Do not weep today. Be sure, you shall not receive Our help. My text was already recited to you, but you turned away.

9

It is He who created ears, eyes, and the heart for you. Yet few demonstrate their gratitude.

It is He who brought you forth on earth, and you shall be led back to Him.

It is He who gives life and brings death, and the difference between night and day is from Him. Do you still refuse to reason?

Muhammad! Say to them, 'To whom does the earth belong, and everything in it? Do you know?'

Without doubt, they shall say, 'Allah!'

Say, 'Why, then, do you not learn a lesson from it?'

Say, 'Who is the Maker of the seven heavens and the universe in all its greatness?'

Without doubt, they shall say, 'Allah! Allah made all things.'

Say to them, 'Do you not want Him as your Protector? Why do you let yourself be misled?'

10

We brought them the truth, but they are liars.

Allah has not taken a son, and there is no other God besides Him. Otherwise, every God would champion his creation above that of the other. But Allah is exalted above everything they ascribe to Him.

Allah knows everything that is hidden and everything that is visible.

He is exalted above all things.

Muhammad! It is within Our power to reveal to you all that We have said.

Say, 'God, I shall seek refuge in You when Satan whispers to me.'

11

When the trumpet is blown on the day of judgement, bonds of kinship between people shall cease to exist. And people shall no longer ask after one another.

Those whose scales are heavy shall be happy.

And those whose scales are light have brought injury on themselves. They shall dwell in hell for eternity.

Their faces shall be burned and disfigured by fire. A voice shall say, 'Were Our texts perhaps not recited to you, and did you not call them lies?'

They shall say, 'God! We had gone astray. Take us out of this hell.'

God shall say, 'Silence! Do not speak to me, but remain in hell! Or do you think that We made you without reason, and you shall not be brought back to Us?'

No, the unbelievers shall not find happiness.

Say, 'My Creator! Forgive and be merciful. You are the most forgiving.'

75

Wait

Those who see God's signs, kneel to praise Him.
Such are the believers; they are not arrogant, and they get up
early in the morning to bow before the Creator of the universe.

In the name of Allah
He is love
He gives
He forgives

1
'Alif Lam Mim.
This is a book that was sent, and without doubt it is from the Creator of the world.
But they say, 'Muhammad made it himself.'
No, Muhammad! It is the truth from your Creator so that you might warn your people, to whom no prophet has come before. Continue to warn them; perhaps they shall choose the right path.

2
It is Allah who created heaven and earth and all that lies between, in six days. Thereafter, He sat down on His throne. You have no redeemer besides Him. Do you still refuse to listen?

3
From heaven He arranges matters on earth. Thereafter, everything returns to Him on a day that lasts as long as a thousand years according to your calculations.
He knows the visible and the invisible. He is magnificent.

4
Everything He made, He made good.
He made humans out of clay. Then He made them sturdy, and blew something of His spirit into them; and He made eyes, ears, and a heart. Then He made their offspring from a droplet.
See how scant your gratitude is.

5
And they ask, 'Is it really possible for us to return to life when we are completely lost in the earth?'
Of course! But they do not believe that they shall meet Allah. Muhammad, say, 'The angel of death shall snatch your soul, and you shall be brought back to the Creator.'

6
And My promise shall be fulfilled. I shall fill hell with jinn and humans. Taste the fire, for you had forgotten your appointment with this day. Now We have also forgotten you. Taste, therefore, the eternal fire, because of what you have done.

7
Only those who kneel to praise Allah when they are reminded of Our signs and those who are not arrogant believe in them.
They rise from their beds to invoke their Creator in hope and fear, and they give from what We have given them.
No, no one knows how much light shall sparkle in their eyes as a reward for what they have done.
Is one who believes the equal of someone who does not believe? They are certainly not equal.
Those who do good deeds shall dwell in gardens. But those who refused to listen shall end up in the fire. And if they try to escape, they shall be thrown back with the words, 'Taste the fire that you denied.'

8

Before the great punishment comes, We shall give them a taste
of it in this life. Perhaps they shall reflect.
But who is more stubborn than those who were warned but
turned away nonetheless?
We shall have our revenge on them.

9

Do they perhaps not see that We already destroyed many peoples before their time? Do they not reflect when they pass the
ruins of their houses?
Do they not see that We caused water to fall on the arid earth
and caused vegetation to grow on it, which they and their animals eat? Do they refuse to reflect?

10

They say, 'Muhammad! If you speak the truth, tell us when the
day of judgement shall come?'
Say, 'The day of judgement shall certainly not be to your
advantage.'
Then turn your face from them and wait. They too shall wait.

76

The Mountain

*Allah swears by At-Tur, referring to Mount Sinai, where Musa
encountered God.*
'Musa! It is I. Your God. Take off your shoes!'

In the name of Allah
He is love

He gives
He forgives

1
By the mountain.
And by a book.
Inscribed on rolled-out parchment.
And by a refurbished house.
By the lofty heavens without a roof.
By the sea that is full of fire:
God's punishment shall come to pass.
And no one can hold it back.

2
Woe to the liars on the day the heavens grow restless and the mountains are set in motion!
This is the fire in which you refused to believe.
Is this fire real, or is it just another trick? Perhaps you cannot see it properly?
Enter it! It no longer makes a difference whether you are patient or not.

3
Those who feared shall enter paradise.
And they shall recline on couches arranged for them in rows.
We shall unite them with female companions, with strikingly beautiful eyes.
There they shall eat fruit and poultry, and their cups shall pass from hand to hand. This shall not lead to meaningless gossip or the commission of sins.
And the youthful servants shall treat them as if they are hidden pearls.

4

Oh, Muhammad! By the clemency of God, you are not a man possessed nor are you a soothsayer. So caution them!

They say, 'He is a poet. Let us wait and see what death does to him.'

Say, 'Wait, then! I too shall wait.'

5

Or they say, 'His stories are his own invention. They are all from him.'

No, Muhammad, they do not believe.

Let them bring a text, then, that is equal to the Qur'an, if they speak the truth.

Were they perhaps created from nothing? Or are they their own creators?

Or were they the ones who created the heavens and the earth?

Or do they perhaps possess the treasures of God?

Or do they perhaps have a long ladder to climb, to listen in on the secrets up above?

Or do they have access to the book *In the Beginning*, which is with Us, and do they copy everything from it?

Or are they devising a dark plan? Their cunning, however, shall always be used against them.

6

If a piece of the sky falls, they say, 'It is a cloud.'

Leave them be, Muhammad! Until the day of judgement seizes them, after which they shall fall unconscious to the ground, and no one shall be able to help them.

We see you, Muhammad! Have patience. Until Our judgement.

7
Praise the Creator when you rise!
At night, and at the moment the stars disappear.

77

The Kingdom

In the name of Allah
He is love
He gives
He forgives

1
Happy is He who has the kingdom of the world under His control.
He has power over all things.
It is He who created death and life to put you to the test, and to determine which of you is the best.
He is the beloved Victor.

2
It is He who made the heavens in seven different levels.
His creation lacks nothing.
Look and see if you can find an error in His work.
Look again and see if there is a crack.
Look again twice over, until your eyes are tired.

3
Truly! We have adorned the air of heaven with lanterns.
And We use those lanterns to ward off the satans.
Whether you speak with one another in secret or in public, He

knows the content of your conversations.
He is tender. He is all-knowing.
It is He who tamed the earth for you.
So walk across the earth and eat of His gifts.
In the end we shall all return to Him.

4
Do you think that you are truly safe; that He who is in heaven
shall save you if the earth suddenly begins to quake?
Do you think that you are truly safe; that He who is in heaven
shall not send a storm of sand?
Then it is time you got to know the sound of My warning.

5
Do you never look up at the birds above your head? How they
spread their wings and how they fold their wings?
Is there anyone other than the beneficent Allah who lets them
glide through the air?
He understands all things.

6
Muhammad, say,
'It is He who created you.
'And made eyes, ears, and a heart for you.
'Yet your ingratitude is immense.'
Say, 'It is He who created you from the earth.
'And He who causes you to return to Him.'

7
Muhammad! They ask when the last judgement shall come.
Say to them, 'I do not know. Only Allah knows. I am merely
a cautioner.'

Say, 'He forgives. We believe in Him, and we have placed our trust in Him. And you shall soon find out who is in error.'

Muhammad, say to them, 'If water goes into the ground and disappears, who among you is capable of bringing it back as delicious flowing water?'

78

Al-Haqqa

What is al-Haqqa?
It is a new word that Muhammad has laden with meaning.
The sura explains when the day of judgement shall dawn, what it shall look like, and how people shall recognise it.
An angel shall blow on a trumpet loud enough for all the dead of the world to hear.
And the dead shall rise up and leave their graves.
Some shall be happy and imagine they are destined for paradise, but others shall be sombre and suspicious because they know what is awaiting them.

In the name of Allah
He is love
He gives
He forgives

1
Al-Haqqa.
What is al-Haqqa?
It is something that shall take place.
But how can you know when it shall take place?

2

When a single blast is sounded on the trumpet, the great event has arrived.

The earth and the mountains shall be violently shaken and destroyed in one blow.

And heaven shall split open and fall to the ground in pieces, for on that day nothing shall hold together.

The angels shall take their place on either side of heaven.

And the throne of Allah shall be carried by eight angels.

3

Then you shall be brought to Him; and no secret shall remain hidden to you.

Those who have the record of their life pressed into their right hand shall say with a happy heart, 'Come! Read this. I was certain that I would see the results of my deeds.'

They shall be shown a beautiful life in gardens where the fruit of the trees is within their reach.

And a voice shall say to them, 'Salaam! Eat and drink! All this is for your good deeds.'

4

But those who have the record of their life pressed into their left hand shall say without cheer, 'Woe unto me; if only this had not been given me. Would that I was ignorant of what it contains. Oh, if only I had remained in my grave forever. My possessions did not profit me, and my power has vanished.'

A voice shall say, 'Take them and bind them. Carry them off to hell and attach them to a chain, seventy ells long, for they did not believe in God, and they did not give to the needy.

'Today they are without friends. They also have nothing to eat except this yellowish fluid of which only the criminals will drink.'

5
I swear by everything you see and everything you do not see
that the words of the beloved messenger are the original words.
They are not the words of a poet.
Why do you not believe?
They are also not the words of a soothsayer.
Why do you not believe?
His words are a message sent from the Creator of the universe.
If Muhammad had added something of his own to Our words
We would have grabbed him by his right arm and cut his aorta.
And no one among you would have been able to save him.

6
This is a book, a warning for those willing to listen.
And We know that there are people among you who consider
it a lie.
And We know that it is a pang of conscience for the unbeliev-
ers.
But it is the truth, the inevitable certainty.
Therefore, praised be the name of the Creator.

79

The Stairway to Heaven

*Allah urged Muhammad to be patient, 'Wait, Muhammad!
Wait!'*
*Muhammad persisted in his conviction that Allah was going to
punish the unbelievers severely.*
*His opponents pestered him, put him under pressure, and said,
'May your Allah drop stones from heaven. Let Him stone us if
He can.'*

Muhammad had nothing to say when they challenged him in this way. He simply repeated to himself, be patient, Muhammad.

His patience, however, did not last forever.
In Mecca he waited because he was still weak and had no power.
In Medina he put an end to his waiting. He had exhausted his patience. He took up his sword and started to fight the unbelievers.

In the name of Allah
He is love
He gives
He forgives

1

They ask about the punishment that is to come.
Which no unbeliever can prevent.
It is the punishment of Allah, who controls the stairway to heaven.
The angels and the spirits shall climb it on a day that shall last five thousand years.
So be patient, Muhammad.
For them, the punishment is far away.
For Us, it is very close.

2

It shall happen on a day on which the sky shall appear as molten metal.
And the mountains as tufted wool.
And none shall express concern about the fate of their kin, although they shall be able to see one another clearly.
Sinners shall be prepared to sacrifice their sons to free themselves.

To sacrifice their wives and brothers.

And even their parents, who were their refuge.

And everyone left on earth.

Out of the question!

It is a flaming fire.

And it tears the skin loose from your heads.

And it takes hold of everyone who refused the faith.

Everyone who amassed possessions and gave away nothing.

3

Humans are restless creatures.

When they are confronted with misfortune, they show no patience.

And when they encounter good fortune, they become miserly.

Except those who pray.

And those who persevere in their prayers.

And those who set aside a portion of their wealth for the needy.

And those who believe in the day of judgement.

And those who fear the punishment of God.

And those who sleep only with their wives or their own female slaves. For this, they shall not be blamed. But those who covet a woman outside this rule are transgressors.

And those who deal honestly with what is given them in trust.

And those who keep their promises.

And those who testify justly.

They are the ones who shall gladly be welcomed into the gardens of paradise.

4

Muhammad, why do the unbelievers hurry toward you from everywhere?

Is it perhaps because they want access to the gardens of happiness? Out of the question.

Truly, it is We who created them, and they know well enough what We made them from.

We swear by the Creator of the east and the west that We are powerful; that We shall replace them with a better people.

5

Muhammad! Let them gossip and entertain themselves until the promised day.

The day on which they shall hurry from their graves, as if they were going to offer sacrifice to their idols.

They shall look in fear at the ground, and the dust of humiliation shall be on their faces.

This is the day that was promised them.

80

The Announcement

In the name of Allah
He is love
He gives
He forgives

1

What do they ask one another?
They ask about the great news.
And what is their problem?
Nothing. They shall know soon enough.
And again, they shall know soon enough.

2
Did We not create the earth as a cradle?
And the mountains as giant pegs?
We created you in pairs.
We designated sleep for your rest.
We made the night as a garment for you.
We made the day so that you might go in search of bread.
We made the heavens above your heads with seven different
levels, with a radiant lantern therein.
We cause rain to fall in abundance from the clouds, to bring
forth plants and grain and mature gardens.
The day of judgement has its appointed time.
The day on which the trumpet is blown.

3
And those who feared shall find happiness on that day.
They shall enter gardens with grapevines and girls of equal age
with young breasts.
And filled cups.
This is a reward from Allah; an appropriate gift.

81

The Angels of Death

*God swears by the angels who come to collect the souls from the
bodies of the dead.*
*He swears by those who shall extract the soul from the bodies of
unbelievers with some violence.*
*And by those who shall extract the soul from the bodies of believ-
ers with care.*
He swears by all sorts of angels of death.

In the name of Allah
He is love
He gives
He forgives

1

By those who extract the soul with violence.
And by those who extract it with pleasure.
And by those who glide.
And by those who are in command.
And by those who are skilled.
The day on which the earth begins to quake without ceasing.
On that day, hearts shall tremble and eyes shall be lowered to
the ground.
The unbelievers say, 'Shall we really return to this earthly life?
Even if our bones are broken?'
They say, 'If that is true, we shall all return broken.'

2

Are you more difficult to create, or the heavens He has made?
He built its platform high and adorned it.
He made the nights dark and the days light.
He made the earth great and expansive, and He caused water
to flow and grass to grow for you and for your animals.
And He made the mountains solid.

3

Muhammad, they ask all sorts of questions, but you are unable
to give them an answer.
You are merely a cautioning messenger.
Allah knows all things.

82

The Day of Punishment

In the name of Allah
He is love
He gives
He forgives

1

When the sky is torn asunder.
When the stars fall.
When the seas flow together.
When the graves are thrown open.
Then everyone shall know what they have done and what they have neglected to do.

2

Oh, human! What has made you so arrogant toward your Creator, He who made you, who gave you balance, who formed you as He desired? Do not think that you can escape the day of punishment.
There are angels keeping an eye on you; they know what you are doing, and they take note of everything.

3

What do you know about the day of punishment?
Again, what do you know about the day of punishment?
It is a day on which no one is allowed to do something for someone else.
It is the day of Allah.

83

The Splitting

In the name of Allah
He is love
He gives
He forgives

1

When the sky splits open.
And listens to its Creator.
As it should.
And when the earth is broken open.
And listens to its Creator.
As it should.
Oh, human!
You do your best on the way to your Creator.
And you shall encounter Him.

2

All those who get the report of their life pressed into their right hand shall be given an easy settlement.
They shall walk in good cheer to their family.
But all those who get the report of their life pressed into their left hand shall immediately begin to lament.

3

But no!
I swear by the red light of the sun at the beginning of the evening.
And by the night and by everything it conceals.
And by the moon when it is full.
That you shall be taken from one era to another.

But how is it possible that they still refuse to believe?
That they refuse to bow down when the Qur'an is recited to them?
Allah knows what they are thinking.
Muhammad! You! Warn them!

84

Rome

Muhammad speaks about Rome, but he means Byzantium. The Persians had defeated the Byzantine Empire, but Muhammad predicted that the Persians in their turn would be forced to submit.
And indeed, the Persian Empire was destroyed in the space of three weeks, not by the Byzantines, but by the young army of Islam.

In the name of Allah
He is love
He gives
He forgives

1
'Alif Lam Mim.
The Romans have been defeated in a neighbouring land. But after their defeat, they shall be victorious again within a few years. The decision belongs to Allah, sooner or later. And on that day the believers shall be happy.
It is Allah's promise and He always keeps His promises, but most people do not know this. They only have a glimpse of life from the outside.

2

Do they not ponder to themselves that Allah truly created the heavens, the earth, and what lies between for a fixed period of time?

Have they not travelled the earth to look at what the outcome was for others? They were more powerful. They ploughed the soil deeper and built more. Prophets and miracles also came to them. Yet it was not Allah who did them an injustice, they brought it upon themselves.

3

Allah initiated creation; thereafter He shall bring it all back. You also shall be carried back to Him.

So praise Allah as you enter the evening and the morning.

The praise of the heavens and the earth is His; likewise in the afternoon and evening.

Allah brings forth life from death, and He expels the dead from among the living. He brought the earth to life when it was dead. You shall be raised up after death in the same way.

4

One of Allah's signs is that He made you from earth, and there-after you spread out over all the earth.

One of His signs is that He made partners for you from your own midst so that you might find rest with them. And he introduced love and friendship among you.

One of His signs is that He made the heavens and the earth as well as the various languages and colours. There can be no doubt that this contains a lesson for those who reflect.

One of His signs is that you sleep at night and go in search of His abundance in the day.

One of His signs is that He shows you thunder as fear and as hope; and He causes water to fall from the sky to bring the earth back to life after its death.

There can be no doubt that this contains a lesson for those who reflect.

One of His signs is that the heavens and the earth are under His command. And when He summons you, you shall emerge from under the earth.

It is He who brings forth the Creation and causes it to return. And He does so with great ease.

His creation will not change. This is an abiding faith, but people do not know.

Turn to Him. Fear Him! And praise Him!

One of His signs is that He sends the winds as harbingers of good news, to allow you to taste His abundance and to set the ships in motion at His command, to allow you to go in search of His favours. Perhaps you shall thus be grateful.

5

It is Allah who dispatches the winds to shift the clouds. He disperses them as He sees fit. He tears them to pieces; you see raindrops appear in their midst, and He causes them to fall on whomever He sees fit. He thus makes them happy, even if they had lost hope.

Look at the traces of Allah's clemency; how He called the earth back to life after it was dead.

It is Allah who calls the dead back to life. He can do all things.

6

Yet if We send a warm wind and they see the ground turn yellow, they lose their faith anew.

But Muhammad! You cannot make the dead hear nor the deaf when they turn away.

You cannot help the blind onto the right path when they go astray.

7

Allah made you weak and thereafter made you strong. And after strength, weakness returns and old age comes.
Allah does whatever He sees fit. He can do all things.

8

Muhammad! We have mentioned all sorts of examples for the people in this Qur'an, but if you come to them with a miracle they shall say, 'You are a liar'.
So be patient! And know that Allah's promise is true. And do not let them put doubts in your mind.

85

The Spider

In the name of Allah
He is love
He gives
He forgives

1

'Alif Lam Mim.
Do people perhaps think that they shall be left in peace once they say, 'We believe', and they shall not be tested?
We also exposed others who came before them to a test. Allah knows the liars, and those who are genuine.
Whoever looks forward to the encounter with Allah knows that the appointed time shall come. Allah hears all things.

2

Muhammad! We advised humans to treat their parents well. But if they insist that you place someone on the same level as Me, you do not have to obey them. You shall all return to Me, and I shall show you what you have done.

3

It is true. We sent Nuh to his people, and he dwelt in their midst for a thousand years save fifty. Then they were overtaken by a flood, but We saved Nuh and the people on his ship. And We made his deliverance into a symbol for everyone on earth.

4

Ibrahim said to his people, 'You serve idols that have no power to give you bread. Serve God! Fear Him and ask Him for your bread. And thank Him, for you shall all be brought back to Him.'
All Ibrahim's people could say was the following, 'Kill Ibrahim! Or set him on fire!'
But God saved him from the fire. There is a lesson in this for those who reflect.

5

Muhammad! A prophet only has one obligation: to pass on the message.
Say, 'Do you never think about how Allah accomplished creation, and how He causes everything to return?'
It is so easy for Allah.
Say, 'Travel round the earth and see how He makes the return possible.'
Allah can do all things.
And you in the heavens and on the earth have no other refuge than Allah.

6

And Lut!

He said to his people, 'What you are doing is vile, something no one before you in the world has ever done. Do you sleep with men? Do you cut off the path of nature? Do you engage in improper things in your circles?'

His people's answer was vicious, 'Let your God punish us, if you speak the truth!'

We caused a punishment to descend on his people, and We destroyed them. There is a lesson in this story for those who reflect.

7

And Shuayb! He said to the people of Madyan, 'Do no evil on earth. Serve God and wait for the last day.'

But they branded him a liar.

They were struck by an earthquake, and they were thus found dead in their houses the following morning.

The same is true for the people of 'Ad and Thamud! You can see it from the ruins of their houses.

Likewise with Qarun and Pharaoh and Haman, to whom Musa came with clear signs, but who continued to commit crimes on earth.

We seized each of them for their sin, and they could not escape.

Among them were those against whom We sent a sandstorm.

Among them were those who were seized by the shriek of death.

Among them were those We pulled deep into the ground.

Among them were those We caused to drown.

Yet it was not Allah who did them an injustice; they did themselves an injustice.

The story of these people can be compared with the spider who builds a house, and thinks it is the strongest house in the world.

We make comparisons, but only those with knowledge shall understand them.

8

Allah created the heavens and the earth and this contains a lesson for those who reflect.

Muhammad! Recite from what has already been revealed to you from the Book, and perform your prayer.

It is true! Prayer fends off what is reprehensible. This is the most important thing.

Think of Allah. He knows what you are doing.

9

Muhammad! We sent the book to you. Before then, you could not read a book or write.

Yet they say, 'Why did his Creator not send him a miracle?'

Say, 'The miracles of Allah are with Allah. I am merely a cautioner!'

Is it not enough for them that We sent you the book that is recited to them?

Without doubt, there is a lesson therein for those who reflect.

Say, 'Allah is a witness; that is sufficient.'

10

Oh, you unbelievers! My earth is vast and wide. So serve Me!

Everyone shall sample the taste of death. Then you shall all be returned to Me.

Those who believe and do good deeds shall enter the beautiful, lofty chambers of paradise, under which rivers flow, and they shall dwell there for eternity.

11

Allah takes care of you, and also of the animals, for there are many animals that cannot take care of themselves. Allah knows all things. He hears all things.

Muhammad! If you ask such people who it was who made the heavens and the earth, who tamed the sun and the moon, they shall certainly answer, 'Allah.'

How, therefore, can they opt for a wrong path?

And if you ask who it is that causes water to fall from the sky on the arid earth in order to revive it, they shall certainly say, 'Allah.'

Say, then, 'All glory be to Allah!'

86

Those Who Give Short Measure

In the name of Allah
He is love
He gives
He forgives

1

Woe to those who tamper with the scales.

When they weigh something of others for themselves, they weigh the full measure.

But when they weigh something of themselves for others, they give short measure.

Do they not know that they shall return one day after their death?

The day on which humanity shall stand before the Creator of the world.

2
But it is not so simple.
The accounts of the transgressors are recorded in Sijjin.
Do you know what Sijjin is?
It is a written document.
Woe to the transgressors on that day.
Those who say, when Our signs are recited to them,
'Fables, all of them, from ancient peoples.'

3
But likewise it is not that simple.
Records on the pious are recorded in Illiyin.
And do you know what Illiyin is?
It is a written document, and its witnesses are near to Allah.
The pious shall be led to couches.
You shall see their faces radiate with happiness.
And they shall be given delicious wine to drink, the seal of
which is musk.
It comes from the spring of Tasnim, from which only those
near to Allah drink.

4
The unbelievers once ridiculed the believers.
When they passed them, they winked at one another and said
unperturbed, 'They are erring spirits.'
And when they returned to their homes they made jokes
about them.
But today the believers ridicule the unbelievers who yearn-
ingly gaze at the couches.

87

The Cow

'The Cow' is one of the most important suras in the Qur'an, containing many of the laws that believers strive to observe.
The text also relates to a turbulent period in Muhammad's life, especially concerning his confrontation with the Jews who challenged and humiliated him.

In the name of Allah
He is love
He gives
He forgives

1
'Alif Lam Mim.
This is a book that has no place for doubt. It is a guide for the devout, for those who believe in the secret, who pray, who give to others a portion of what We have given to them.
And for those who believe in this book and in the other books that were revealed in the past, and who firmly believe in life after death.
Such people shall be helped by Allah, and shall find their way.

2
For the unbelievers, it makes no difference if you warn them or not. They are deaf, dumb and blind. Their story is like the story of those who kindled a towering fire. When their surroundings are illuminated, God suddenly extinguishes their fire, leaving them in the dark and unable to do anything. They are deaf, dumb, and blind, and nothing can help them.
Or when the rain pours in torrents and the thunder is hor-

rendous; they put their fingers in their ears for fear of death. If lightning brings a moment of light they run on, and when darkness returns they stand still, terrified.

3

God can do all things. He made the earth as a garment for you and the sky as a roof over your heads. And He caused water to fall from heaven and produced fruit from it. Allah is One. Muhammad! Recount the good news to those who believe you when you say that there are gardens set aside for them, under which rivers flow. That there will be pretty male and female companions for them, and they will have a dwelling there for eternity.

4

How did you dare deny God when you were dead, when He gave you life? He shall cause you to die, and he shall call you back to life; then you shall return to Him.
It is He who made everything on earth for you. Then He created the sky and built seven heavens. He knows all things.

5

Israelites, do you ask people to do good deeds, and forget to include yourselves?
Do you not reflect when you read Torah.
Oh, Israelites, do not forget: I chose you above all others and gave you everything.
Fear the day on which no one shall help the other.
Think back to the time We liberated you from Pharaoh who had tortured you, who killed your sons, and let only your daughters live.
Do not forget that we parted the sea for you, that we saved you, and let Pharaoh drown.

Remember how you agreed on forty nights with Musa. As soon as he was gone you started to praise the calf.

We gave Musa a book to point you in the right direction.

Do not forget that you said, 'Musa! We refuse to believe until we have seen God with our own eyes.'

It thundered, and you saw the lightning with your own eyes.

And when Musa asked for water for his people We said, 'Strike the rock with your staff.' Then water began to flow from twelve places.

We said, 'Eat and drink of what We have given you, but do not be a source of misery.'

You said to Musa that you wanted more, and you could not be satisfied with one sort of food. You asked for vegetables, cucumbers, garlic, lentils, and onions.

Musa said, 'Do you want something that is worth less than what you have received?'

They thus called God's rage upon themselves. They grew poor and humiliated.

6

The Jews say, 'The Christians are not genuine.' And the Christians say, 'The Jews are not genuine.' Yet they both read the same book.

God shall judge them after their death.

There are no greater criminals than those who destroy mosques and prevent the name of Allah from being heard in them.

They shall be punished in this life and also after their death.

7

The east and the west belong to God. Wherever you align yourself, you align yourself to God.

The Christians say, 'God has a son.' That is not true. Allah is pure. Everything on earth and in the sky is from Him. No one is His son.

He is the Creator of the earth and the heavens. If he desires something, all He has to say is, 'Be', and it is.

8

The ignorant say, 'Why does Allah not talk to us without an intermediary? And why does He not show us a miracle?'
Muhammad! In days gone by, the ignorant said the same.
Their home is hell. You shall not be held responsible for them.
The Jews and the Christians will never be happy with you unless you follow their faith.
Muhammad! Tell them, just to be sure: there is but one way, the way to Allah.
And if you follow them nonetheless, with the knowledge you have received from Us, then nothing can protect you against Us.
Oh, Israelites, think of everything I have given you, and how I chose you above all others. And fear the day on which no one shall protect you.

9

Just as Ibrahim built the Kaaba with Isma'il and said, 'God! Accept this from us. And make our descendants a believing people, and show them the way they should follow. Choose a prophet from among them who shall lead them with the book and with wisdom to a better life. You are all-knowing!'
So! Wherever you come from, align yourself toward the Sacred Mosque, the Kaaba.
And wherever you are, align yourself toward the Kaaba.
Fear no one, but fear Me.
Remember Me, therefore, and I shall remember you.

10

You who believe! Seek help through prayer and patience. God remains with those who are patient.

Those who have died for God are not dead. They are still alive, but you do not know it.

11

We put you to the test through fear, hunger, damage to your property, and injury to your bodies, but those who show patience have Our blessing.

Those touched by death and injury say, *"Inna li-llahi wa-'inna 'ilay-hi raji'un.* We belong to God and we shall return to God.' They are the ones who have found their way.

12

You, believers!

Eat of all the pure foods We have given you.

I forbid you corpses, blood, pork, and animals that are not slaughtered in the name of Allah. But those who have no choice, and are not transgressors, and do not act out of greed, may eat such things, for God is giving and forgiving.

Believers! It is your duty, if you have wealth, to leave a last will and testament. You are obliged to provide for your father, your mother, and your kin.

If someone tampers with a testament, it shall be deemed an offence. God sees all things.

Believers! It is your duty to fast.

Those who cannot fast: provide a poor person with food.

Fasting is good for you. Ramadan is the month in which the Qur'an was revealed as a guide. If you are sick or travelling, you can fast later. God desires to make it easy for you, not difficult.

Muhammad! If people ask about Me, tell them I am close to them during the month of Ramadan. If they call out to Me, I shall hear them, and if they ask for something, I shall grant it.

Believers!

You are permitted to sleep with your wives during the nights of Ramadan. Your wives are your shirts, and you are their shirts. Sleep with them, therefore, and ask of them what God has permitted you. Eat and drink until the white threads of morning separate from the black threads of night.

13

Muhammad! They ask questions about menstruation. Tell them it is suffering. Abstain from women, therefore, until they have washed themselves and are pure again.
God loves those who are pure.
Your wife is your field. You may enter your field as you please.
Muhammad! They ask you about wine and gambling.
Tell them that both contain great sin as well as much advantage for humankind.
But their sin weighs heavier than their advantage.

14

God is the king of those who believe.
Those who do not believe are on the side of Taghut, the devil.
Have you not heard the story of King Namrood, who disputed with the prophet Ibrahim about God?
Ibrahim, 'My God is He who gives life and causes death.'
Namrood, 'I do the same. I kill and I give life.'
Ibrahim, 'God causes the sun to rise in the east. You, Namrood, cause the sun to rise in the west if you can.'
Namrood was stunned into silence.
God can do all things.

One day Ibrahim turned to God and said, 'Let me see how You bring the dead back to life.'
God said, 'What do you mean? Do you not believe Me?'
Ibrahim said, 'Yes, I ask this only to reassure myself.'

God said, 'Catch four birds, kill them, cut them to pieces, mix them up, and place portions thereof on various different mountains. Call on them, and they shall fly to you.'
God is all-knowing.

15

Believers! Give away part of what you possess.
Giving is like sowing, you scatter a grain of seed and it comes back to you as seven ears, each containing a hundred new grains for you.
God is exceptionally generous.
Those who give are like an orchard on the slope of a hill. It receives much rain and produces twice as much fruit.

Give something of what you own and of what your soil gives you.
Do not dare give away the worst part, give the best part. God sees everything.

88

The Spoils of War

When Muhammad first went into battle with his enemies, he promised his followers victory and rich rewards. They win the war, but the cost in lives on their side is considerable, and the spoils are not worth mentioning. An argument thus ensues.
Prior to the second attack, Muhammad asks God to send angels to reinforce his young and inexperienced army. God grants his request and sends a thousand angels who appear at the front one by one. The enemy is roundly defeated, and Muhammad's army reaps rich rewards.

In the name of Allah
He is love
He gives
He forgives

1

In the name of Allah, He is kind and forgiving.

Muhammad! They ask about the spoils. Say, 'The spoils belong to God and His messenger. Fear and do not argue among yourselves.'

Recall that God promised that the spoils from one of the two attacks were for you. But you opted for the easy option, the defenceless caravan, while God wanted to spread His word and destroy the unbelievers to the last of them.

2

Recall what God said when you asked Him for reinforcements and He heard you, 'I shall reinforce you with a thousand angels, one following the other.'

He only did so to reassure you. Without His will, a victory would have been impossible.

Recall that He dazed you thereafter with a gentle curtain of sleep, and He caused water to fall from the sky to wash you.

God said to the angels, 'I stand behind you. Go! Fight! Reinforce the believers. And I shall shortly fill the hearts of the enemy with fear.

'Strike! Cut their throats and cut off the tips of their fingers!'

Those who resist God and His messenger are punished in the same way. God's punishment is severe.

3

You, those who believe! If your enemy confronts you and they are numerous, you must never flee. Those who do can expect hell as their home.

Unless you flee in order to attack once again.

Unless you flee to join another group.

Know this! You are not the one who kills them. God kills them. You are not the one who shoots an arrow. It is God who shoots.

Do not forget! When you were a small group, poor and afraid that the unbelievers would drive you from your homes, He came to your assistance. He gave you shelter, food, and spoils. So praise Him.

Do not forget! The enemy did not cease in devising wicked plans to kill you, to put you to flight. But He is the most intelligent deviser of plans.

4

If you believe in God and in what He did during the battle, know that a fifth part of the spoils of every war is for God, his emissary, his kin, the orphans, and the poor.

Do not forget! You were on the near side of the valley, and they were on the opposite side, and the horsemen and the caravan were below you. Then you made a mutual agreement to attack them, yet you did not do it. But God had decided to put an end to it, to kill those who had to be killed and spare those who had to be spared. God hears all things. God knows all things.

Do not forget! God made them appear in your thoughts and in your sight to be small in number, whereas they were numerous. If he had shown them in their true magnitude, you would have been afraid and there would have been dissension among you, such that you would no longer dare to fight. He protected you. God knows what goes on in human hearts.

5

Know this! When you started the war, He made you appear few in number in their eyes because He wanted to put a definitive end to it.

Know this! It is He who arranges all things.
So continue to fight when the enemy confronts you, even if they are many.
Those who count on God should know that God is invincible.
The angels shall strike the unbelievers in the face and on the back, and when they come to get them they shall say, 'Later you shall taste the fire!'
God is cruel when He punishes.

6

Do not let the unbelievers think they are easily done with Us.
Their only escape is past Us, there is no other way out.
So be ready at all times, with every possible force, with horses, with weapons, and with provisions, to frighten God's enemies and others besides them, of whom you do not yet know.
And if they are inclined to peace, you also should incline to peace and rely on God in doing so.
God hears all things.
God knows all things.

7

Muhammad! Urge the believers to fight.
Know this! If twenty of you persevere in battle, you shall be able to take down two hundred.
And if one hundred of you persevere, you shall defeat a thousand.
God has made it a little easier for you, because He knows that you have a weakness. So continue to fight with determination! If one hundred of you fight with determination, they shall defeat two hundred of them. And if a thousand of you fight with determination, they shall defeat two thousand.
God is with those who persevere.

8

Those who have accepted the faith and left house and home to fight for God, and those who have given them food and shelter, are comrades, and they form a unity. You do not have to accept responsibility for those who believed but did not want to leave, unless they go to Medina after all or ask for protection against the unbelievers.

If you do not listen to these warnings, a great commotion shall take hold of the land. Because those who do not believe, form a front.

Those who have left everything behind and those who have offered them shelter, they are the true believers. They can expect forgiveness and untainted food.

God knows all things.

89　　　　ٱ

The People of Imran

Zakariya, Maryam, and her mother Anneh belonged to the people of Imran.
Maryam gave birth to Isa, the new prophet. Muhammad reframes the story in an Arabic form.

In the name of Allah
He is love
He gives
He forgives

1

'Alif Lam Mim.

There is nothing on earth or in the sky about which God knows nothing.

The possessions and children of the unbelievers cannot protect them from God's rage. The unbelievers shall all be used as wood to stoke the fire of hell.

Exactly what God did with Pharaoh. God punishes without mercy.

Tell the unbelievers they shall soon be on their knees in hell, and hell is a horrendous place.

2

People like pleasant things, such as women, sons, and abundant property, gold, silver, thoroughbreds, livestock, and land. These are all life's pleasures, and God does not begrudge you such things.

But Muhammad, tell them this, 'Do you want more, even better than this?

'There are gardens for the believers under which rivers flow, where they shall dwell for eternity with pure male and female companions.'

3

God is firm and even-handed. Angels and genuine scholars testify that there is no God besides Allah.

The only religion chosen by God is Islam.

Ask those to whom a book has been given and the Christians if they will accept Islam or not.

If they submit, they are following the right path. If they do not, you need say nothing more. Allah sees all things.

Muhammad, tell them, 'If you love God, follow me!

'God will love you. He hears all things, He is all-knowing.'

4

And so it continued until the wife of Imran said, 'God, I dedicate what I am carrying in my belly to You. Accept it, God. You are all-wise and You hear all things.'

But when she gave birth she said, 'God, I have brought a daughter into the world. A son is not the same as a daughter. I have called her Maryam. I seek refuge in You for her and her descendants.'

God beheld Maryam and He entrusted her to Zakariya.

Each time Zakariya visited Maryam he noticed she had fruit and other provisions with her.

He said, 'Maryam, where did these come from?'

Maryam said, 'God sent them. He gives to whomever He desires.'

5

Then Zakariya prayed and said, 'God, You hear everything. Grant me good descendants, Your offspring.'

In the midst of his prayer, Zakariya was told by angels that he was to be granted a son who would be called Yahya.

Zakariya said, 'God, how can I have a child at my late age? My wife is no longer able to bear children'

God said, 'God can do everything.'

Zakariya said, 'Give me a sign.'

God said, 'The sign shall be that you shall be unable to speak to anyone for three days, except with gestures. And remember God.'

6

Muhammad! We are now telling you one of the secrets of the unseen. You were not present when they cast their pens to determine who was to be granted guardianship over Maryam. And you were likewise not present when they doubted.

7

Zakariya was still praying when the angels visited Maryam. 'Oh, Maryam, God has chosen you. He has news for you in His name. You shall give birth to a child, and his name shall be Isa son of Maryam, and he shall converse with the people from the cradle.'

Maryam said, 'God, how can I bear a child if no man has touched me?'

They said, 'God can do whatever He desires. He decides, then He says, "Be!" and it becomes, and it is.'

And He shall give him the book. The messiah shall be sent as an emissary to the Israelites, and he shall say, 'I shall show you a miracle from my God, 'I shall make a bird from clay and it shall fly. I can make the dead live. So follow me!'

8

For Allah, Isa is the same as Adam. God created Adam from the earth and said, 'Be!' And he became. And he was.

If you do not believe me, let our sons and your sons, our women and your women, ourselves and yourselves, gather together. Let us turn toward God and call His curse upon those who lie.

9

God is king of heaven and earth, and He can do all things.

For those who reflect, a miracle is hidden in the creation of the day and the night, and how they alternate. And for those who remember God standing, lying on their back, or on their side. And for those who know that all this was not made for nothing.

90

The Parties

The lion's share of this sura is devoted to Muhammad's wars with the army of Mecca and his difficulties with the Jews, who wanted nothing to do with Muhammad's Qur'an. He told the Jews that the content of the Qur'an was the same as that of the Torah and Bible, but they stated that this was not true; that their God had nothing to do with Allah. Muhammad flew into a rage, 'Everything is the same, but you have changed many of the Torah texts, you have removed many parts of the original texts. You have hidden segments, and forgotten them.' The remainder of the sura deals with women and women's rights. It is this sura that determines that women should wear a veil.

Muhammad went too far with women, and constantly sought new female companions. He falls in love with yet another woman, this time the wife of his adopted son Zayd. Stubborn rumours abound, and Allah introduces new measures.

Allah cautions him, 'Enough, Muhammad!'

In the name of Allah
He is love
He gives
He forgives

1
Prophet! Fear God; do not listen to the hypocrites.
And follow what has been revealed to you. Allah knows what you are doing.
Trust in Him! He is a trustworthy protector.

2

Believers! Do you remember Allah's intervention when the enemy attacked from all sides? Then We sent a storm and angels as invisible warriors. Allah sees everything you do.

Do you remember? When you were assailed from above and from below; when your eyes crossed with fear, and your hearts pounded in your throats; when you started to invent all sorts of things about Allah.

That was the moment of trial and you were severely shaken.

3

Muhammad, say to them, 'Running away from death or from battle shall do you no good. You shall only enjoy rest for a short time.'

Say, 'Who shall protect you against Allah if He has something good or bad in store for you?'

Allah knows those among you who sabotage and those who say, 'Count on us!' but do not really fight when battle commences.

As soon as they are confronted with danger, they roll their eyes in fear, but once danger has passed, they speak harsh words to receive their spoils.

These are the ones who do not believe. Allah knows them, and He makes their deeds ineffective. Allah does so with the greatest ease.

4

Allah withdrew the unbelievers in their rage so that they were unable to achieve anything. He is strong.

He brought down the people of the Torah from their strongholds. And he put fear in their hearts, allowing you to kill a group of them and capture another group of them. They had helped the enemy.

He made you heirs to their land, their houses, and their property, together with a land on which you had never set foot before. Allah has power over all things.

5

You, Muhammad, say to your wives, 'If you desire this life and its benefits, come then, I shall pay you, and graciously let you go. But if you desire Allah, His messenger and the life hereafter, Allah has a great reward for you.

'Wives of the prophet! Each of you who does something unseemly shall be punished with twice the severity. It is so easy for Allah. And each of you who does something good shall be granted twice the reward.

'Wives of the prophet! You are not to be compared with other women. So do not speak enticingly, lest you kindle desire in the heart of someone weak. Speak appropriately. Stay in your homes and do not expose your beauty as women did in former times, in times of ignorance.

'Wives of the prophet! Obey God and His emissary. Allah intends only to protect you against evil.'

6

Muslim men and Muslim women, devout men and women, sincere men and women, patient men and women, humble men and women, chaste men and women, men and women who remember God, Allah has a great reward in store for them.

7

It is inappropriate for a man or woman of faith to make their own decision after Allah and His prophet have issued a decree on a given matter.

Those who do not obey Allah and His prophet undoubtedly go astray.

Muhammad, when you said to your adopted son Zayd, 'Keep your wife by your side and fear Allah,' you hid something in your heart that Allah was later to reveal. You were afraid of the people, while you should have been afraid of Allah.

And when Zayd broke contact with his wife, We united you with her as your wife so that there would be no impediment for other men to marry the wife of their adopted son if she was divorced from him. Allah's will must be implemented.

The prophet should have no doubt about what God has prescribed for him. It is the will of Allah, which was also observed in the past.

Wives! Muhammad is not the father of your husbands; he is a messenger from Allah and the last messenger. And Allah is aware of everything.

8
Believers, remember Allah frequently.

Praise Him in the morning and the evening.

He greets you, and His angels do the same to guide you from darkness to light.

He is kind to those who believe.

Their greeting is, 'Salaam!' on the day they shall encounter Him.

And He has set aside a fine reward for them.

9
You, prophet!

We sent you as witness, as messenger, as cautioner, and as proclaimer of good news.

Also as one who summons to Allah in His name, as a light-giving lantern.

Proclaim to believers that they shall be granted a great gift from Him.

And do not listen to unbelievers and hypocrites. Ignore their ugly language and put your trust in Allah. He arranges all things.

10
You who believe!
If you marry a woman of faith and no longer desire her thereafter, you do not need to take a period of waiting into consideration if you did not go to bed with her; give her rather an appropriate gift and graciously let her go.
You, prophet!
We have permitted you wives.
The wives to whom you have given their dowries.
And female slaves, given you by Allah as spoils of war.
And the daughters of your uncles on your father's side.
And the daughters of your uncles on your mother's side.
And the daughters of your aunts on your father's side.
And the daughters of your aunts on your mother's side, who have accompanied you.
Every woman of faith who wants to give herself to the prophet.
This rule applies to you alone and not to other men.

11
Muhammad!
You are free to leave each of your wives or to keep them as you wish. And you are free to desire them anew as you wish. You commit no sin in any of these instances.
The goal is that they should feel happy and not sad, content with what you give them.
Allah knows what you have in your heart. Allah knows all things and He is patient.
Muhammad! You are not allowed to have additional wives, and you may not exchange them for other wives, not even

if you find them beautiful and want to have them, with the exception of your female slaves.
Allah sees all things.

12
You, believers!
Do not enter the houses of the prophet unless you are invited to dinner.
Do not go early and wait until dinner is ready, but enter when you are invited to enter.
And when you have eaten, leave and do not sit there talking.
This hurts the prophet. He is too embarrassed to say it to you himself, but Allah is not embarrassed. He speaks the truth.
And if you have something to ask his wives, ask it from behind a curtain.
It is better for your heart and theirs.
It is not fitting for you to disturb the prophet of Allah. And you are not permitted to marry any of his wives after his death.
Allah disapproves of this.
And you must do nothing covert in his house.
Fear Him. He sees all things.
Allah and His angels greet Muhammad.
You who believe, greet him also and say 'Salaam'!

13
You, Muhammad!
Tell your wives, your daughters, and women of faith to cover their head with a veil. They shall thus remain unrecognised, and no one shall harass them.
If the hypocrites of Medina do not put an end to their gossip, We shall allow you to intervene against them.
They are cursed. Wherever they are, they must be put to death or taken prisoner. This is Allah's will and it shall not change.

14

Believers!

Fear Allah! And speak untainted language!

Those who obey Allah and His prophet shall achieve great happiness.

We invited the heavens, the earth and the mountains to be representatives, but they refused the task, they were too afraid. Humans accepted it.

But they are ignorant and cruel.

91

Those Who Are Put to the Test

Muhammad and his followers fled from Mecca to Medina, the city that was to become the centre of his rule.

As knowledge of him spread, more and more people joined his ranks.

One interesting event was the flight of a group of women from Mecca who left behind their husbands and escaped to Medina to be with Muhammad.

Many of the women were spies in the service of the Council of Mecca and they tried to marry one of Muhammad's followers to get closer to the prophet and to spy on him.

Muhammad had asked his followers expressly to keep an eye on these women, but they were welcome nonetheless, if they swore by Allah that they were not conspiring with Mecca, that they had fled because of their violent husbands, that they had not come to seek a husband among Muhammad's men, and that they had only escaped on account of their faith in Allah.

One of the women was a prostitute by the name of Sareh. She had left Mecca and entered Medina with blistered feet. She met Muhammad in person and said to him, 'I earned my living by dancing in public, but I wanted to stop. Lately, all I could think of was you and your Qur'an. I want to join you.'

She swore three times by Allah, by His Qur'an, and by His prophet, and thus she gained access to Muhammad's followers. And because she was beautiful, she married one of the men close to Muhammad.

When Muhammad was preparing his army to attack Mecca, the woman fled from Medina to warn the Council of Mecca.

Muhammad found out about it and sent three horsemen after her.

The following day he introduced a new sura, 'al-Mumtahana: She Who Is Put to the Test'.

In the name of Allah
He is love
He gives
He forgives

1

Believers! You who left your houses in Mecca for Me and My satisfaction and went to Medina, do not make friends with My enemies.

They are the ones who have rejected your faith.

They are the ones who banished you and the messenger, only because you believed in Allah.

2

If you wage war for Me, do not seek contact with them in secret.

I know what you do in public and what you do in private.

Those who do so nonetheless, have strayed from the right path.

3

If the unbelievers gain the upper hand, they shall stand before you as enemies; and they shall assail you with their hands and with their words.

They want nothing more than your return to the state of unbeliever.

Fear! On the day of judgement, you shall not be able to help your kin and your children.

Allah alone shall decide their fate, and He is aware of everything they do.

4

It may be that Allah shall establish friendship between you and your enemies.

He can do all things, and He forgives.

He does not prevent you from maintaining good relations with those who have not fought against you, and with those who did not drive you from your houses.

Allah loves those who are just.

5

But Allah forbids you to maintain relations with those who have fought against you and driven you from your houses.

Allah advises against befriending such people.

Those who do so nonetheless, are unbelievers.

6

You, believers! When the women who fled from Mecca arrive, put them to the test.

Allah knows about the truth of their faith.

If you consider their faith to be genuine, do not send them back to the unbelievers; these women now belong to us, and they are unlawful and forbidden to unbelieving men.

Unbelieving men are also forbidden to these women.
But reimburse the costs that their husbands have incurred on their account.

7
You who believe! You are permitted to marry these women, but only after you have paid their dowry.
And do not maintain marital relations with unbelieving women.
Such is the will of Allah.

8
And if your wives go to unbelieving men, ask them to pay the expenses you incurred on their behalf.
Such is the will of Allah.
He is all-wise.
He is just.

9
If one of your wives defects to the side of the unbelievers, and you manage to recover your expenses, share them with the men whose wives ran away but who have been unable to recover their expenses as yet.
Fear Allah.

10
You, Muhammad!
If women come to you to swear fidelity to you, to swear that Allah is one, that they shall not steal, that they shall not commit adultery, that they shall not kill their children, that they have not acquired a child by deceit, and that they shall not ignore your command, then accept their oath of fidelity and ask Allah to forgive them.
Allah is forgiving.

11

Believers! Do not make friends with those who have drawn Allah's anger upon themselves.

They cannot look forward to life after death, just as unbelievers have no hope for those in the grave.

92   🐄

The Women

Muhammad had fifteen wives who shared their bed with him. Their names were Khadija, Sawda, Aisha, Salama, Hafsa, Zaynab, Juwayriyya, Habiba, Safiyya, Maymunah, Fatima, Hind, Asma, Habla and Dosiye.

Muhammad visited each of them in turn, but the wives exchanged turns with one another and sometimes relinquished their turn to one of their sisters.

Muhammad also visited two female slaves—Rayhana and Magus.

He was permitted to keep the women he received as a gift. One of them was called Mariyah, a beautiful gift from the king of Habasha.

He was permitted in addition to sleep with women who offered him their body.

But Aisha, Muhammad's youngest wife, behaved as if she was superior to all the others.

I am privileged for five reasons, she said:

1. *Muhammad was my first husband and my last.*
2. *Muhammad could not endure anyone near him when a sura was revealed, but at such decisive moments he wanted me to be close to him nonetheless.*

3. *When Muhammad's enemies set out to break him on my account, a sura was revealed to him containing fifteen quotations about me. People shall thus remember me for eternity.*
4. *If Muhammad was ill, he always found his way to my house and my bed.*
5. *When Muhammad died, he died in my bed.*

In the name of Allah
He is love
He gives
He forgives

1
People, fear the God who created you all from one single body. Fear! Do not exhaust the possessions of orphans, and do not mix their money with yours. God sees all things. It is a great sin.
If you do not know how to deal with orphan girls, choose one or two or three or four of them, and marry them.
But if you are afraid you cannot treat them fairly, be satisfied with one of them.
Give the women their promised dowry willingly. But if they do not want it and freely give it to you, you are welcome to keep it.
Be careful with orphan girls and treat them justly. Determine whether they are ready for marriage. If they are not, return their property to them. Allah sees all things. Be careful not to consume their money.
And when you return their property, invite a number of witnesses to be present, to avoid potential dispute.
Those who consume the money of orphans consume fire in their bellies.

2

Allah declares the following with respect to children: a son's inheritance is equal to the share of two daughters. If there are only daughters, however, and there are more than two of them, two-thirds of the inheritance is for them. But if there is only one daughter, half the estate is for her.

If the deceased has children, each of his parents inherits a sixth of what he bequeaths.

But if he has no children, his mother receives a third. Unless he has brothers, then the mother inherits a sixth.

This is your duty according to Allah. These are God's rules.

Those who obey His prophet shall enter gardens of happiness under which rivers flow and where they are free to dwell for eternity. But those who refuse to listen shall find themselves in a fire for all time.

3

And with respect to your women; if one of them commits a serious fault, four men must be able to testify to it. Only when they confirm the evidence may you lock her in her room until she dies, or until God offers a way out.

You may chastise them for their ugly deed, but if they show remorse you should leave them be, for God is kind and He forgives.

4

Men, you are not permitted to inherit women against their will. And you must not keep them in your home as your wife. You must not use violence to recover something you gave to them unless they have done something wrong. Treat them well, and if they do not please you, be aware that there are many things in life that do not please us, but God has placed something good in them nonetheless. Allah is all-wise.

5

Men, if you desire another woman instead of your wife, do not ask her to return what you gave her.

Indeed, how can you ask it back if you have slept with her and given her your consent!

6

Men, the following women are forbidden to you:

Your father's wives. To touch them would be a heinous deed. Also your mother, your daughters, your sisters, your aunts, your brothers' daughters, your sisters' daughters, your wet-nurse, your wet-nurses' daughters, your wives' mother, your wives' daughters, your sons' wives, as well as two sisters at the same time, and married women, except the female slaves at your disposal.

7

Men! If one among you is unable to afford to marry a free woman of faith, it is better for him to marry a devout female slave. You belong together. And God is aware of your genuine decisions.

Choose, then, one of them who is chaste, who has not had contact with another man in secret. And if you marry her and she later commits adultery, half the punishment applicable to a free woman is to be applied to her.

This rule is for those who are afraid to sin.

God desires to make everything easy for you, for humans are weak. God is all-knowing.

8

Men are above women, for God chose the one above the other, and because they have their wealth at their disposal.

The best women are those who obey, and who guard over what

lies hidden in them. God knows all things.

But if there are women whose obedience causes you concern, speak with them first, caution them. If that does not work, distance yourself from them in bed. And if that does not help, strike them.

If they obey you thereafter, you may not afflict them further. God is great!

But if you fear potential conflict, ask a member of her family and a member of your own family to mediate. God is all-knowing.

9

God treats no one unjustly, and if you do a good deed He shall reward you twofold in return. God gives.

You cannot hide anything from God.

God explicitly asks you to return the property of others that is in your custody. That you are just in your judgement of others. Listen to God. He hears all things. He sees all things.

10

We shall cause those who ignore Our words to burn in the fire. Each time their skin is completely burned they shall be given a new skin so that they shall be able to feel the actual punishment. God can do all things.

But for those who follow Us there are gardens of happiness under which rivers flow, where they are free to dwell forever with male and female companions who stand ready for them in the shade of the trees.

11

Muhammad, tell them that the pleasures of this life are limited; that it is better in the hereafter.

That they shall not be treated unjustly at any moment.

That wherever they are, even in fortified lofty castles, death shall reach them.

Tell them that every favour they encounter comes from God, but that all the evil they endure comes from themselves.

There is no God besides Allah. It is He who shall gather you together for the day of judgement. This is beyond every possible doubt. Who is more honest than Allah?

12

Believers! Be on your guard for the charlatans, those hypocrites. They hope you shall become unbelievers, just as they are unbelievers. So do not befriend them unless they fully associate themselves with you and join you.

But if they turn away, and if they do not leave you alone, and if they do not offer you peace, and if they intend to use violence, grab them wherever you find them and kill them. God has given you a free hand against such people.

13

Believers, if you go on a journey for God, be on your guard.

All those who leave their homes and accompany the believers shall be given many opportunities. And there shall be shelter for them wherever they are.

And those who leave their homes for the prophet of God and meet their death shall receive extra reward from God. God is giving.

And if you are on a journey and you fear they shall strike while you are praying, shorten your prayer and take your leave; the unbelievers are your enemy.

14

Muhammad, if you are standing in the midst of your followers and you want to pray with them, keep your sword at your side.

Your followers should also carry their swords. And you should arrange it in such a way that a group is standing behind you when you bow during your prayer, to keep watch.

The unbelievers are waiting patiently for the moment you neglect your weapon, allowing them to attack you by surprise. God has devised a severe and mighty punishment for the unbelievers.

15

Believer! When you are finished praying, continue to think about God when you stand up again, when you sit, and when you lie on your side.

What God says is true and no one is more just than He.

Everyone who commits a crime shall be punished. And everyone, man or woman, who does a good deed shall make their way to paradise.

Everything in the heavens and on earth is from God, and He has dominion over it all.

16

Muhammad, they ask you for clarity concerning women.

God speaks without ambiguity. And the rules are written in the book that is recited to you; it speaks about the orphan girls whose property you consume, with whom you do not want to marry.

Be sincere with the orphans, for God sees what you do.

If a woman notices that her husband has taken his distance from her, that he is ignoring her, it is better for both to come to an arrangement; reconciliation is the best way, but humans are inclined to be greedy.

You will never be able to treat your wives equally, even if you wanted to, but you must never suddenly ignore one of your wives or leave her if you find yourself drawn to another woman.

In so doing you would leave her in a situation of uncertainty while she is still your wife. It is better to seek peaceful solutions. God sees all things.

Oh, people! If He should so desire He could destroy you all and put others in your place. He can do all things.

17

Hypocrites are intent on misleading God, but God misleads them.

During prayer they get to their feet lazily and without interest; they are insincere; they do not think about God.

Believers! Do not take the unbelievers as your friends.

Hypocrites shall be cast into the fire on the lowest level of hell, and no one shall ever help them.

God is averse to ugly words unless they come from someone who has been treated unjustly.

God is all-knowing. He hears all things.

18

Those who believe in the Torah demand that you cause a book to come down for them from heaven.

They asked Musa something even stranger. They asked him to let them see God.

Then they were all struck by a devastating bolt of lightning.

They then accepted the calf as God, although they had seen clear signs. But We granted them forgiveness and We gave Musa a clear mandate.

We lifted Mount Tur high above them, because that is what they wanted. And We said, 'Bow down and enter the door with humility.'

We said, 'And you must not transgress on the Sabbath!'

And We made a firm covenant with them, but they broke it and did what they wanted.

On account of their lies and their lack of faith, and on account of their breaking the covenant, and because they killed the prophets without the least justification, and especially because they uttered mean and malicious words about Maryam, God has sealed their hearts.

They say, 'We killed Isa, the son of Maryam.'

But they did not kill him, and they did not crucify him. That is how it appeared to them, but they are mistaken. It is an illusion. They certainly did not kill Isa.

God took him up to heaven. God can do all things.

19

You who believe in the Bible, do not go too far in your faith. And say nothing but the truth about God.

Isa is the son of Maryam and the emissary of God. God sent His word upon Maryam and it became flesh.

So submit to God and His emissaries and do not say, 'The Almighty is three in one: the Father, the Son and the Holy Spirit.' Desist with this. It is better for you.

God is one. Having a child is far from Him.

The firmament of heaven and the earth belong to Him. And His rules are clear.

He is all-knowing.

93

Divorce

Women lived in difficult circumstances, because they had no rights, and it became even more difficult for them when their men no longer wanted to live with them.

The men would thus arrange a divorce unilaterally and send

their wives away empty handed.
Muhammad uses this sura to try to create some order in the
resultant chaos.
He introduces clear rules and states that those who do not adhere
to them are enemies of Allah.

Muhammad himself had fifteen wives. He slept with thirteen of
them, but not with the remaining two when they grew old. He
took them into his home to take care of his children. He did not
divorce any of his wives.

In the name of Allah
He is love
He gives
He forgives

1
Oh, messenger!
If you want to divorce your wives, do so when they are having
their monthly period. Calculate the time with precision.
Fear Allah, and do not expel them from their dwellings.
It is better that they do not leave, except when they have done
something unacceptable.
This is a clear stipulation from God.
Those who contravene this stipulation harm themselves
unjustly.
You do not know whether Allah will bring about progress in
your case.

2
When the end of their waiting time approaches, show them
courtesy and let them stay at home, or divorce her in a respect-
able way.

Have two honest individuals among you bear witness. This is genuine testimony before Allah, a warning for those who believe in Allah and in the day of judgement.

He leaves a way out for those who fear Allah.

And He shall provide their bread from a completely unexpected corner.

For those who put their trust in God, God is enough.

Allah knows what everyone does, and He has established a measure for all things.

3

The women among you who no longer expect a period have a waiting time of three months.

This also applies to women who have not yet had their period.

The waiting time for pregnant women lasts until they have given birth to their child.

Allah makes it easy for those who fear Him.

This is the stipulation Allah has sent down to you.

He shall forgive the sins of those who fear, and He shall reward them.

4

So give them a dwelling according to your abilities, similar to the dwellings in which you yourselves live, and do not hurt them or make it more difficult for them.

And if they are pregnant, take care of them until their child is born.

And if they breastfeed their child, pay them for it, and try to reach a just solution.

But if it becomes difficult for you both, have another woman feed the child.

The wealthy should give of their wealth with generosity to their divorced wives.

The poor should make a contribution from what God has given them.
Allah asks no one more than what He has given them.
He shall thus make the problem bearable for you.

5
It is Allah who created the seven heavens and the earth.
His command descends upon it so that you might know that He is powerful.
He embraces all things with His knowledge.

94

The Light

Muhammad takes one of his wives with him during every war, and this time it is Aisha's turn. But on the way home, as the caravan is about to continue after a brief stop, the fifteen-year-old Aisha hides behind a sand dune and the caravan departs without her. Muhammad's enemies assail him, and poets mock him, 'Muhammad, your young Aisha has had a rendezvous behind the sand dune.'
This very event prompted Muhammad to introduce rigorous laws for women.
Since then, women have been expected to cover themselves and stay indoors.

In the name of Allah
He is love
He gives
He forgives

1

This is a sura We have revealed, which We have made obligatory.

We have passed on clear signs that you might learn from them. Every woman and every man who engages in illicit sex is to receive one hundred lashes. And if you believe in Allah and in the day of judgement, do not have compassion with them.

A group of believers should be present when they are being reprimanded.

The lecherous man is only allowed to marry a wanton woman or an unbeliever.

And the wanton woman is only allowed to marry a lecherous man or an unbeliever.

2

Those who accuse decent married women of adultery and do not come forward with four witnesses are to receive eighty lashes. You must not accept their testimony in the future. They are at fault.

And those who accuse their own wives of lechery with only themselves as witness must swear four times in the name of Allah that they are speaking the truth, and the fifth time they must say, 'May Allah's curse rest upon me if I am lying!'

But the punishment due to the woman must not be carried out if she swears four times in the name of Allah that her husband is lying, and if she says the fifth time, 'May Allah's rage come upon me if my husband is speaking the truth and I am lying.' Allah is forgiving. Otherwise it would be difficult for you.

3

There are some among you who have spread gossip.

If Allah had not been merciful, you would have been stricken with a severe punishment in this life and also in the life hereafter.

You took such gossip on your own lips and you passed it on with your mouths without the least understanding. You considered it unimportant, but for God it was loathsome.

When you heard it, all you would have had to say was, 'It has nothing to do with me; I have nothing to say about it. Praise be to You. This is a serious accusation.'

Those who are happy to see gossip spread among the people shall be punished severely in this life and in the life hereafter. Allah knows, but you do not know.

4

Those who accuse decent women, who know no evil, of debauchery shall be cursed in this life and in the life hereafter. A severe punishment awaits them.

On a given day, their tongue, hands, and feet shall testify to what they have done. On that day, God shall determine what they deserve, and they shall understand that Allah knows the truth.

5

Wicked women are for wicked men, and wicked men are for wicked women; good women are for good men, and good men are for good women. They are cleansed of everything said about them by others. They can expect forgiveness and they shall be treated well.

6

Oh, you who believe! Do not enter the houses of others without asking or without greeting those who dwell there with 'Salaam!' This is better for you. Perhaps you shall learn from it. And if you find no one at home, do not continue without first acquiring permission.

And if someone says to you, 'Turn back,' turn back. Such is pure. Allah knows what you do in public and what you keep hidden.

7

Muhammad, tell male believers that they should lower their eyes and preserve their chastity. Such is pure for them. Allah knows all things.

And tell female believers that they should lower their eyes and preserve their chastity; that they should not expose more of their adornment than is naturally visible; that they should drape their veils over their breasts; that they should expose their adornment to no one but their husbands, their fathers, their sons, the sons of their husbands, their brothers, the sons of their brothers, the sons of their sisters, the women of their own faith, their male servants who have no need of women, and children who pay no attention as yet to the female body.

Muhammad, tell the women that they must not stamp hard on the ground with their feet, lest the hidden adornment of their feet be exposed.

8

Believers! Help the people who work for you to marry each other, including your virtuous male and female slaves.

If they are poor, God shall make them rich from His abundance. Allah is all-embracing and all-knowing.

Those who do not have the opportunity to marry must persevere in their chastity until Allah makes them rich from His goodness.

Give your male slaves a letter of emancipation if they ask for their freedom, and give them something of your gifts from Allah.

And do not force your female slaves to sleep with someone else so you can earn money from them.

We have sent you clear signs and examples of the people who disappeared before your time, and We have given lessons for those who desire to learn.

9

Allah is the light of the heavens and the earth.

You can compare His light to a niche with a lantern in it. The lantern is in a glass, and the glass radiates like a brilliant star. The lantern burns with the oil from a sacred tree, an olive tree, neither easterly nor westerly. The oil already radiates light without fire touching it. Light upon light.

10

The deeds of unbelievers are like a mirage in the desert. Those who are thirsty see water, but when they reach the place they find nothing. Rather, they find Allah who settles accounts for their deeds, and Allah tallies swiftly.

Alternatively, they are like darkness in a deep sea covered with waves, with other waves on top and clouds above them both. Darkness upon darkness. When someone reaches out a hand, He can barely see it. There is no light for them.

11

Have you never noticed that everything in the heavens and on earth praises Allah, including the birds with their outstretched wings? Each has its own prayer. Allah knows all things.

12

The kingdom of the heavens and the earth belong to Allah.

Have you not noticed that Allah causes the clouds to move, assembles them, then presses them together until you see huge raindrops form in their midst? And how He causes hail to fall from the clouds? He strikes whomever he desires with it, and avoids whomever He desires.

13

Allah alternates day and night. This contains a lesson for those able to observe it.

And Allah made every animal from water. Some lie on their bellies, some walk on two legs, and others on four legs. Allah makes whatever He desires. Allah can do all things.

14

You believers! Have your male and female slaves, and the minors among you, ask three times for permission to come inside if you have taken off your clothes to wash for morning, midday, and evening prayer; three moments at which you are not fully dressed.

At other moments there is no problem, since they are always present in your vicinity.

This is how Allah makes His signs clear to you.

15

When your children leave their childhood behind, they also must ask permission when they enter a place, just as others did before them.

16

Older women who can no longer expect to marry are permitted to remove their chador, as long as they do not intend to parade their adornment. But it is better for them to remain covered. God sees all things. God knows all things.

17

The blind are not to be blamed, the lame are not to be blamed, the sick are not to be blamed, and you yourself are not to be blamed if you eat in your own house, in the house of your father, in the house of your mother, in the houses of your brothers, in the houses of your sisters, in the houses of your father's brothers, in the houses of your father's sisters, in the houses of your mother's brother, in the houses of your mother's sisters, in the house for which you have the keys, or in the house of a friend.

It is up to you if you eat alone or with others.

But if you enter a house, call out 'Salaam'. It is blessed and God considers it beautiful.

Allah thus makes His signs clear for you. Perhaps you shall learn from them.

18

Know this! Everything in the heavens and on the earth belongs to Allah.

He knows what you are doing, and when you shall be brought back to Him.

He knows all things.

95

The Dispute

There was an outdated regulation that allowed a man to leave his wife without a formal divorce. This regulation was called the 'Zihar', or the 'Back Law'.

According to this law, the man was to say to his wife, 'Your back is like the back of my mother. I am no longer allowed to go to bed with you.'

It was a profound insult, with which a man suddenly left his wife with the excuse that her body was forbidden to him.

One of the women thus rejected by her husband turned to Muhammad with her complaint.

Muhammad said to her, 'It is the law; you are now forbidden to him.'

The woman started to argue with Muhammad, 'How dare you say such a thing. I've been with that man for forty years. Give me advice. I cannot leave it like this.'

But Muhammad had no advice for her.

The woman pressured Muhammad to put her in touch with Allah.

But her dispute with Muhammad resulted in nothing. She returned to her house deeply saddened, ate nothing, did not sleep, wept, and called upon the help of Allah.

A few days later Muhammad introduced a new sura: al-Mujadila. *The Dispute.*

In the name of Allah
He is love
He gives
He forgives

1
Muhammad!
Allah heard the woman who had an argument with you about her husband and brought her complaint to Him.
He hears you. He knows all things.

2
The men among you who use the Back Law to divorce their wives should know that their wives are not their mothers.
Their mothers are the women who bore them.
These men speak ugly words. They are lying.
Yet Allah is forgiving.

3

But the men who have used the Back Law and now regret it, preferring to have their wives back, must set free a male slave before they can be reunited.

This is what Allah advises you, and He is aware of everything you do.

4

If someone does not have a male slave to liberate, instead he must fast for two consecutive months before they can be reunited.

And if this too is impossible, he should feed sixty needy people.

This is a stipulation from Allah.

Those who do not implement it shall be severely punished.

And those who resist God and his messenger shall be humiliated. Just like those who were humiliated before them.

We sent down clear signs to that end.

5

Believers! When you are asked during the meetings to make room, make room. Thus, Allah shall make room for you in the gardens of paradise.

And if you are asked 'Stand up', stand up. Allah shall thus elevate you to a higher status.

He is aware of everything you do.

6

Believers! If you want to share a secret personally with the prophet, give something away first, before you go to visit him. It is better for you this way.

But if you have nothing to give away, Allah is forgiving.

96

Forbidden

If Muhammad slept with other women when he was away from home, it would cause problems with his own wives. They would argue with him or ignore him in bed.
One day when he is about to get into bed with his young wife Aisha after having slept with a pretty female slave, she starts to cry and sleeps with her back to him the entire night.

Muhammad's second young wife was named Hafsa and Hafsa had a beautiful female slave by the name of Maryam al-Qibtiyya. When Hafsa was away, Muhammad slept with Maryam in Hafsa's bed.
Hafsa returned unexpectedly and caught them. She was so angry that she summoned Muhammad and all his wives and started a massive argument.

The following day, and with a bitter taste in his mouth, Muhammad forbade himself from sleeping with other women.
He later regretted his decision and reproached himself for giving in to pressure from his wives. He breaks his vow.

In the name of Allah
He is love
He gives
He forgives

1
You, messenger!
Why do you forbid yourself something Allah permits you? Do you do so perhaps to satisfy your wives?

Allah is kind and forgiving.
Allah gives you room to break your vows.
He is your creator. And He knows all things.

2

It transpired thus. Muhammad confided a secret to Aisha, one of his wives. But she passed it on to Hafsa, one of his other wives. And Allah made it public.
Muhammad told part of what he knew to Aisha and withheld the other part.
She said to him, 'How do you know this? Who told it to you?'
Muhammad said, 'He who knows all things informed me.'

3

If you, both wives, turn to Allah and express remorse, then it was an error of the heart, and He shall forgive you.
But if you conspire together against His messenger, He shall protect His messenger.

4

If Muhammad divorces you, perhaps his Creator shall grant him still better wives. Chaste, believing wives who listen, who are not arrogant, who pray, who fast, women who are widows or still virgins.

5

Believers!
Protect yourselves and your family from a fire of which people and stones are the fuel; a fire guarded by stern, malevolent angels who listen to Allah and do what He commands them.

Oh, unbelievers, do not show remorse on the day of judgement.
You shall nonetheless be punished for what you have done.

Oh, believers!
Show remorse from the bottom of your hearts. Perhaps He shall forgive your sins, and He shall take you to the gardens of paradise under which rivers flow.

6
You, messenger!
Fight the unbelievers and the hypocrites and oppose them with all your might. They shall all end up in hell.
And it is a dreadful place for them.

7
Allah offers two examples of unbelieving women.
The wife of the prophet Nuh was an unbeliever, as was the wife of Lut. They were the wives of two of Our best people, but they both deceived their husbands.
Nuh and Lut thus remained silent when God severely punished their wives. These women were told, 'Both of you! Enter into the fire with the others!'

8
Allah also offers an example of a believing woman.
The wife of Pharaoh. She lived in a difficult situation and said to God, 'My Creator. Grant me a dwelling with You in paradise. And free me from Pharaoh and what he is doing.'

9
And Maryam, the daughter of Imran, is another good example. She maintained her chastity and We breathed Our soul into her. And she fell pregnant with Isa.
She believed the words and the books of God, and she listened.

97

The Earthquake

In the name of Allah
He is love
He gives
He forgives

1
When the earth is shaken up by the last quake.
And it throws off its burdens, the dead.
And people say, 'What is wrong with it?
On that day, the earth shall reveal its secrets on the command of Allah.
On that day the people shall be brought forward in different groups, and they shall be shown their past deeds.
Whoever has done even the slightest good shall behold it.
And whoever has done even the slightest evil shall also behold it.

98

Iron

Iron is hard. Allah taught the prophet Dawud to smelt iron and make a suit of armour from it.

In the name of Allah
He is love
He gives
He forgives

1

Everything that exists on earth and in the heavens, give praise to Allah.

He is the beloved Victor.

He is the King of the heavens and the earth.

He gives life and brings death. He can do all things.

He is the beginning and the end, the internal and the external.

He has knowledge of all things.

2

It was He who created the earth and the heavens in six days.

Then He sat down on His throne.

He knows what goes into the earth and what comes out of it.

And what comes down from heaven and what ascends to heaven.

3

He is everywhere you are, and He sees everything you do.

He covers the night with the day, and He covers the day with the night.

And He knows the secrets of every heart.

4

Believe in Allah and in His messenger, and give!

It is true! Those who give can expect a great reward.

What has happened to you that you still do not believe in God?

It was He who sent the Qur'an as a guide to His servant, to lead you from darkness into light.

Know this! Allah is kind to you.

5

But what happened to you, that you still refuse to give on account of Allah, whereas the inheritance of the heavens and the earth is due to Him?

Those who gave themselves and fought for victory against Mecca are not equal to everyone else. They are higher in rank than those who only gave and fought after the victory.

Allah knows all things.

To those who give others a pure loan, He shall repay it twofold.

6

On the day you see devout men and women while their light radiates from their right and their left side, it is a good omen. They shall make their way to the gardens of happiness, and they shall dwell there forever.

On that same day, the hypocrites, male and female, shall say to the believers, 'Will you not wait a while so that we can make use of a little of your light?'

They shall be told, 'Go back! Seek light for yourselves.'

A wall with a door in it shall be constructed between them. On the inside of the door you shall see glory, but on the outside of the door you shall see punishment.

The hypocrites shall call out to the believers on the other side of the wall, 'Were we not with you?' They shall answer, 'Yes, but you were deceived by your desires and misled by your dreams. You constantly questioned everything, and you followed Satan until death took hold of you.'

7

Know that Allah brings the earth back to life after its death. He has set forth His signs with clarity for you so that you might learn from them.

8

Know that this life is a game of amusement, magnificence, pride, and the desire for more possessions and more children. It can be compared to the rain that pleases the farmer, because it brings growth to his crop. But afterwards the plants dry up, you see them turn yellow, and they become stunted and thorny.

This present life is only a deceptive pleasure, similar to the life of such plants.

Hurry, therefore, to the gardens of happiness; they are for eternity, and their dimensions are those of the heavens and the earth.

9

Never lament, therefore, about what you have lost.

And do not rejoice on account of what you have received.

Because Allah has no love for the haughty.

Especially not for those who give nothing.

He Himself is in need of nothing. He gives.

Men and women who give pure loans shall be rewarded twofold.

10

We sent iron, durable in strength and useful for people in many ways.

Allah gives, and His giving knows no bounds.

99

Muhammad

Isa once said to his apostles, 'After me an Arab prophet shall come named Ahmad (Muhammad) and he shall be the last prophet.'

'How shall we recognise this Ahmad?' the apostles asked.

'He bears the sign of the moon on his left shoulder,' Isa answered.

Muhammad was born in Mecca five-hundred and seventy years later.

His mother's name was Amina.

The birth was joyless for Amina, because her husband had just died.

But the midwife called out, 'Amina, do not cry. Your son has a sign of the early moon on his shoulder. It shall bring wealth and happiness.'

Muhammad was born into the Quraysh tribe, one of the most important in Mecca. For centuries, the chief of the Quraysh tribe was appointed key keeper of the Kaaba. The function enjoyed considerable respect and afforded the chief access to the secrets of the Kaaba.

Muhammad's grandfather was the key keeper and as a child Muhammad regularly went with him to the Kaaba, which Ibrahim and his son Isma'il once built as a dwelling for God.

It now contained countless idols.

In the name of Allah
He is love
He gives
He forgives

1
Allah shall despise the deeds of those who refuse the truth and lead people away from His way.
But He shall forgive the faults of those who believe.

2
Believers! When you engage in battle with unbelievers, kill them with a deathblow.
If you prevail, imprison them and bind them firmly.

And when the battle is fought, set them free with or without a ransom.

This is how it shall be, and it is God's rule. Had He so desired, He could have taken revenge against them.

And those who have killed for Allah shall be rewarded for their deed. They shall be brought to paradise.

3

Did the unbelievers not travel the earth without seeing how those who did not listen met their end? God destroyed them all.

The unbelievers make use of the pretence of life. They eat and sleep like herd animals.

Muhammad! We have destroyed many cities that were bigger and stronger than the city that allowed you to escape. And there was no help for them.

4

The believers shall enter the gardens of happiness, where rivers of pure and healthy water flow, and also rivers of delicious milk, delectable wines, and rivers of pure honey, and where there is every sort of fruit.

Is eternity dwelling in such gardens to be compared with eternity dwelling in hell?

5

The unbelievers refuse to reflect on the Qur'an and have closed their hearts.

How shall they feel when the angels come to take their souls while beating their backs and faces?

Is it because they follow idols, which angers Allah? And hate what is dear to Him?

6

This present life is play and amusement. But if you believe and fear, He shall reward you.

7

Give away part of your wealth, and do not be miserly. Those who are miserly are miserly toward themselves.
Allah needs nothing, but you are needy.
And if you do not listen, He shall establish another people in your place. And they shall not be like you.

100

Thunder

Muhammad referred to himself as an Arabic prophet and the world's last prophet. He brought all of the Arabic tribes together under the green flag of his movement.
Muhammad was six when his mother died, and his grandfather took on the task of raising him. He was twenty-five when he married the wealthiest woman in Mecca; she was fifteen years older than him.
Muhammad regularly climbed Mount Hira at night, and he was forty when he returned home one night shaking, terrified, and sweating. He said to his wife, 'The inhabitants of heaven have contacted me.'
From that moment onward, he set out on a mission that was to last twenty-three years.
The people in Mecca put him under pressure, saying he was not a prophet and was unable to work miracles.
Muhammad responded helplessly, 'I do not know why I cannot perform miracles. Only God knows why.'

When the authorities in Mecca wanted to kill him, he fled to Medina. His gentle words seemed to have been to no avail, and his patience had yielded nothing. When he arrived in Medina, he took up arms and his words grew hard, 'You want a miracle from me? The Qur'an is my miracle. It is the mother of all the books in the world. My sword shall give answer to those who contradict it.'

In the name of Allah
He is love
He gives
He forgives

1
'Alif Lam Mim Ra'.
These are the verses of the book. And everything sent by God is true, but most do not believe it.
It is God who caused the heavens to rise up without visible supporting pillars. Thereafter He sat on His throne and He tamed the moon and the sun, such that each followed a fixed course. He regulates the world and its functions.

2
It is He who extended the earth and made mountains and rivers; and He made every sort of fruit in two portions as one pair; and He caused the night to cover the day.
And on earth there are stretches of ground, side by side, and vineyards, and cornfields, and date palms, alike and unalike, which all receive water as a single whole. These are signs for those who reflect.

3

Those who do not believe, say, 'Why was a sign not sent down with him from his Allah?'

But Muhammad! You are merely a messenger, and for each people there is only one messenger.

God knows what a pregnant woman is carrying, how wombs decline and how they grow. For Him, everything has a measure.

4

It is He who knows what is hidden and what is visible.

It makes no difference to Him if people speak in secret or out loud, or move about in the dark of night or in the light of day. He knows all things. There are angels who walk in front and behind human beings to observe everything.

5

It is He who uses lightning to instil fear and hope; and He sends the heavy clouds.

The thunder praises His glory, and the angels praise Him out of fear, and He sends lightning with which He takes whomever He pleases. Allah is cruel in His punishment!

The idols they praise instead of God do not hear them. You can compare it with a man who puts his hands in a spring of water to drink but sees that the spring is dry.

6

Everything in the heavens and on earth praises God, willingly or unwillingly; also their shadows in the morning and the evening.

Muhammad! Ask them, 'Who is the Creator of the heavens and the earth?'

And say, 'Allah!'

Ask them, 'Why, then, do you prefer idols that do not even have power over themselves?'

And say, 'Are the blind the same as the sighted? Are darkness and light equal?'

Say, 'Allah is the Maker of all things. And He is One. He is the most powerful!'

He causes water to fall from the sky to make the rivers foam and flow. Foam also rises from everything thrust into fire, to make jewels or tools. God thus separates truth from falsehood. The foam is lost, but what is useful remains. Allah thus compares one thing with another.

7

Those who show patience before God, perform the prayers, have averted evil with good, and have given away a portion of what We have given them, shall be granted a good final destination. They shall find themselves in the gardens of happiness, where angels shall approach from every side to welcome them, 'Salaam to you for your patience. Oh, what an excellent end.'

But those who have spread destruction on earth shall be cursed. A terrible end awaits them.

8

Muhammad, say to them, 'He is my Allah! And there is not God besides Him. I place my trust in Him and shall return to Him.

'And even if there is a Qur'an that sets the mountains in motion, causes the earth to fall apart and the dead to speak, there shall still be some who do not believe in it.'

9

To those who believe, gardens of happiness are promised under which rivers flow, where fruit and shadow are eternal.

Muhammad, say to those who do not believe, 'I have been commanded to serve Allah and not to associate an equal with Him. I call everyone to Him. And I shall return to Him.'
We have thus revealed the Qur'an as a judgement in Arabic. And if you continue to follow your desires, even after the knowledge that has come to you, you shall be without protection against God.
Allah destroys what He pleases and establishes what He pleases.
And the book *In the Beginning* is with Him.

101

He is Exalted

The unbelievers said, 'Muhammad is an ear. The Persian poets taught him such things.'
God said, 'We taught him! We who give. We who forgive.'
Allah uses the word 'him' to refer to both Muhammad and humankind because He made humankind. And He taught humans to speak.

Allah continues His account of the creation of humankind.
But He first mentions Muhammad, and only then humans.
Moreover, He also taught other beings to speak: the moon, the sun, the stars, the seas, the ships, and the camels too. They venerate Allah.
Nevertheless, He granted humankind a special place in His creation. He sent messengers to them. If they listen, young maidens leaning on green cushions, sitting on elegant carpets in magnificent tents await them in paradise.

In the name of Allah
He is love
He gives
He forgives

1

He taught Muhammad the Qur'an.
He made human beings. He taught them to speak.
The sun and the moon move according to His calculations.
The trees and the plants bow before Him.

2

He constructed the sky, made it lofty, and He drew up the rules
for measuring and weighing, to prevent you from employing
the measure wrongly.
So be honest with the scales and do not be miserly.
And He made the earth for living beings.
On earth there is fruit and date palms.
And fragrant spices and grain.
You! Humans and jinn! Which of your Creator's gifts do you
still deny?

3

He created humankind from clay, like earthenware.
And He created the jinn from a flame of fire.
Which of your Creator's gifts do you still deny?

4

He is the King of the east and the west.
Which of your Creator's gifts do you deny?
He brought together the two seas, but there is a barrier between
them to prevent them from flowing together.

Both produce pearls and corals.
Which of your Creator's gifts do you still deny?

5
And the great ships that sail across the sea like mountains belong to Him.
Which of your Creator's gifts do you still deny?
Everything on earth shall die in the end. Only the beloved face of God remains.
Which of your Creator's gifts do you still deny?
Everything on earth and in the heavens belongs to Him. And He is engaged with them every day.
Which of your Creator's gifts do you still deny?

6
You, jinn and humans! We shall soon settle scores with you.
Oh, jinn and humans, if you are able to leave earth and heaven, do your best. But without My command you cannot leave.
Which of your Creator's gifts do you still deny?

7
A scorching fire without smoke and a scorching smoke without fire shall be let loose on you, and you shall be unable to hold it back.
Which of your Creator's gifts do you still deny?

8
When the sky bursts open and becomes like hot oil and a red flower, on that day jinn and humans shall not be questioned about their sins.
Which of your Creator's gifts do you still deny?

9

The guilty shall be recognised by their marks. Then they shall
be dragged to hell by their forelocks and their feet.
And they shall walk back and forth in boiling water.
This is the hell you declared to be a lie.
Which of your Creator's gifts do you still deny?

10

But for those who feared there are two gardens.
Their trees have many branches.
Which of your Creator's gifts do you still deny?
Two springs flow in each garden.
Which of your Creator's gifts do you still deny?
And there is every variety of fruit in pairs.
Which of your Creator's gifts do you still deny?

11

Those who find themselves in these gardens shall sit on car-
peted couches, lined on the inside with brocade; the fruit shall
hang low on the trees, making it easy to pick.
Which of your Creator's gifts do you still deny?

12

And there are young maidens with their eyes cast down, with
whom neither human nor jinn has slept.
They are like rubies and coral.
Which of your Creator's gifts do you still deny?

13

There are two additional gardens.
Deep green.
With two leaping springs.
And there is fruit, and there are date palms and pomegranate
trees.

Ravishing maidens too, beauties set apart in tents.
They recline there on green cushions and splendid carpets.
Untouched by human or jinn.
Which of your Creator's gifts do you still deny?
Allah is Sublime. Blessed be His name.

102

Humankind

After Allah made the human Adam from clay, He left him sitting where he was for seven days. He then sent him a chair of red gold adorned with jewels, a garment of silk, and a crown.

Adam put on the garment, set the crown on his head, and sat down on the chair. Allah asked seven hundred thousand angels and Satan to kneel before Adam. All the angels kneeled, but Satan remained standing.

'I refuse,' he protested. 'I am superior to humankind. You made me from fire, and him from a layer of dark earth.' He pressed his hand against Adam's stomach and said, 'The human's stomach is empty inside. He is incomplete. This is his weak point. He is vulnerable. Why do You choose him above us?'

'I gave him a hunger for knowledge,' Allah replied, 'and I left behind something of Myself in him.'

'What?! What did You leave behind in him?' the seven hundred thousand angels asked.

'Love, perhaps,' the angel Jabra'il speculated.

The angels lifted Adam in his chair onto their shoulders and carried him to paradise.

Creation at that point was twelve hundred and forty years old.

(According to Abu Ishaq Ibrahim ibn Mansur Nishaburi)

In the name of Allah
He is love
He gives
He forgives

1

Was there ever a period in which humankind was not note-worthy?
We made humans from a mixed drop.
We made them seeing and hearing to put them to the test.
We sent them on the right path, whether they were grateful or not.
And for the deniers We have readied a blazing fire and chains.

2

But good people shall be granted a place in paradise.
They shall take their rest reclining on couches in the delightful shadow of the trees, where there is no notion of heat and cold.
And the shadows shall stay close to them with fruit within their reach.
Silver plates and bowls shall be offered them, with pitchers and goblets of magnificent finely-formed glass.
They shall be given a drink that tastes of ginger, from a spring named Salsabil.

3

Boys shall pass among them who remain forever young. If you look at them, they will remind you of scattered pearls.
And when you walk around, you shall see a great kingdom with endless prosperity.
They shall wear transparent garments of green silk with silver bracelets, and their Creator shall pour them pure wine.
And He shall say, 'This is your reward. I thank you for your good deeds.'

4

Muhammad! We revealed the Qur'an to you in portions.
Wait patiently, therefore, for the judgement of your Creator,
and do not listen to the sinners.
Remember Allah in the morning and the evening.
Kneel before Him for part of the night.
And pray to Him for part of the night.

103

Proof

This is a sura from Medina that was revealed during Muhammad's struggle with the Jews.
By this time, Muhammad had acquired standing in Medina. He was an authentic prophet, a man with a sword, but the Jews wanted nothing to do with him. They had made up their minds, 'He is not a prophet, and his Qur'an is a lie.'

In the name of Allah
He is love
He gives
He forgives

1

The unbelievers, those who have a book, the Jews, and the servants of idols who do not have a book, refused to relent until clear proof was presented to them:
'Muhammad is a messenger from Allah who recites pure texts, in which great words are spoken.'

2

Those who had a book were not divided at first until the decisive word came to them.
All they were asked was to serve Allah, to give, and to follow this pure faith.
This is the best religion.

The unbelievers who have a book and those who do not have a book shall be united in hell.
There they shall dwell for eternity.
They are the worst of creation.

104

Expelling

The leader of the Jewish tribe Banu Nadir was one of Muhammad's sworn enemies.
While Muhammad was visiting this Jewish tribe, its leader devised a plan to kill him, but Muhammad found out about the plan and managed to escape.
Muhammad ran out of patience with the Jews, and he made a decision he had wanted to make for a long time.
He gave the Jews one day to leave the city. Each family was free to take as much property with them as a single camel could carry. They were obliged to leave their money and gold behind.
The Jews ignored the command and withdrew behind the city wall, closing the gate.
Muhammad waited for a week, but they remained in their houses and refused to leave.
'The longer you resist, the more severe your punishment shall be.'
Now three families were expected to share a single camel. This

was a new command from Allah.

The Jews did not listen, and they managed to persevere for two more weeks.

Muhammad did something he should not have done. He set fire to their date palms and thus destroyed their date crop. This hurt the Jews and broke their resolve.

'If you refuse to leave, I shall set fire to your houses. Now you must leave everything behind. This is a new command from Allah.'

The Jews were no longer able to stand their ground. They destroyed their own houses, pulled the windows from the walls, and spoiled their own belongings to be sure that nothing was left behind for Muhammad's followers. They then left their city empty handed.

But as they left, the women beat their drums loud and hard and cheered, to show Muhammad that he could not break their spirit.

Debate emerged among Muhammad's followers; they should not have burned living trees. Muhammad introduced a new sura, 'Allah prescribed it. When necessary, living trees and dead trees are the same.'

In the name of Allah
He is love
He gives
He forgives

1
Everything that exists in the heavens and on earth, give praise to Allah.
He is a wise Victor.
It is He who drove the unbelievers from their housing and their familiar surroundings in large numbers.

2

They did not think they were obliged to leave. They thought their walls would protect them from Allah.

But Allah's punishment came from an unexpected corner.

He placed fear in their hearts so that they destroyed their own houses with their own hands and with the hands of the believers.

You who see! Draw a lesson from this.

3

If Allah had not decided to banish them, He would have punished them even more severely in this life.

The punishment of fire awaits them.

Because they continue to resist Allah and His messenger.

Truly, those who resist Allah shall be punished severely.

4

Believers! Consider the beautiful date palms you destroyed and the other date palms you left unscathed; all this took place with the approval of Allah, for He thus intended to humiliate the protesters.

Believers! All of the livestock that Allah granted to His messenger as booty is not for you, because you did not fight for it.

This victory came about as a result of the fear Allah drove into their hearts.

Allah gives His prophets dominion over whomever He pleases. He has power over all things.

5

Therefore, the spoils that Allah made available to His messenger belong to Allah, to the prophet, to his closest family, and also to the poor, the orphans, and the travellers. In this way it shall not find its way into the hands of the wealthy.

6

Take what the messenger gives you.
And stay away from what he denies you.
Fear Allah.
Because His punishment is severe.

7

If We had sent down this Qur'an on a mountain, you would have seen the mountain demonstrate its humility and split asunder for fear of Allah.
These are the examples We set forth; perhaps they shall learn from them.

8

He is Allah.
He is one, the King.
He is giving and forgiving, and knows about everything visible and invisible.
He is kind, the Victor and the Founder of peace.
He is the Mighty One, the Powerful One, and the Giver of safety.
He is the Maker of all creatures.
He has the most beautiful names.
Everything in the heavens and on earth gives praise to Him.

105

Hajj

Muhammad maintains always and everywhere that he is illiterate, that he is incapable of inventing or writing down the recitations of the Qur'an by himself.

He repeats incessantly, 'Nothing is from me, everything is from Him.'

In the name of Allah
He is love
He gives
He forgives

1
You!
Fear the earthquake of the hour on the day of judgement. It shall be horrendous.
It is a day on which you shall see mothers forget their infants and pregnant women dropping their burden. You shall see drunken people, but they are not drunk. It is because of the day. The punishment of Allah is very severe.

2
Oh, people! If you doubt the resurrection, recall that We made you from earth, thereafter from seed, thereafter from a clot of blood, and thereafter from a formless lump of flesh, to thus reveal Our power to you.
We leave it for a fixed period in your mother's belly. Then We let you out as a child and We make you grow up.
Some among you die, and some grow so incredibly old that they forget everything they ever learned. And you see the lifeless earth, but as soon as We cause water to fall on it, it comes back to life. It becomes green again and brings forth all sorts of beautiful plants.

3
The hour is coming and it is beyond question. And God shall raise the dead from their graves.

Those who have done good deeds shall be brought to the gardens of happiness under which rivers flow.
Allah can do all things, and He does what He pleases.
Those who think that Allah will not help them in this life or in the hereafter should tie a rope around their necks, pull it heavenward, then cut it off. Let them see, then, if this deed has quelled their anger.

4
Do they perhaps not see that everything in heaven, everything on earth, the sun, the moon, the stars, the mountains, the trees, the animals, and many people too bow down before Allah?
Why do they not learn a lesson from this?

5
Garments of fire have been made for those who desire to remain unbelievers. And boiling hot water shall be thrown over their heads, such that their skin and everything in their bellies shall be cooked.
And iron cudgels have been set aside for them. Each time they flee from fear and sorrow, they shall be brought back with the words, 'You still have to taste this.'
But the believers shall be brought to the gardens of happiness under which rivers flow. They shall be given golden bracelets there. They shall be adorned with pearls and their garments shall be of silk.

6
Muhammad!
This is how it was until We directed Ibrahim to the site of the Kaaba. And We said, 'Hold no one equal to Me. And keep my house clean for those who walk around it, for those who stand

up, and for those who bow. And proclaim the hajj to human-kind. They shall come to you from distant regions, on foot or on lean camels.

'Let them first wash themselves, and let them offer sacrifices, before they walk in a circle around the Kaaba.

'Those who devise another besides Allah shall be carried off by birds or by the wind to a distant abandoned place.'

7

We have considered the sacrifice of large camels as a sacred sign for Allah, and there is something good in it for you.

Call on the name of Allah when the sacrificial camels are chained and ready, and when they are pushed to the ground on their sides. Eat of them, and give of their meat to those who ask for it and to those who do not.

We tamed the camels for you. Their flesh and blood is not for Allah but for you. So give praise to Allah.

Muhammad! They pronounce you a liar; in the past they pronounced all the other prophets liars. I indulged them; I seized them thereafter unexpectedly. See how I punished the others in the past.

How many cities have I not already destroyed, because their inhabitants committed crimes? How many walls and roofs have not already collapsed? How many wells are not already dry and damaged, and how many lofty castles have not been left abandoned?

Have such unbelievers never travelled the earth to understand with their hearts and hear with their ears?

They urge you to hasten the punishment. Without doubt, Allah shall keep His promise. But a single day for Allah is as a thousand years according to your calculations.

Muhammad! Say to them, 'People! I am only a clear-speaking

cautioner. And I say what I have to say.'
Allah is kind. He forgives.

8
He causes night to pass into day and day to pass into night.
He is Great, Sublime.
Do you not see that Allah causes water to fall from the sky, with which the earth is revitalized and made green? He is indeed all-knowing and tender.
Everything in heaven and on earth belongs to Him. He is Rich and He has need of nothing.
Do you not see that He tamed everything on earth for you, including the ships that sail the sea on His command alone? That He holds up the stars lest they fall to the ground?
But humankind is ungrateful.
It is He who gave you life. He shall bring you death, and He shall restore you to life.
Muhammad! Summon the people to your God, therefore. And if they argue with you, say, 'Allah is aware of what you do! And everything is mentioned in the book *In the Beginning*.'

9
You, people! Shall I tell you something?
The idols you worship instead of God are not even capable of creating a fly, even if they all worked together to do so. And if a fly takes something from them, they are incapable of taking it back. Flies and idols are both weak.
Allah is strong!
Praise Him.
Fight for Him!
And seek refuge in Him.
He is your Creator!
What a beautiful Creator!

106

The Hypocrites

The word munafiq, *hypocrite, was a neologism, used by Muhammad for the first time.*
It refers to a group of people who said to his face, 'We are with you, Muhammad,' but spoke ugly words behind his back.
This sura was a reaction to a statement of a clan leader by the name of Abdullah bin Beni.
He had said to Muhammad, 'I follow you, and whatever you command I shall do it. I shall pray, give, vast, and fight with you against your enemy.'
But when Muhammad was away, he turned to his clan and said, 'You can compare Muhammad with a dog you keep at home; you feed it and care for it, until it suddenly devours you!'

Such people enraged Muhammad, and he called them invisible enemies; more dangerous than the enemies who fought him openly with a sword.

In the name of Allah
He is love
He gives
He forgives

1
Muhammad! When the hypocrites visit you, they say, 'We testify that you are a genuine messenger of Allah.'
But Allah testifies that they are liars.
Allah has no need of their testimony. He knows that you are His messenger.
They swear to conceal themselves so they can keep others

away from the path to Allah.
Look and see how evil their deeds are.

2

This is because they first accepted the faith and then returned to being unbelievers.
Their hearts are sealed, and they no longer understand it.
If you look at them, their bodies surprise you. Even when they are talking, and you are listening to them.
They look more like dressed up beams of wood.
They consider every cry to be against them.
How can they be so lost?
Muhammad! Be careful! They are your enemies.
May Allah curse them.

3

When they are told, 'Come! The messenger of Allah shall ask forgiveness for you,' they turn their faces, and you see them walk away full of pride.
It makes no difference to them if you ask forgiveness for them or not, Allah shall not forgive them.
He does not guide hypocrites.

4

They are the ones who say, 'Give nothing to those who are with Muhammad. They might thus run away from him.'
They say this, whereas the treasures of the heavens and of the earth all belong to Allah, but the hypocrites do not understand.
They say, 'If we return to Medina, the powerful there shall dismiss the weak.'
But the hypocrites do not understand that the honour is for Allah, for His prophet, and for his followers.

5

Oh, you who believe! Do not let your possessions and your children distract you from thinking about God.

Those who do so are losers.

Oh, believers! Give before death seizes you.

Give of what We have given to you.

Allah shall not hold back anyone's death.

And He knows what you are doing.

107

The Rooms!

The people always talked at the top of their voices and often called one another names. They did not let Muhammad finish his sentences and talked over him, making his voice inaudible.

Muhammad improved his people's manners and regularly introduced new rules.

People walked into one another's houses unannounced, like camels. Muhammad established a rule, 'Do not do this! If you enter someone's house call out audibly, "Salaam!" so that those who live there know they have a visitor.'

He proclaimed each change in the form of a new revelation. The present chapter deals with conversation: speak calmly, control yourself, and know that Allah's word always has priority. Therefore, talk in such a manner that His word can be clearly heard.

In the name of Allah

He is love

He gives

He forgives

1

Oh, you who believe! Do not raise your voice above that of the messenger, and do not speak as loudly as you do when you converse.

Those who speak calmly in the presence of the messenger are those who shall be rewarded by Allah.

2

Muhammad! Those who shout to you from behind the door to the room lack understanding.

It would be better for them to wait until you receive them outside. Yet Allah is forgiving.

3

Oh, believers! If a bad person comes to you with a message, be careful to ensure it is accurate so that you do not hurt people out of ignorance, and regret what you have done.

4

Know that the messenger of Allah is among you. If he were to give ear to all your requests, it would create problems for you. But Allah has made the faith in your hearts something pleasant; and sin and anger something unpleasant.

5

People! If two groups of believers quarrel with each other, conclude peace between them. But if one of them goes beyond what is lawful, you must fight that group until they submit once again to the will of God. Judge between them without bias. Allah loves the just.

Believers are brothers to one another. Spread reconciliation among your brothers. And fear Allah.

6

Oh, people! It should not be so that one group insults the other group. Perhaps one group is indeed better than the other.
Women likewise should not insult other women. Perhaps some women are better than others.
People! Do not speak evil of one another.
And do not give one another insulting nicknames. Those who do are wicked.

7

Believers! Distance yourself from suspicions, for many of such conjectures are sinful.
Do not interfere with one another's affairs. And do not gossip behind each other's back. You are brothers. Is it right for people to devour the flesh of their dead brother with pleasure? Such a thing is disgusting.
Fear Allah. He forgives!

8

Oh, people. We created you male and female, and we made you into different peoples and tribes so that you might know one another better.
Truly! The most devout among you is the most cherished by Allah. He knows all things.

9

The Arab desert dwellers said, 'We believe!'
Say to them, 'You do not believe completely, for the faith has not reached your hearts.'
Say, 'Or do you perhaps want to teach Allah what faith is? While He knows everything in the heavens and on earth.'

10

Muhammad! They think you should be grateful to them, now they want to follow you.

Say to them, 'No gratitude from me. On the contrary, you should be grateful that Allah has led you to faith, if you are sincere.'

Allah knows the secrets of the heavens and of the earth. He sees all things.

108

The Day of Remorse

This sura focuses on the incessant debate among Muhammad's opponents concerning life after death.
Those who believe in this return shall be rewarded with paradise, but those who doubt it can expect hell.

Muhammad also states that Allah created the world in six days and on the seventh day He shall be finished with everything. On that day everyone shall be called back.
Muhammad sees each day as a thousand years. He tells his followers, 'When I was born, six thousand years of life had already passed. There is not much time left. The seventh day is approaching; that is why I am the last messenger.'

In the name of Allah
He is love
He gives
He forgives

1

Everything that exists in the heavens and on earth, give praise to Allah.
His kingdom is true and it is fitting for Him to be praised.
He can do all things.

2

It is He who created you, although some of you are believers and some are unbelievers.
And Allah knows all that you do.

3

He created the heavens and the earth in truth. He created you in various forms, and He made beautiful faces for you.
And in the end all things shall return to Him.

4

He knows what is in the heavens and on the earth. He knows what you conceal, and what you do in public. He knows the heart's secrets.
Have you not heard the stories of the unbelievers of old? How We punished them, and how they met their downfall?
When their messengers came to them with clear signs they said, 'A mortal is intent on leading us? Must we listen to you?' They thus became unbelievers.

5

The unbelievers think that they shall never be reawakened after they die.
Say to them, 'On the contrary. By my Creator! You shall be called back. And you shall be informed of what you have done. For Allah, it is easy.'

Believe, therefore, in Allah and His messenger and in the light,
the Qur'an that was sent by Him.
He knows everything you do.

6

The day on which He assembles you for the last judgement,
that day is the day of remorse.
The sins of those who believe in Allah and do good deeds shall
be forgiven, and they shall be brought to gardens under which
rivers flow. And there they shall dwell for eternity.
It is a beautiful place for them.
But those who deny Allah's signs shall find themselves in the
fire, and there they shall dwell for eternity.
It is a miserable place for them.

7

Obey Allah and obey His prophet. But if you refuse to listen, Our prophet's only duty is to pass on the message clearly.
Nothing more.
There is no God besides Allah, and believers should put their
trust in Him alone.

8

Believers! Some of your wives and some of your children are
indeed your enemies. Beware of them.
But if you forgive them nonetheless, Allah shall also forgive
them.
He is love. He forgives.

9

Believers! Your possessions and your children are a burden to
you.
With Allah there is great reward.

Fear God, therefore, listen, and give.
Those who give a pure loan because of Allah shall receive twice as much in return from Him.
He is friendly.
He appreciates.
He shall forgive you.
He sees the visible and the invisible.
He is the wise All-Knowing One.

109

The Row

This sura was revealed in Medina when Muhammad was engaged in fierce combat with his enemies, sword in hand.
He had issued orders to kill the unbelievers without mercy in battle, but some of his fighters hesitated.
Muhammad, 'Strike them dead without pity. Unless they call out, "la 'ilaha 'illa llah!" Then they are ours and you may not kill them.'

The sura also speaks about Isa when he performed miracles to convince the Israelites; when he made a bird from clay and let it fly away, but the Israelites said, 'Lies! Blatant sorcery, all of it.'

The sura also contains a statement that has had essential importance to Muhammad's mission. He quotes Isa as having proclaimed the coming of the messenger Muhammad.
Isa speaks of Ahmad who is to come, who shall succeed him.
With Ahmad Isa meant Muhammad, for both names have the same meaning.

But this proclamation is not in the Bible, and Muhammad was thus angry with the priests of his day.
He claimed that they had distorted the Bible for their own ends, that they had removed many essential texts, and added many sinful passages.

Muhammad thus insisted that the priests had taken out the correct proclamation of Isa, and had invented the trinity.
'The Bible is no longer the original Bible,' he said.
Isa is not the son of Allah.
Isa was not crucified.
Isa did not rise from the dead.
But Isa did proclaim that Muhammad would come, that he would be the last messenger.

In the name of Allah
He is love
He gives
He forgives

1
Everything in the heavens and on earth give praise to Allah. He is kind. He is wise.
Oh, you who believe! Why do you say things you do not do?
Allah sees it as hostility when you say something but do not do it.
Allah loves those who fight shoulder to shoulder in a row on His path as if they are a solid wall.

2
Isa, the son of Maryam, said, 'Oh, Israelites! I am God's messenger for you. To confirm what was contained in the Torah before my time, and to proclaim the good news that a messen-

ger is to come after me whose name is Ahmad.'

But when he came to them with clear words they said, 'This is pure wizardry.'

3

Tell me, who is more unjust than the one who invents lies about Allah?

They are intent on extinguishing the light of Allah with their words, but Allah shall cause His light to catch fire. Whether the unbelievers like it or not.

4

He sent His messengers on the right path, with a true faith to exceed all other religions.

Although the unbelievers do not like it.

5

Oh, you who believe! Be God's helper, just as Isa the son of Maryam said to his apostles, 'Which of you shall help me on the way to God?'

The apostles said, 'We are all God's helpers.'

Then some of the Israelites followed Isa and others refused.

We helped the believers against their enemies, and they thus gained the upper hand.

110

Friday

Two subjects are treated in this text.
First the Jews, and this time in an unequivocal manner.
The Jews did everything they could to make a fool of Muham-

mad, to undermine his mission, and to write him off as illiterate. Here Muhammad strikes back with force.

He says to the Jews, 'If you love God so much, wish to die so you can live with Him in His paradise. But you, Jews, do not do such a thing, because you are so enamoured of this life, of trade, of money, and of gold, that you commit many crimes.'

The second subject is the Friday prayer, 'Close the shops and pray. Go in search of your bread only after that!'
The Islamic world was prepared to obey this command from Muhammad.
After fourteen hundred years, Muslims still close their shops and go to pray in large numbers on Friday.
Friday prayer also had (and has) a political purpose. The leader addressed (addresses) the people and gave (gives) his opinion on important issues in local and global politics.
The minbar that was used during Friday prayer used to be the most important podium.
Muhammad devised the Friday prayer, and it is still experienced across the Islamic world with the same original intention.

In the name of Allah
He is love
He gives
He forgives

1

Everything in the heavens and on the earth give praise to Allah.
He is the beloved, wise King.
It is He who chose a messenger from the midst of an illiterate people, to pass on His signs to them, purify them, and teach them what is wise.

Truly, they were once a people astray.
And He sent other messengers to other peoples.
He is a wise Victor.

2

It is a gift from Allah that he grants to whomever He pleases.
Allah gives and His gift is great.

3

The story of those to whom the Torah was given and of those who did not observe it is like the story of a donkey carrying books.
The donkey has no idea what it is carrying.
Yes, it is an unpleasant comparison for those who deny the signs of Allah.
And Allah shall not guide a criminal people.

4

Muhammad, say to them:
'Oh, you Jews! If you think that you alone are God's friends then wish for death, if you speak the truth.'
But they shall not do such a thing on account of what they did with their hands in the past.
And Allah knows all things.

Muhammad, say to them, 'The death from which you flee shall certainly catch up with you and take hold of you. Then you shall be brought to the All-Knowing One, who knows both the visible and the invisible.
'And He shall show you what you have done in this life.'

5

Oh, believers!

When you are called to Friday prayer, hurry, then, to remember Allah.

Leave your businesses. Know this! It is better for you this way. Disperse only when the prayer is over, and go in search of your bread from His infinite clemency.

Remember Allah. Perhaps you shall thus find the right path.

6

Muhammad! But as soon as they see merchandise and entertainment again, they hurry away and leave you standing alone. Say to them, 'What is with Allah is better than trade and amusement.'

111

The Peace Treaty

Muhammad's absolute victory, the conquest of Mecca, was not yet complete.

The message of Muhammad's mission focussed entirely on idols. He refused to accept them and found it shameful that the people served gods made of stone.

He wanted to conquer Mecca with a view to smashing the idols and handing the Kaaba over to his Allah.

After years of conflict, he reached a compromise with the rulers of Mecca. They decided to leave one another in peace for the time being. Muhammad agreed to stop his attacks on the caravans that came from Mecca.

Muhammad's comrades were furious with him for agreeing to such a peace treaty, but they swore fidelity to him nonetheless.

Muhammad knew that the treaty was the beginning of his absolute victory. He had the cow's tail in his hand, now he wanted the entire cow. And he knew he would get what he wanted.

After concluding the peace treaty, Muhammad and his followers were free to travel to Mecca to visit their families. They were also at liberty to enter the holy place.

Muhammad saw it as a great victory.

He said to his followers, 'I know what you do not yet know.' What he meant was the approaching conquest of Mecca.

In the name of Allah
He is love
He gives
He forgives

1

Muhammad! We have provided a new breakthrough in your mission. And We shall guide you to a clear victory.

It is Allah who grants rest to the hearts of believers.

The soldiers of heaven and earth are His. He is knowing. He is wise.

2

Muhammad! We sent you as proclaimer of good news and as cautioner so that they might believe in God and His prophet, that they might honour Him, revere Him, and praise Him in the morning and in the evening.

Those who swear fidelity to you swear fidelity to Allah, and He lays His hands on their hands.

But those who break their word break it to their own disadvantage.

3

The Arab desert dwellers who did not want to fight shall say 'We are sorry. Our family and our possessions held us back. Ask forgiveness for us.'

They profess this with their lips, but in their hearts it is different.

They thought that the prophet and his followers would not return to their houses and their kin. But they were wrong, and they became a lost people.

4

Say to the desert dwellers, 'We have kindled a blazing fire for the unbelievers.'

God forgives whomever He pleases and punishes whomever He pleases.

When you and your men are on their way to take possession of the spoils of war, they say, 'We follow you.'

Say to them, 'No! You cannot follow us, for Allah has so decided!'

And they shall say, 'You begrudge us this.'

Say to the desert dwellers who have remained, 'Soon you shall be asked to fight against a criminal people. If you participate, Allah shall reward you. But if you refuse, as you have often done, He shall punish you severely.'

5

Truly, Allah was pleased when your followers swore fidelity to you under that tree. He knew what they were thinking, brought rest to their hearts, and he was to reward them swiftly with a clear victory.

There is yet another victory with great spoils, which you are still to receive, but Allah has placed His hand on it. Allah is mighty.

6

The people in Mecca had committed sins. They held you back when you attempted to enter the Sacred Mosque, and prevented your offerings from reaching their destination.

If there had been no believers in Mecca, and if they would not suffer damage, and if the unbelievers were standing apart, We would have given orders to invade the city, to punish those unbelievers painfully.

7

Truly! Allah almost fulfilled the dream of His prophet so that you are free, after agreeing peace, to enter the Sacred Mosque in safety and without fear, your heads shaved and your hair cut short.

Allah knows what you do not yet know. And He shall soon grant you victory.

It is He who sent His prophet with a guiding book and a true religion so that this faith would prevail over every other religion.

Allah is witness; that is enough!

8

Muhammad is the messenger of Allah. And those who are with him are hard to unbelievers but kind to one another.

You see them bowing and kneeling before Allah, and the traces of their prayers are visible on their faces.

In the Torah and in the Bible they are described as seeds that germinate and gradually grow bigger and stronger. When their branches are firm, they surprise the farmers and make them happy.

Allah has promised believers a great reward.

112

The Table

The disciples of Isa said, 'Oh, Isa, son of Maryam, can your lord send down a table to us from heaven?'
Isa said, 'Fear God, if you believe in Him.'
They said, 'We want food, and we want to know that you are telling the truth.'
Isa said, 'God, our Lord, send a table down to us.'

Muhammad uses this discussion between Isa and his disciples to explain the rules concerning food.

In the name of Allah
He is love
He gives
He forgives

1
Believers, fulfil your obligations.
The meat of herd animals is permitted, but some are forbidden. You are not allowed to eat the following:
Animals that died a natural death.
Pork.
Blood of an animal.
And the meat of an animal over which Allah's name was not invoked during slaughter.
The meat of suffocated and strangled animals and those beaten to death with a stick or a stone, or animals that have fallen to their death from a height.
And meat that has been eaten away by a wild animal.
And the meat of an animal that was offered to idols.

Nevertheless, if someone is forced to endure hunger, God is forgiving.

It is shameful for you to indulge in such meat.

But if you find yourself in a situation of necessity then God forgives. He is kind.

2

Muhammad, they ask what is permitted from all that is edible.

Say: All pure food and drink.

And everything your hunting animals catch.

And the animals you have tamed with the knowledge God gave you.

But do not forget that you must invoke the name of Allah when you slaughter them.

Today, all pure food is permitted, including the food of those who have a book. And your food is permitted them also.

3

And you are free to marry chaste women from among those who have a book, on the condition that you pay their dowry, you treat them well, and you do not visit another woman in secret.

4

Believers! When you go to pray, wash your face and wash your hands to the elbows. And rub your moist hands over your head and from your big toe to your ankles.

But if you are sick and cannot wash yourself, or on a journey and there is no water, or if you are sleeping with a woman and you find no water, you may press your hands onto some clean earth and rub your face with your hands. This is sufficient, since God does not want to make it difficult for you. He only wants you to be clean.

And fear God! He knows what you do.

5

Those who say that Isa, the son of Maryam, is God on earth are certainly unbelievers.

Say to them, 'Who has the power to hold God back if He decides to remove Isa and his mother and the entire population of the earth?'

Allah has dominion over earth and heaven and everything that lies between.

6

Musa said to his people, 'Remember God's benevolence in choosing prophets from among you, and in making some of you kings, and in giving you what He has not given to another people.

'My people! Enter the holy land that God promised you, and do not turn your back on it, otherwise you shall be losers.'

They said, 'Musa! A formidable people live in the land, and as long as they are there, we shall not enter it. Only after they leave shall we go in.'

Two pious men among them, whom God loved, said, 'Trust God if you believe. Enter through the gate. Once you are inside, victory shall be yours.'

They said, 'Musa! As long as they are there, we shall not go in. Go first, and fight against them with your God. We shall wait here.'

Musa said, 'God! I have lost control over my people; the only authority I still possess is over myself and my brother. Separate the two of us from these people.'

God said, 'If this is so then it shall be forbidden to them. For forty years, they shall wander the earth. Do not be concerned, therefore, about those who do not listen. And tell them the story of Habil and Qabil, the two sons of Adam. When they each offered sacrifice and that of Habil was accepted but that of Qabil was not, Qabil said to Habil, "I shall kill you!"

'Habil said, "God only accepts the sacrifices of good people. Even if you hold out your hand to kill me, you should know that I shall not hold out my hand to kill you. Because I fear the God of the world.

"I hope you carry the sin of your deed and my sins on your shoulder so that you shall find yourself in hell. That is what you deserve."

'The evil spirit of Qabil forced him to kill his brother.

'And he became one of the losers.

'Then God sent a crow to dig a hole in the ground with its beak and claws, to show Qabil how to hide the corpse of his brother in the ground.

'When he saw the crow he said, "Woe is me. Am I capable of hiding the corpse of my brother in the ground like that crow?"

'And he was filled with remorse.'

Therefore, We have made it clear to the Israelites that killing another human being is like killing all of humanity, except when it is to revenge a murder, or when it concerns the killing of those who sow corruption on earth.

And if someone lets another live, it is as if all humanity is allowed to live.

The punishment of those who fight against God and His prophet, and of those who sow corruption on earth, is death or hanging, or the severing of hands and feet, one left, the other right. Or expulsion from the land.

But if they show timely remorse, God is forgiving.

7

Believers, do not make friends with those who tell jokes and laugh when you are praying. It does not matter if they believe in a book or if they are unbelievers.

And do not make friends with those who begin to joke and

mock when you are called to prayer.

Such people lack understanding.

Muhammad, say, 'Why do you do this? Why so much hate? Is it solely because we believe in God and in the book that descended upon us, and in the books that were sent down before us? It is because all of you are sinners and have lost the way.'

Say, 'Shall I tell you about those whom God has punished without mercy? About those God has cursed, those who have kindled His anger, those who believe in idols? God transformed them into pigs and monkeys with tails.

'They are the most erring spirits.'

Believers! When such people are with you, they say, 'We also believe.' But they visit you without faith, and they leave without faith.

God knows all things.

Many among them commit sins; they are despots, usurers who earn their money through usury.

What they do is particularly bad.

Why do their rabbis and scholars not discourage them from using sinful words, earning money, and spending money they earned fraudulently?

Their deeds are impermissible.

And the Jews say, 'God's hands are tied. He has limits, He cannot give much.'

Their own hands are tied!

May they be cursed for what they say.

God's hands are wide open. And He gives to whomever He pleases.

God does not like troublemakers.

But if those who believe in a book follow us, We shall forgive their sins and bring them to the gardens of happiness.

8

Some say that Isa, the son of Maryam, is God on earth. They are unbelievers.

But Isa himself said, 'Israelites, worship God who is my God and your God.'

To those, therefore, who devise someone equal to Allah, paradise is forbidden. They shall find themselves in hell.

Those who claim Allah is one of three are unbelievers. There is only one God.

And if they do not put an end to the claims, they shall be thrown into the fire.

Isa is none other than an emissary of God, who was preceded by other emissaries.

And his mother was a good woman, and they both ate food like other people.

See how we explain everything for them, and see how they still refuse to listen.

God hears all things.

9

Believers! Appreciate the good food that God has given you, and do not transgress His rules.

Eat what is permitted, and fear God.

Believers! Wine, gambling, lotteries, and idols are all the affairs of Satan. Avoid them, therefore.

Satan is intent on using wine and games of chance to sow hatred among you. Satan thus wants to keep you preoccupied so much that you no longer have time for God and prayer.

10

If you are on pilgrimage, seafood and hunting at sea is permitted, but hunting on land is forbidden.

God punishes without mercy, and He is kind at the same time.

The prophet is only an emissary, but God knows everything you do in public and in private.

Muhammad! Declare that the wicked and the decent are not alike, even if the number of the wicked surprises you.

Do not ask about things that will distress you when you hear the answer. Save your questions until the words of the Qur'an descend anew. Therein shall be your answer.

God leaves the past for what it is. He forgives.

11

Believers! Hold firm in your faith, even if the entire world is in error. Those who go astray cannot hurt you if you are on the right path.

We shall all return to Allah in the end.

If one of you is faced with death, two witnesses from among you should be present, for you to pass on your last word. But if death comes to you on a journey, two others who are not from among you can serve as witnesses. And if you doubt their honesty, you must ask them to swear by God after the prayer that they shall not sell their honesty for any price and that they shall not falsify the divine testimony.

God does not lead bad people.

12

One day, God shall assemble all the prophets together and say, 'How did you treat your people?'

They shall say, 'God, we do not know. You know every secret.'

God said to Isa, 'You, son of Maryam! Recall what I gave to you and your mother, when I caused you to speak in the cradle as by a miracle.

'Recall that I taught you, and gave you wisdom, and the Torah, and the Bible.

'And recall that you turned a flower into a bird with My will, that you blew into it, and that it then flew like a bird.

'That you healed the blind and lepers with My will.

'Recall that you brought the dead back to life from their graves with My will.

'And when you showed your miracles to the Israelites, I took you under my wing and protected you from the violence of those who said it was nothing but sorcery.'

And thus it continued until the disciples said, 'Isa, son of Maryam, can your God send down heavenly food for us?'

You said, 'Fear your God, if you are believers.'

But they said, 'We want to eat of it until our hearts are satisfied and we know for certain that you are telling us the truth. Thus we shall be witnesses.'

Isa, the son of Maryam, said, 'God, send down food for us from heaven, as a miracle from You and a feast for us and for our descendants.'

God said, 'I shall do what you ask, but if one of you remains an unbeliever, I shall punish that person as I have never punished anyone before.'

And thus God said to Isa, 'You, son of Maryam, did you say to the people that they may praise you and your mother as two gods besides God?'

He answered, 'It does not befit me to say such a thing. You would certainly have known if I had spoken thus, for you know everything I keep within, and I know nothing about You. You know every secret. I have said nothing to them, other than what You asked me to say. I said, "Praise God who is my God and your God."

'When I was alive, I was in the midst of them and I was a witness. And when You brought my death, You were their guard and You were witness.

'If you punish them, they are Your subjects. And if you forgive them, You are the Mighty One.'

God said, 'Today is a day on which the deeds of the true shall benefit them. Gardens of happiness under which rivers flow have been set aside for them, and they shall dwell in them for eternity.'
God can do all things.

113

Contrition

Muhammad is no longer the lonely man he used to be. He is no longer the man who fled from Mecca to Medina, no longer the man who had nothing but a group of barefoot female slaves to follow him.
Muhammad is now a general, a deviser of cunning plans to defeat the enemy.

The present sura is about contrition. And Muhammad is une-quivocal, 'Believe in Allah. Show regret. Leave everything behind, and come!'
He is angry, he decides what will happen, and he is convinced that he shall conquer Mecca. His dream is within reach, and he thus speaks the language of a victor.

In the name of Allah
He is love
He gives
He forgives

1
Herewith the termination of a treaty concluded by Allah and His messenger with the servants of idols!

You are permitted to stay in the land for four more months, but know that there is no way out for you, know that you cannot flee from Allah.

God unmasks unbelievers.

This is an announcement from God and His messenger! God and His emissary have reached the limits of their patience with those who continue to praise gods of stone.

It is better for you to show contrition. You still have time!

But when the four holy months have passed, kill the worshippers of idols wherever you find them! Be on the lookout for them everywhere! Take them hostage!

But if they show remorse, perform prayer, and relinquish a portion of their wealth, let them go free. God is forgiving.

2

Why should God and His emissary respect the treaty with those unbelievers?

Why should it be so? If the unbelievers gain the upper hand, they do not respect a single contract, no single bond of kinship. They concur graciously with their lips, but in their hearts they refuse. Most of them are unreliable.

They sell God's word for a pittance, and they prevent people from following His way. The way they behave is very wrong.

They want to have nothing to do with believers. They are transgressors.

3

Will you not fight against those who do not fulfil their promises, who break their promises?

Why should we not fight against those who drove the messenger of Allah from his home, those who maltreated you?

Are you afraid of them?

Fear Allah alone!

Fight them until God punishes them by your hands and unmasks them.

Fight them! God shall help you to defeat them.

And He shall thus alleviate the pain of believers. And He shall take rage and unrest from their hearts.

God is all-knowing!

4

Those who have accepted the faith, left their homes without their possessions, and fight in person for God, they enjoy the highest rank in God's eyes

God shall reward them with the gardens of happiness, where they shall dwell forever.

You who believe! Do not seek contact with your father and your brothers if they chose unbelief over belief.

Those who do so are not with Us.

5

Muhammad, say to them, 'If your father, your brothers, your sons, your wives, your clan, the possessions you have amassed, the business that you worry might go bankrupt, the houses in which you feel at home, mean more to you than God and His messenger, wait, then, until Allah comes with His punishment!' God does not lead such people.

6

Allah has helped you in many battles. At Hunayn, for example, when you were numerous, were astonished at your great number, and were assured of victory. Yet it did not help you, and it did not go as you expected. The earth in all its vastness became too narrow and cramped. You turned, determined to flee.

Then Allah gave rest to the heart of His messenger, and He sent help; an army of angels you did not see. His punishment

of the enemy was exceptional.
This was revenge on those who do not believe!

7

Oh, you who believe! Unbelievers are impure! Do not let them enter the Sacred Mosque. And if you fear poverty, because they do not trade with you, God shall make you rich with His indulgence, if it pleases Him.

Believers! Fight against those who have a book but do not believe in Allah or in the last day.
The Jews say, 'Uzayr is God's son.'
The Christians say, 'Isa is God's son.'
What they claim is wrong. May God take their lives. How can they choose such a path, stray so far?
There is no one besides Him. Allah is alone.
Allah is One.

8

Believers! Know this! Many priests and monks devour the possessions of the people by deception, and mislead them on their way to God.
Warn those who amass gold and gold coins, and refuse to give any of it away for God, that a severe punishment awaits them.
A day shall come on which their gold and money shall be heated in the fire of hell, thereby burning their foreheads, their sides and their backs.
They shall be told, 'Taste! This is precisely what you amassed for yourselves.'

9

Know this! God divided a year into twelve months, when He made the earth and the sky. Four of those months are sacred, the forbidden months.

Know this! Our religion is the right religion. Fight the unbelievers together, therefore, as they fight you.

God remains with you.

10

Oh, you who believe! What has happened to you?!

Why do you stay pinned to the ground like lead, when you are asked to go to the front and fight for Allah?

Do you prefer this life to the life hereafter? This life is worth nothing when compared with the life hereafter.

If you do not join the fight, He shall punish you with a painful punishment. He shall remove you and bring forth another people in your place.

Allah can do all things!

11

If you do not want to help His prophet, Allah shall help him as He did before, when some wanted to kill him, and he fled to the mountains with Abu Bakr, a companion.

They sought refuge in a cave. He said to his companion, 'Do not be discouraged. Allah is with us!'

God sent down His rest upon them. A spider appeared and closed the entrance to the cave so that the men who were pursuing them were unable to see them.

Allah can do all things!

12

Muhammad, say, 'You shall be given nothing beyond what God has decreed. He is the Protector.'

They swear by God that they are yours, but they are not yours. They are just afraid. If they find a cave, a cavern, a place to hide, an underground tunnel they can enter, they crawl into it with haste.

Some among them are hurtful to the prophet. They say, 'He is an ear. He listens to everyone, and he believes what he hears.' Say to them, 'He is an ear, but he listens to Allah, and his listening is good for you.'

Those who insult the messenger shall be punished painfully. The hypocrites are afraid that a sura shall be revealed against them, in which their hearts shall be exposed.
Say to them, 'You may laugh, but Allah shall reveal what you fear.' If you ask them, 'Why do you behave so?' they shall say, 'We did not ridicule anyone. We talked with one another and made jokes to amuse ourselves.'
Hypocritical men and women belong together. They are lascivious. Allah has cursed them.

13
God has promised believing men and women gardens under which rivers flow, where they shall dwell in fine houses for eternity.
Muhammad, fight against the unbelievers and the hypocrites, and treat them harshly, for hell awaits them.

14
If a sura is revealed, 'Believe in Allah! And fight with His emissary!' the rich among them shall say, 'Let us stay at home with those who sit at home.'
They are happy to stay at home; their hearts are sealed like a hypocrite's, but they do not notice it.
They refuse to fight for Allah. They say they cannot endure the heat.
Say to them, 'Later you shall taste how hot it is in hell.'
Let them laugh less and weep more on account of the retribution that awaits them.

Muhammad! If they ask you once again if they may join you in battle, say, 'You may not, especially not with me. You shall not fight with me against any enemy, for it was you who first wanted to stay at home. Stay at home, therefore, with those who ought to stay at home.'

Muhammad! Never pray for the corpse of any one of them, and never go to their graves, for they renounced God and His emissary, and they died unbelievers.

15

The poor and the sick are not expected to make a contribution. There is also nothing against those who came to you to ask for a horse so they could join you, and you said, 'I do not have a horse. And I can find nothing for you to ride.'

They went away with tears in their eyes.

They have no guilt, but the problem is with the rich who have everything but want to stay at home nonetheless.

Among the Arabs from the desert and the Arabs in Medina, there are many hypocrites who are insincere by their very nature. You do not know them, Muhammad, but We know them. We shall punish them twice over, and a further immense punishment awaits them thereafter.

And there are others among them, who have admitted their mistakes and shown remorse. Perhaps God shall forgive them. Allah is forgiving.

Take part of their property as a donation, thus making them pure, and pray for them. Your prayers shall give them rest. Allah hears all things.

16

It does not befit Muhammad and the believers to ask forgiveness for those who serve idols, even if they are their family members. And especially not for those who are certainly destined for hell.

The prophet Ibrahim only asked forgiveness for his father because he had promised him he would, but when it became clear that he was an enemy of God, he cut himself off from his father. And he bore his pain with patience.

17

Allah has purchased the lives and property of the believers in exchange for a place in paradise. They can thus kill and be killed for God.
And who fulfils his promises better than Allah?
Be happy, therefore, with your dealings with Allah.
This is the great triumph.
The earth and the sky belong to God's kingdom. He gives life, and He takes life.
And you have no one except Him.

18

It is not fitting for the inhabitants of Medina and the Arabs from the desert to ignore Muhammad's command to fight.
They should not remain behind and leave him alone.
Or that they prefer their own lives above the life of Muhammad.
Those who fight for Allah suffer no pain, tiredness, thirst, or hunger.
Each step taken by the believers against the unbelievers shall be rewarded. If the believers attack the unbelievers and enrage them, take from them, inflict damages; all of it is seen, all of it shall be rewarded.
So, you who believe! Fight against the unbelievers close to you.
Let them taste your toughness.
And know that Allah is with you!

19

If a sura is revealed, the unbelievers look at one another, 'Does anyone see us?'

And if no one sees them, they turn their faces and disappear.
'Is anyone coming?'
And if no one comes, they start to laugh out loud.
They are sick in their hearts; they pile impurity on impurity.
They shall die unbelievers.
Do they not see that they are put to the test once or twice a year, through sickness and famine? They learn nothing from it. They show no remorse.

20
A prophet has come to you, one of your own, someone who suffers pain for you, someone who is concerned about you.
Muhammad! If they still continue to ignore you, say, 'Allah is enough for me. He is One. I rely on Him. And He is the Maker of the universe.'

114

Victory

When Muhammad conquered Mecca he did not hesitate for a second to enter the Kaaba and destroy the idols.
He smashed one of the images himself and left the rest to his followers. After the rubble was cleared away, he purified the Kaaba and rededicated it as the House of Allah.
Hubal, the largest of the idols, was kept back. Later, when Muhammad built the first mosque in Mecca, he gave orders for the idol Hubal to be buried in front of the door so that everyone entering the mosque would walk over it.

In the name of Allah
He is love

He gives
He forgives

1

Muhammad! When victory comes,
and you see the multitudes who accept faith in Allah,
praise then your Creator and ask Him for forgiveness.
He forgives.

115

The Messenger

In the name of Allah
He is love
He gives
He forgives

When Muhammad passed away his happiness was at its height.
He was afflicted by fever and when his temperature dropped he
appeared to be extremely weak.
He leaned against the wall of the inner courtyard, exhausted.
He wanted to be taken to the house of his youngest wife Aisha;
he wanted to die in her bed.
Aisha looked at him and gently wept.
Before long Muhammad rested his head on Aisha's lap and mur-
mured something.
'What did you say, my love?' Aisha asked.
Muhammad looked at her, his eyes filled with tears.
He smiled and died.
Aisha pulled her green transparent veil over his face and said
softly: 'The messenger is gone.'

Contents

Kader Abdolah has restored the chronological order of the suras to allow the reader to follow the development of both Muhammad and his Qur'an. His elderly uncle came across an extremely old list in the family library with the correct sequence. It was contained in the first Persian translation of the Qur'an, made by the renowned Qur'an expert Tabari, who published his translation under the title *Tafsir al-Tabari* or the *Exegesis of Tabari* 1000 years ago. His translation is an ancient, jewel-encrusted monument, which Kader has used extensively in his own work.

sura	Qur'an	sura	Kader Abdolah's Qur'an
1	Al-Fatiha	5	Al-Fatiha
2	Al-Baqara	87	The Cow
3	Al-'Imran	89	The People of Imran
4	An-Nisa'	92	The Women
5	Al-Ma'ida	112	The Table
6	Al-'An'am	55	The Cattle
7	Al-'A'raf	39	The Elevations
8	Al-'Anfal	88	The Spoils of War
9	At-Tawba	113	Contrition
10	Yunus	51	Yunus
11	Hud	52	Hud
12	Yusuf	53	Yusuf
13	Al-Ra'd	100	Thunder
14	Ibrahim	72	Ibrahim
15	Al-Hijr	54	The City of al-Hijr
16	Al-Nahl	70	The Bees
17	Al-Isra'	50	The Night Journey
18	Al-Kahf	69	Kahf
19	Maryam	44	Maryam
20	Taha	45	Taha
21	Al-'Anbiya'	73	The Prophets

SOURCES

De Koran translated into Dutch by Fred Leemhuis. A fine, honest and reliable translation. First edition 1989.

De heilige Qor'aan. A careful translation. Under the auspices of the late Hazrat Mirza Bashir-Ud-Din Mahmud Ahmad. First edition 1953.

De Koran. A daring Dutch translation intent on staying closer to Muhammad's prose. Translated by Prof. Dr. J.H. Kramers (1891-1951), revised by Asad Jaber and Fr. Johannes J.G. Jansen.

And the noble Qur'an.
a) *Al Qur'an Al Karim*, a masterful translation with explanation by Mohieddin Mehdi Elahi Ghomsheie.
b) *Qur'an Karim*, a fine translation with explanation by Bahaeddin Ghoramshahi.
c) *Qur'an Majid*, the old Persian translation with explanation by Ghadjeh Abdollah Ansari.
d) *Qur'an*, the magisterial medieval translation in the *Tafsire* of Tabari.
e) *Explanation of the Qur'an* by the medieval philosopher Abdollah Anasari.
f) *The Qur'an*, the old, original version, much annotated by my uncle Aga Djan.
g) *The Life of Muhammad, the Prophet of Islam* (Persian) by M.A. Ghalili.
h) *Muhammad, a prophet we must get to know again* (Persian) by Zabiholah Mansoeri.

1. *The Last Prophet* (Persian) by Abbas Shoeshtari.
2. *The Prophet* (Persian) by Zeinolabedin Rahnema.
3. *Islam in Iran* by the Russian author Ilyia Petrochovsky.

4. *Aisha After the Death of Muhammad* by Zabiholah Mansoeri, based on the book by the German writer Kurt Fischer.

5. *Forms of Government in Iran after Islam* by Gh. Ensafpoer.

6. *Twenty Years of Muhammad's Life* by Ali Dashti.

7. *The Light of the Qur'an* by Mahmoed Taleghani.

8. *Latajef altawajef* by Ahamad Golchin Maani.

9. *De Statenbijbel* (Dutch standard version)

10. *The Torah.*

11. *The Avesta* by Zarathustra.

12. *Nahjul Balagha* by Ali ibn Abi Talib, the prophet Muhammad's son-in-law.

13. An explanation of *Nahjul Balagha* by Djawad Fazel.

14. *Medieval History* by Beehaghi.

15. *A Thousand Years of Persian Prose* by Karim Keshawarz.

16. *Two Centuries of Silence* by Gh.H. Zarrinkoeb.

17. The medieval *Book of Travels* (to Mecca and Medina) by Naser Ghosro.

18. Explanation of a couple of suras from the Qur'an by Mehdi Bazarghan.

19. Explanation of sura 'Al Fatiha' by Ayatollah Motahari.

20. The books of Ali Shariati on Islam in Iran.

21. *Almodjam*, a study of old Arabic poetry.

22. *Research in Ancient Iran and Avesta* by M. Mirshahi.

23. *Aieen Moghan*, a study of old Persian religions by Hashem Razi.

24. Soware ghiaal, images in Persian poetry.

25. *The History of Persian Social Life* by Morteza Rawandi.

26. The medieval explanation of the Yusuf & Zulayka love story in the Qur'an.

27. *The Lives of the Prophets* in Persian translation.

28. 'The Life of Ibrahim', in *Tafsire*, Tabari's explanation of the Qur'an.

29. The medieval explanation of the story of Dawud and Sulayman in the Qur'an by Ghazai Razi.

30. *The Story of the Prophets from Adam to Muhammad* by A.M. Gharmaroedi.
31. Yusuf & Zuleika from *Haft Orang* by Nezami.
32. *Dawud and Sulayman* from the series *Masterpieces of Persian Prose*.
33. *Asrar Altohied* by Mohammed bin Monnavar.
34. *Zahak* from Shahname Ferdosi.
35. *Ibrahim* from *The Lives of the Prophets*.

ACKNOWLEDGEMENTS

My gratitude is due to Kader Abdolah for his elegant prose, and to Nadia for her meticulous editing and relevant expertise. Thanks also to my co-translator Niusha Nighting, who managed to make work such a pleasure at many a turn. And for those around me who waited with patience as I walked with Kader in the gardens of the Qur'an, thanks and thanks again.

NOURI NIGHTING